DREAMING THE IMPOSSIBLE

Mihir Bose is a British-Indian journalist and author who was the first Sports Editor of the BBC. In nearly 50 years in journalism he has worked for the *Sunday Times*, the *Daily Telegraph* and written on sport, business and social and historical issues for the *Financial Times*, *Daily Mail*, *Independent*, *Sunday People*, *Evening Standard*, *Irish Times* and *History Today* and broadcast for Sky, ITV, Channel Four News and was the first cricket correspondent of LBC Radio. He is the author of 37 books. His *History of Indian Cricket* won the 1990 Cricket Society Silver Jubilee Literary Award. *His Sporting Colours* was runner-up in the 1994 William Hill Sports Book of the Year.

DREAMING THE IMPOSSIBLE

THE BATTLE TO CREATE
A NON-RACIAL SPORTS WORLD

MIHIR BOSE

First published in 2022 by

ARENA SPORT
An imprint of Birlinn Ltd
West Newington House
10 Newington Road
Edinburgh
EH9 1QS

www.arenasportbooks.co.uk

Copyright © Mihir Bose, 2022
Foreword Copyright © Roy Hodgson, 2022

ISBN 978 1 913750 06 3
eBook ISBN 9781788855341

British Library Cataloguing-in-Publication Date
A catalogue record for this book is available on request from the British Library.

Designed and typeset by Biblichor Ltd, Edinburgh
Printed by MBM, East Kilbride

To Debi, Somen, Edwin, Hamish, Arthur, Antonia and Edward –
may they see the dream come true.

CONTENTS

Turning the Sports World Upside Down

Our Rulers' Struggles

The Frozen Media World

Towards a New Jerusalem

ACKNOWLEDGEMENTS

This book has come about because of Peter Burns of Arena Sport. Incidents of racism in sport were on the increase and we had been discussing the question of race, sport and society. I had suggested that perhaps I should reissue my book, *The Sporting Alien,* published 25 years ago, which had looked at these matters. While Peter and his team liked the book, he suggested that I should look at the whole subject again. At that stage nobody outside China knew of Wuhan and the perils held by its lab and its wet market, and George Floyd was still alive. Within months, the world had changed like never before and Floyd's death and the rise of the Black Lives Matter movement completely transformed the debate about race and sport. So my first thanks are to Peter.

Neville Moir, my editor at Birlinn, has guided the book with a deft touch and Ian Greensill, not put off by editing a previous book of mine on India, willingly took this one on and has done an admirable job.

I have always seen it as a failure that I could not persuade Roy Hodgson to join my London club, the Reform. He prefers the Garrick but I cannot thank him enough for sparing the time to write a very generous foreword which means a lot to me.

Naynesh Desai, as ever, was willing to take time off from his busy schedule to advise and guide me.

Over the years, I have interviewed many people in sport. In the course of writing this book, I have gone back to many of them and interviewed many others. The number of people I have spoken to covers a vast field. To all of them, I owe my thanks for sparing me their time and providing valuable insights into sport, race and society. The entire list is too long to mention everyone. I would like to thank in particular: Michael Holding, Mo Farah, Pat Cash, Raman Subba Row, Moen Ali, Chris Powell, Luther Blissett, Garth Crooks, Brian Stein, Colwyn Rowe, Trevor Westley, Dwight Marshall and David Gower, Rimla Akhtar.

The most recent interviewees include: Isa Guha, Ebony Rainford-Brent, John Barnes, Azeem Rafiq, Lilian Thuram, Brendon Batson, Mark Bullingham, Ricky Hill, Chris Hughton, Alex Williams, Tim Lamb, Solly Adam, Taj Butt, Tom Harrison, David Morgan, Mark Butcher, Scott Lloyd, Alan Pardew, Alan Smith, Chris Lewis, David Bernstein, David Davies, Devon Malcolm, John Gosden, Justin Layne, Chris Davidson and his team at Beech Hill Primary School, Anwar Uddin, Adrian Forbes, Nas Bashir, Paul Camillin, Paul Barber, Mahdi Chowdhury, Pete Bassi, Riz Rehman, Sanjay Bhandari, Stuart Barnes, Sue Day, Tom Loizou, Zulfi Ali, Michele Dorling, Mark Doidge and John Holder.

Majid Ishaq was, as always, ready to take time off from his busy City work painting a picture of the interaction between business and sport which is little known.

Thanks also to Ben Wiseman of the LTA and Graham Jepson for providing me with excellent tennis pictures.

It was, as always, a pleasure to talk again to David Pleat for his unique perspectives on football and society.

My old colleagues from the *Daily Telegraph* – Simon Briggs, Nick Hoult and Oliver Brown – allowed me to pick their brains and their contact books. Matt Hughes, Alyson Rudd, Barney Ronay, Jonathan Liew, Jonathan Northcroft and Sanjiev Johal were very generous with their time providing me valuable insight into race, journalism and British society. Anthony Clavane, whose book *Does Your Rabbi Know You're Here?* is a classic, Arunabha Sengupta, David Robson, my old editor at the *Sunday Times*, and Paul Newman, like me a Tottenham sufferer, also shared their thoughts. Joseph Harker of the *Guardian* provided me unique insights into journalism and race.

I would like to thank Harry Hall of Haus Books, for letting me use my writings from my book, *The Lion and the Lamb*. My old colleague Doug Wills, Editor Emeritus of the *London Evening Standard*, very kindly agreed to allow me to use material from interviews I had conducted for the paper.

Jeremy Butterfield was his usual unflappable self.

Covid has meant that I have not been able to have any face-to-face interviews but have relied on the use of the phone, Zoom, Teams and Skype. The need to use technology, which I did not even know existed before Covid, has meant that I have had to rely even more on Rose Chisholm, whose help and patience was invaluable, all the more so as my ideas on technology were formed in the typewriter age.

As ever my wife Caroline was the rock who made sure I kept to the course despite the fact that it often meant she herself was diverted from her busy work as well as writing her own book which I am convinced will be a bestseller. My daughter Indira has provided wonderful insights into how her generation sees the question of race.

Of course none of these people are responsible for the errors and omissions that remain. They are my responsibility and I can only hope there are none.

London
January 2022

FOREWORD

by Roy Hodgson, former England manager

Mihir Bose has used his vast experience, his contacts with top people in the world of sport and his considerable skill as a journalist and author to produce a topical book which sheds much-needed light on the intolerable abuse and the many injustices which our black and Asian sportsmen and women have had to endure for so long.

The varied and interesting stories the book contains highlight the many myths and prejudices that have confronted talented black and Asian sportsmen throughout the years and which, in many instances, still do today.

A theme that occurs in so many stories, especially those relating to the particularly brutal period of the 1970s and '80s, concerns the advice players of that era received in order to help them deal with racial abuse. Basically, it amounted to being told to 'get on with it' and 'rise above it'. On no account should it ever be allowed to affect their game or be taken into any account whatsoever!

Incredible and simplistic solutions offered for an ugly and unacceptable state of affairs and the governing bodies of that era and those that have followed to the present day cannot escape criticism that not enough was done to change it.

The emergence of anti-racist organisations, such as 'Kick It Out' and 'Black Lives Matter', combined with such initiatives as 'taking the knee' by Premier League footballers, have helped to raise awareness which is long overdue but may help to provide a better platform and environment for black and Asian sportsmen and women of the future.

In the final chapters of this fascinating book, Mihir looks deeper into the lack of opportunities at management and boardroom level for the BAME (black, Asian and minority ethic) community. He questions why there are still so few Asian players breaking through to the professional ranks, especially in the world of football. Mihir also discusses with the leading administrators of British sport questions about white privilege and institutional racism which are now so much a part of our public discourse as a result of the rise of the Black Lives Matter movement. Some of their responses are enlightening.

I congratulate Mihir for undertaking the monumental task of researching the historical abuse and prejudice that has blighted British sport for so long and for allowing us to 'dream the impossible' and to believe that this will not be so for ever.

INTRODUCTION

The Coon, the Baseball Bat and Enoch Powell

Forty years ago a train used to run on Saturday nights from Nottingham to London. It left Nottingham at 19.03 and arrived at St Pancras just after 21.30. It was an unremarkable train. The first-class coaches, which were usually at the front, consisted of cubicles set off down a corridor. This was marked first class from the second class (the term standard class had not yet come into use) in a much more class-conscious manner compared to present-day trains where all compartments blend into one long corridor and what distinguishes first from second is more the quality of the furnishings and the fact that the seats in first class are more spacious. When I first encountered the train the cubicles had some of the feel of the trains in *Brief Encounter*, exuding an air of seclusion and intimacy. Over the years, and particularly on winter nights, they also conveyed some of the danger and fear of an alleyway. If they had first held out hope of adventure, they later threatened menace.

But their full significance did not become clear to me until I took a fateful trip – returning from covering a football match for the *Sunday Times* – when they made a horrifyingly indelible impression on me.

The first time racism had revealed its football face to me was on 21 March 1981. I was on my way to Norwich to cover their game against Arsenal. The match was unremarkable but I had persuaded John Lovesey, sports editor of the *Sunday Times*, that this would be suitable for an experiment in reporting. I had read in *Time Out* how most journalists and directors watched football from a seat in line with the centre circle rather than behind the goal as the terrace supporters did. This, said the writer, gave them a middle-class bias as opposed to the supposedly more genuine working-class view provided from behind the goalposts. I wrote for *Time Out* but I knew it could occasionally come out with pretentious rubbish, particularly when those who did not write on sport ventured into this area. But it did strike me that depending where you watched a football match, you might have a different perspective, not in a class sense but as a way of looking at the game.

So, I suggested to Lovesey that we send not one but five reporters to a match. Get one to stand with the hard-core terrace supporters, another with the manager in the dugout, a third with the chairman and the fourth with the season ticket holder in the main stand. These four journalists would report the match through the eyes of their chosen subjects. In addition there would be the normal match reporter sitting in the press box to provide the usual match report. With a page devoted to this one match, the reader would get a feel of how different people, all of them supporters of the same team, saw the game and the whole exercise would indicate that a football match had many dimensions. It would also address the charge made against us journalists that our reporting never corresponded to the match as seen by the supporters and was more often a figment of our preconceived ideas.

Lovesey was attracted to the idea but I felt devalued the concept somewhat by allowing the match reporter 900 words or so while the four of us had no more than 250 words each, instead of the equal space I had envisaged. Nevertheless, it was a major feat to make this the main feature and persuade a national newspaper to send five reporters, including Brian Glanville, the paper's legendary football correspondent, and Rob Hughes, the number two football reporter, for this fairly ordinary league match against Arsenal.

So, fairly full of myself, I travelled down to Norwich on the train with Glanville, Hughes, Chris Lightbown and Denis Lehane. I had been assigned to sit in the directors' box with the Norwich chairman, Sir Arthur South; Lehane was with a season ticket holder; Lightbown, who was seen as the voice from the terraces, with a young terrace supporter; and Hughes with Ken Brown, the Norwich manager. Glanville was to do the match report.

Norwich was a town I always liked visiting and the train journey, which I made often, was a delight. The walk to Carrow Road took us past the canal and I chatted happily to Lehane and Lightbown as we moved along with hundreds of supporters. By this time a large crowd had gathered outside the ground and they seemed to be in good spirits. There was just one moment that jarred. As I made my way to the entrance marked

'Directors', I heard a cry: 'Get your copy of the *Bulldog*, get your colour supplement.' I turned to see a man with close-cropped hair, wearing a bomber jacket on the arm of which was the NF insignia, selling copies of a paper marked *Bulldog*. Lehane and Lightbown heard the cries as well and they seemed somewhat embarrassed. To me it was by now part of the environment round a football ground. I was, after living in this country since the sixties, well aware of racism and had learned to accept such things.

I soon forgot about the incident as I tried to portray the match through Sir Arthur South's eyes. All of us had been provided with excellent crib sheets on our subjects by Rob Hughes who had already been to Norwich and done a fair bit of preliminary work. He had picked out both the season ticket holder and the terrace supporter – Bert Horrex, a 65-year-old who sat in Block C, seat eight, and had been going to Carrow Road since 1937, and Mark House, a 13-year-old who used his pocket money to watch Norwich. Hughes, who had interviewed all of them, had carefully noted down Sir Arthur's confession that he did not know anything about football but he knew men. He never interfered with the manager and did not know the team until he arrived at the ground. If Steve Walford, whom Norwich had recently bought, committed an error, then the first time it happened he would not say anything. But if he repeated the mistake he would ask Brown if he knew he had this tendency. Was that why Walford was available rather cheaply, his price knocked down from the original asking price of £400,000? This, in those pre-Premier League days, was big money.

Sir Arthur lived up to his advance billing and Hughes's notes made it easy for me to write Norwich versus Arsenal as seen by the knight. More interesting in some ways was the insight the whole experience provided in a world I hardly knew existed. Until that moment I had not realised how class-ridden football clubs could be. I had watched football as a supporter or from the press box. At Norwich, for the first time, I was admitted to the directors' box, the holy of holies in football. It was a world removed from the pen where away supporters were herded. Here there was no frisking, no injunction to wait until the home supporters had left. I was now the chairman's guest and immediately made aware of the almost mystical significance football clubs assign to the word 'chairman'. From the moment the steward met me, saying, 'The chairman is expecting you', never once did I hear Sir Arthur South referred to by his name. Many people spoke to him during the course of the afternoon but it was always yes, chairman, no, chairman, chairman this and chairman that. And the style and opulence of the hospitality available to directors and their guests surprised me. As a football supporter I was aware that football grounds provided more than soggy meat pies and wretched instant coffee. The standards of press box hospitality varied from the sumptuous spread at Arsenal – provided, so the joke went, to compensate for their football – to Nottingham Forest, where a half-time cup of tea was a treat second only to getting an interview with Brian Clough. By the time I came on the scene, Clough had stopped attending post-match conferences. But that afternoon at Norwich I was introduced to the comfort the real bosses of football enjoyed before, during and after a game.

I had not been invited to the pre-match meal that the Norwich board, the visiting Arsenal directors and their guests had partaken of, but I was ushered into the boardroom for a pre-match drink and at half-time there was a magnificent spread supplemented by as much free drink as anyone could manage. In the years since then, and particularly with the formation of the Premier League, the hospitality provided by clubs for the reporters has increased and in some clubs it is truly lavish. But it was at Norwich I was first introduced to it and to a certain kind of well-heeled woman in expensive furs, tasteful but costly jewellery and with what looked like a permanent suntan. Many years later I learned that the tan was very often acquired after hours under a sunbed rather than actual exposure to the sun, but nevertheless the women there were very far removed from the sort of occasional woman of pallid complexion I had seen on the terraces or in the stands.

My mind was full of these wonders of the boardroom when after the match, and having filed my copy, I met up with Lehane and Lightbown to walk, or rather run, back to the station. There was a train at five past five and we were all very keen to get it. We got to the station just as the train was about to pull out. Normally I would have walked the length of the platform to find a first-class compartment but there was no time for that and, following Lightbown's lead, I jumped in the first available compartment with Lehane just after me. As we did so the train left. It was now, as I walked down the aisles towards first class, that I realised the great peril I had put not only myself but all three of us in.

We had got in at the back of the train packed with Arsenal supporters returning to London. As I walked through them they looked at me with faces like thunder. Suddenly, as I went past one large, fat supporter, he looked at me and cried out, 'Coon, coon, hit the coon over the head with a baseball bat.' As he said so he got up and started following me. It was my extreme good fortune that by the time he did I had gained some distance on him and a couple of people had interposed themselves, quite unwittingly, between me and him. But this only seemed to add to his sense of urgency to hit the coon.

So, as the train sped away from Norwich, a strange procession made its way. Lightbown was in front of me, Lehane just behind me, after that a couple of others and then this fat Arsenal supporter crying out, 'Coon, coon, hit the coon over the head with a baseball bat.' I had never heard this song before and it was only later I learned it was a very popular football song. As he sang, the Arsenal supporter was trying to shoulder his way past Lehane and the others to get at me. I quickened my step but I could not really make a run for it. I was going through some very crowded compartments and they were all filled with hard-faced, young men who looked angry and menacing and brought back visions of the skinhead whose fist I had encountered at Holborn station, some months earlier. As the cries of 'Coon, coon, hit the coon over the head with a baseball bat' grew nearer and louder, I feared the Arsenal supporters we were passing through would take up the chant and reach out for me. It was clearly an incitement to provoke such an assault on me, but fortunately for me they didn't. Then, just as the man chasing me brushed past Lehane and reached for me, I stepped into the first-class carriage. And the first person both of us saw sitting there was a policeman – a black policeman.

Whatever the fat Arsenal supporter may have felt about the policeman's colour, this was one 'coon' he could not trifle with. Now, as the policeman put himself between me and him, the situation was completely transformed. The supporter's cries died as if someone had switched off the power and as the policeman started to question him he looked more than a little confused. Beyond the policeman I could see the first-class cubicles where Brian Glanville was sitting with the rest of the football reporters amicably chatting away and totally unaware of what had happened. I have never felt such a sense of relief as I did when I saw them. I sank amidst them with their moans of uncomprehending editors and moronic footballers and felt I had regained paradise.

This overpowering and oh-so-sweet feeling of being rescued obscured everything else. Once the policeman had apprehended the 'coon' basher I had lost interest in him and was quite prepared to let the matter rest. But Lehane, a tough, Irish-born journalist who had reported on the Troubles in Ireland, was most outraged by what had happened and insisted I bring charges. I eventually agreed. Lehane, by now, was in his element. It was he who rang the office – in those days before mobile phones we had to wait until we got to Liverpool Street and found a phone box. John Lovesey told us we could have dinner and charge it to the *Sunday Times* and Lehane decided that we ought to recover in a fish restaurant in Soho that he knew well. There, over champagne and oysters, the man hunting 'coons' was put behind us and the night ended with Lehane recounting his experiences as a journalist.

*

It was winter by the time the case came to court and Lehane and I returned to Norwich to provide evidence. I had doubts about the journey. Would the 'coon' basher be on the train? Would he have his mates with him who might complete the job he was so keen on the previous spring? But I need not have feared. This midweek journey in the pale winter sunshine could not have been more different from the one that spring evening. If he was on the train we did not see him. At Norwich we were met by a very friendly policeman who epitomised all the best in English police work.

When I finally saw the Arsenal supporter he could not have looked more different from the frightening vision I had carried of him since that train ride. Now, instead of jeans and T-shirt he wore a suit, his disorderly hair was slicked down – he had washed it but had not blow-dried it – and he looked an unremarkable if rather overweight young man. It turned out he was a chef who was not always in work and his story, as told to the Norwich court, was a sad one, made all the more pitiable by his extreme contrition. He had got into bad company; now he had straightened himself out and such behaviour would not happen again. His plea of guilty meant we did not have to give evidence and he was fined £20 for using abusive language and threatening behaviour.

Before I had arrived at the courtroom I had been apprehensive about how I would feel when confronting him again. In that crowded train full of Arsenal supporters, and in the middle of his tribe, he had looked like an ogre with me the alien. Now he was the outsider in surroundings that to me were part of the reassuring correction systems necessary in a civilised society. On the train he had behaved as if he was the butcher and I was a mere sacrificial lamb waiting for the slaughter. Now in the courtroom he seemed to be going through such a terrifying sense of bewilderment that I actually felt sorry for him. He was clearly intimidated by the court, the judge and the lawyers in their wigs. I had also never been in a court but I had read any number of books and seen films to feel this was a real-life recreation of how the British judicial system, always fair-minded, worked. When he apologised and promised never to stray again, I almost felt like patting him on the back and saying, 'There, there.' I did not, but I felt both removed from his world and not a little contemptuous of his background and upbringing. The difference was emphasised when at the end of the hearing he slinked away, unable to meet my eyes, while Lehane and I went with the policeman for a very civil lunch and then a leisurely return home to London.

Years later I was to read in Bill Buford's *Among the Thugs* his experience of football violence on a train coming back from Wales. A drunken supporter got into a first-class carriage and tried to set alight a well-dressed man whose clothes and manner indicated his wealth. Buford pictured it as, 'a telling image: one of the disenfranchised, flouting the codes of civilised conduct, casually setting a member of the more privileged class alight'. Lehane saw my battle with the Arsenal supporter in similar terms and since I had only pressed charges on his insistence the punishment meted out and, even more, the supporter's contrition were for him a victory for civilisation. On the train back from Norwich, Lehane, pressing endless drinks from the bar on me, grew increasingly expansive. He was now with the *Daily Express* and long before we reached Liverpool Street he promised me the job as cricket correspondent once he had got his feet under the table there.

All this made that midweek evening train ride a marvellous contrast to the journey back from the Arsenal match. Just as almost everything surrounding that train ride was a nightmare, now everything was reassuring. The gathering autumnal mist that allowed us fleeting glimpses of the passing East Anglian countryside, the elegantly dressed businessmen and women, so perfectly behaved, not only polite and thoughtful to each other but also to strangers, and Lehane's visions of the journalistic worlds we could conquer all made me feel that this was just the England I had always imagined. By the time the train came back to Liverpool Street, the sometime-employed chef was like a Victorian cartoon villain, little connected with my everyday world. I might have glimpsed Caliban on the train back from the Norwich versus Arsenal match but now, six months later, Camelot had re-emerged and everything was all right with the world.

Three weeks later I was on the 19.03 train from Nottingham and these cosy images were shattered, like so much brittle glass. The Arsenal supporter might have reformed but there were many others from different clubs who shared the same tribal instincts, and they all seemed to be waiting to hit the 'coon'. None of them were waving baseball bats but they might as well have been.

I was in Nottingham to cover Forest's game with Leeds and my main concern about the match was that it was unlikely to be used in the London edition of the *Sunday Times*. In those days, long before separate sports supplements, and with only four pages devoted to sports, the *Sunday Times* had reporters, at best, at half a dozen football fixtures. The rest were covered by a round-up written by Jason Thomas, who, as it happened, was a Leeds supporter. Generally, the matches favoured for reporters to be there were north–south matches – Tottenham versus Manchester United, Arsenal versus Liverpool etc. The reasoning was that such matches were of interest both to the readers down south and up north and could be carried in all the editions. Matches such as Forest versus Leeds were held to be of limited interest: at best Midlands and the north and of no interest for southern readers. I knew that the London edition that would drop through my letter box the next day would have no match report by me, my match being replaced by one featuring a London club. I consoled myself with the thought that I would soon be in India covering India versus England.

The game in any case did not deserve wide circulation. Although it was early November, Leeds already looked doomed – they duly went down at the end of the season. The match turned out to be poor, redeemed by the weather which my notes say was brilliant. Forest scored first through Ward in the 22nd minute, Butterworth equalised for Leeds in the 43rd and the Forest winner came in the 53rd minute when Robertson scored from the penalty spot after Graham was adjudged to have handled.

I had hoped to catch the train that left Nottingham at about 17.20 but I knew this was going to be a struggle and when I got to the station I found I would have to wait for the 19.03. With the station dark, dank and uninviting, I found a Chinese restaurant nearby where I had a meal. By the time I returned, the London train was waiting and I headed for the first-class cubicles at the front.

The cubicles – there were six of them – were completely deserted but this did not worry me. I quite liked the solitude. I had Arthur Schlesinger's biography of Robert Kennedy, which had been my book on my football travels that season, and there were newspapers including the sporting pink, as local Saturday evening papers that carried the football match reports were called. Then a staple of the football season they have, reflecting how the football world has changed, long been defunct. I settled down to read, quite happy to be on my own. There was no reason for me to be anxious about the trip. The police had gone but so had the fans and the train looked wonderfully peaceful. It was some time after the train had left Nottingham that I became aware that I had every reason to be very worried – this would not be a leisurely journey back to London. It would prove to be the most traumatic train journey I have ever had, when at times I felt I would not survive.

The first sign was shouts and cries in the corridor leading to the cubicles. Soon I found a boy – he could not have been more than 12 – pressing his face against the door of the cubicle and flattening his nose against the glass in racial ridicule. He was joined by a second who shouted 'Sieg Heil', and then started marching up and down the corridor.

A few minutes later there were more boys – four of them in all – and they slid open the door of my cubicle and entered. They introduced themselves as trainspotters. One of them, a chubby boy who wore plimsolls, resembled, apart from his colour, my own features at that age. He did most of the talking.

'Who are you? What do you do?' he asked.

When I told him I was a sports reporter he turned to his friends and they looked at me as if they could not believe me.

'How do you know anything about football?' he asked. 'Pakis don't know anything about football, do they?'

I let that pass.

Then the chubby boy asked again, 'Who do you work for?'

'*Sunday Times*,' I said. This seemed to throw them and I got the impression that the *Sunday Times* was not a paper they were familiar with.

'What's your name?' asked the chubby boy. When I told him he said, 'What? Not Patel? All you Pakis are called Patel. That is what the Paki who owns the corner shop is called.'

I could have said that Pakis, meaning Muslims from Pakistan, could hardly be Patels who were Hindus from India or East Africa, but felt silence was the best part of valour. However, my silences or occasional monosyllabic responses, far from deterring them, only seemed to encourage them.

Soon the chubby boy asked, 'What do you think of the National Front?' When I made no response he asked, 'What do you think of Enoch Powell?'

I could have said much about what I thought about Powell including his despair when India got independence, having failed to persuade Churchill to intervene and hold on to India, and his 'Rivers of Blood' speech. But I contended myself by saying, 'I understand he is a very fine Greek scholar.' This reply seemed to throw them and for a few minutes silence reigned.

Then they started again. The chubby boy noticed I had a sporting *pink* and asked whether I knew the Manchester United score. He was, he said, a United supporter. I extended the paper to him. He looked at it: '2-1 to United.' But then his face contorted into a scowl. 'That wog Moses scored again.' Remi Moses was a mixed-race player of Manchester United.

By now the boys were getting really tiresome and, with hindsight, I should have asked them to leave. But I felt they posed no physical danger and, believing the less I did the better it would be, I kept quiet.

For a time they left me in peace and even left the compartment. But soon they had returned and now there was a different mood. They no longer wanted to chat, they were acting as my well-wishers out to warn me of the dangers ahead. The chubby boy came in and said, 'There are a bunch of hooligans in the next compartment. Chelsea supporters. They are not in a happy mood.' Chelsea were then in the Second Division and that day they had lost 6-0 to Rotherham. I was aware of the reputation of Chelsea fans and the news that they were on the train threw me into utter confusion. When I had boarded the train I was reassured by the thought that there could not possibly be football fans on it. The Leeds fans would be heading north, the vast bulk of Nottingham Forest fans would hardly be travelling to London and the few that might be must have got an earlier train. I had not anticipated that a journey back from Nottingham could take in Chelsea fans returning from Rotherham. I was not aware that Chelsea fans were anywhere near me and the news the boys brought was like being told as in old cowboy movies that the 'Red Indians' were about to ambush the stagecoach.

The boys seemed to sense this and began to play on my fear. For what seemed like ages, but was probably no more than 15 minutes, they would come in and out of my cubicle warning me of the hooligans in the next compartment and the dangers that lay in store for me. The train was now passing stations so familiar to me from university days at Loughborough. Then, as the train thundered through such stations, I had seen them as reassuring landmarks and hoped the journey would be prolonged. Now I desperately peered through the darkness hoping against hope that I would see signs for St Pancras.

Just before Wellingborough the boys returned and the chubby one said, 'They are going to get you before St Pancras. We are getting off at Wellingborough.' Then with a smile which suggested he had tried to play the Good Samaritan but could do no more to help me, he and his friends were off. As the train left Wellingborough I decided to take what precaution I could and put on my coat and muffler. I opened and reopened the Kennedy book, shuffled the pages of the newspaper, but could not concentrate on the words. I dared not look in the corridor, aware that that was where my nemesis was supposed to come from.

Just as the train left Luton the lights went off, plunging my compartment into utter darkness. I thought this was an accident. I later learned that there were switches in the train which determined people could get at and use to plunge the train into darkness. The Chelsea hooligans had undoubtedly done that. I flicked on my lighter and checked my watch, praying for the minute hand to move faster and St Pancras to come. Just then the lights came back on and as they did so the long-threatening Chelsea mob finally arrived. There were about ten of them, their blue-and-white scarves flaunted across their persons. The leader was a man dressed in a woolly red jumper. He theatrically flung open the door of the cubicle and, dancing a jig in front of me, seized me by my lapels. 'He's mine,' he cried. Then, pressing his face close to me, he said, 'OK, mate, this is a mugging.'

As if on cue the lights on the train began flicking on and off, and as the train plunged in and out of tunnels, there would be brief spasms of light followed by utter darkness. By now the mates of the man who had claimed me had crowded into the compartment, some of them dancing up and down on the seats in front of me. One stood in front of me and started to shadow-box silently, another pushed me about. They all disputed the right to work over what they called 'the wog'.

The man in the jumper released me, or rather pushed me away, and as I sank back to my seat he grabbed my briefcase and scattered the contents round the compartment with a triumphant shout. Another one snatched the lighter from my hand and smashed it against one of the walls, while another grabbed my cigars and yet another asked for my wallet but then seemed to lose interest and started jumping up and down in front of me. All the while they talked amongst themselves. Who did the 'wog' belong to? Who would have him? Who would make the kill? I was now surrounded on all sides by the Chelsea army and felt like a missionary tied before the fire while the natives danced around me. I could feel the flames licking me and it seemed it was only a matter of time before I was tossed in.

I did feel genuinely that I might not live through it and my mind seemed to dwell on curious, irrational things. I had changed the way I took notes for the match, particularly the precious team formation of which the *Sunday Times* was so fond. Had this, I wondered quite stupidly, disturbed the traditional pattern, altered the cosmic waves around me and brought about this unexpected retribution? I also thought of the pair of gloves I had left in the driving compartment of my car at St Pancras, a natty pair that I had recently bought and which I usually carried in the outer pocket of my overcoat. Now I had this vision that after they found me, they would go to my car and unearth the gloves. The story would be headlined: 'The Man Who Left His Gloves Behind'.

Then, suddenly, just when it seemed the Chelsea mob had made up its mind and was ready to roast me, a cry went up: 'Old Bill's coming.' The train was slowing down in its approach to St Pancras. A lookout had noticed that the Transport Police had boarded the train and as if by magic the Chelsea mob forgot about me and vanished. I feared it might be a false hope but to my great relief I saw the train was pulling into the platform. I slowly gathered myself and my things and made my way out. As I did so I could see a fire burning in a toilet behind me.

I was shocked and angry and my first port of call was the Transport Police followed by the stationmaster's office. By the time I got there I was quite worked up, my fury increased by the fact that throughout the two-and-a-half-hour journey I had not seen a single British Rail official. The stationmaster looked at me steadily and said, with a mixture of sympathy and helplessness, 'I am sorry, Mr Bose, but the guard is a human being too; he doesn't like walking up and down the train.'

In those days, the *Sunday Times* offices were at Gray's Inn Road, very near St Pancras, and I got into my car and headed there. The Saturday ritual of Gray's Inn Road meant that the sports department had decamped to a bigger room on another floor and I arrived to find the usual sports room empty. I was glad. I had gone there to tell Lovesey that I did not want to report football any more; it was not worth the hassle. But finding nobody there I sat at a typewriter – one of those heavy typewriters so common in newspaper offices then – and wrote a little note to John Lovesey which, without giving any details, mentioned I had had a bad experience on the train back. I felt curiously better after that.

Lovesey responded very sympathetically and decided that this was a story the *Sunday Times* should feature. He assigned Dudley Doust, the sports feature writer, to it. The article he produced – 'Journey into Terror on the 19.03 from Nottingham' – was a masterpiece of recreation. Lovesey ran it as the lead item on the sports feature page, although one *Sunday Times* editor thought it ought to have been on the front page of the paper.

The following Saturday I drove to Ipswich to report their game against Swansea City and the whole experience was so totally different that I was reassured. I then spent some weeks in India covering the England tour. Within days of my return I was back on football – the FA Cup match between Swansea and Liverpool, which saw Liverpool win 5-0 – and I did take the train to Wales. But, fortunately for me, I had the vast, comforting bulk of Ken Montgomery – to whom I stuck like glue, both on the way up and back – to protect me.

But the incident on the Nottingham train had marked me. After that I grew reluctant to take trains and did not take one for almost five years until the beginning of the 1985 season when I travelled to Manchester City to see Tottenham play. Whatever match I was assigned to, I drove, even if it meant driving up and back to Swansea in a day. At times, towards the end of these 400- and 500-mile return trips, I was in danger of falling asleep on the motorway and once or twice I even nodded off – but nothing could make me return to the train. For me they carried a dread and a menace that were almost unspeakable.

I also now planned my football trips as if I was a general preparing for battle. The more I analysed the incident the more it was evident that I had fallen victim to the remnants of the Chelsea army that had travelled that day to Rotherham. The police had escorted the main army safely back to London but that still left scattered bands to terrorise the countryside and it was one of these bands I had encountered. They were like a guerrilla army

INTRODUCTION

and since I was clearly their natural target my objective on Saturdays was to avoid the sort of ambush I had suffered on the 19.03 from Nottingham.

Whatever match I was covering I always checked where teams like Chelsea, West Ham and Leeds, all of whose fans had established a reputation for their racism and violence, were playing and took detours to avoid their possible paths. I always went very early, often arriving at the town some three hours before the match. And after browsing through yet another small town bookshop I would drive up to the ground, at times even before the stewards had arrived. Sometimes I had to wait until they unlocked the gates. But I knew by getting in so early I could park my car as near to the ground as possible. My objective was to cut down the distance I had to travel from the ground to my car after the match. My experiences of both the train journeys from Norwich and Nottingham had convinced me that the greatest danger I faced on a Saturday was not when travelling from London during the day, but on the return journey at night. It was then that I was likely to fall prey to a mob like the Chelsea one and next time I might not be so lucky.

Today, of course, the *Sunday Times* article would have provoked a huge storm on social media, but then, the article created no media waves in this country. However, in India it made the front pages of the papers and I had anxious calls from parents and friends. In this country I received some letters. One person, who had experienced abusive chanting from Manchester United supporters in a game with Spurs, sent me copies of letters he had written to Martin Edwards. Eddie Norfolk, writing on behalf of the Association of Provincial Football Supporters in London, commiserated and Monica Hartland invited me to a dinner of the association. However, one person wrote saying I had got it all wrong and that, despite being called a 'coon' and a 'Paki', it was not about race. What had motivated the assault was that I was travelling in first class and my assaulters resented that.

However, nobody from Arsenal or Chelsea responded. Neither did the Football League, then a unified body, or the Football Association. I had some sympathy from fellow journalists but it was very muted and the Football Writers' Association or the Sports Journalists' Association did not react in any way. Looking back I can see my journalistic colleagues, all white, just could not understand what had happened. For them a journalist being targeted for the colour of his skin was something they could not imagine because they would never be in such a situation. This was summed up by how John Thicknesse, cricket correspondent of the *Evening Standard* responded when I arrived in India for England's cricket tour a few weeks after my experiences at the hands of the Chelsea mob. The news of my assault had been front page news in the *Times of India*, the paper I had grown up reading, and as we gathered just before the first Test in Bombay, as the city was then called, he said, 'I see you made the front page of the *Times of India.*' He was clearly bemused this could have happened. Then I thought nothing of it. Now I can see why this Harrovian would have found it bewildering. He had always been kind to me and as far as he was concerned he saw me as no different from any other journalist. That the colour of my skin set me apart was something he just could not comprehend.

I have long overcome my fear of going to football matches, although every now and again a football supporter does make me feel like I am an outsider who does not belong. But that is very rare and not violent as in 1981. Football, particularly, with the advent of the Premier League, has changed out of all recognition. The wider world outside football has changed even more. But how closer are we to creating a non-racial sports world? Indeed, is this a realistic objective? Is it like the idea much trumpeted after Barack Obama's election, that a black man in the White House meant we had entered a post-racial world? That proved to be a myth. Is the desire to create a non-racial sports world also a search for a mythical world? It is the answer to that question I have set out to discover, talking to various people in sport, many of whom had not even been born when I had my experiences in 1981.

LOOK BACK IN SORROW

ONE

SUFFER IN SILENCE

'I have never thought of being black when going into a football match. I don't think of myself as being black. I didn't find it odd that there were no black people in the crowd. Sometimes I felt a little bit uncomfortable, that there should be more black people. But the number of people who are black in a crowd doesn't mean anything. What matters is people wearing your colours.'

The man telling me that was Luther Blissett, a legend at Watford, who played 14 times for England and then went on to play in Italy. Our conversation was taking place just before Euro 96 with the country convinced that racism was history, football was coming home and the game would unite people of all colours and creeds. After all, it was 18 years since Viv Anderson had become the first black player to play for England. In those months before Euro 96, began Blissett was one of a number of footballers, coaches and school administrators I talked to. Their views feature in this and the next chapter before we move on to how sports people feel about race in the second decade of the 21st century. For Blissett not to see colour may seem that we have a non-racial sports world, but I found when talking to him that this was also because Blissett was part of the generation told by his white managers that he should just put up with racism.

For Blissett, who came from Jamaica, football came naturally:

'I just liked playing football. Never saw it as a problem. Went to Willesden High, which has produced black sportsmen like Chris

Lewis, [Phillip] DeFreitas, not far away was John Kelly, where Mike Gatting, Ricky Hill and Brian Stein came from. As black players are athletic – we are a lot quicker – lots of the black players are forwards, get down the wings and cross, or get behind them. It is the pace that makes us different. When I started there was Clyde Best, Ade Coker, Brendon Batson and Laurie Cunningham. I was one of the forerunners. I did hear comments like black players are fine when the sun is out, not when it gets cold or, if you kick them you won't see them. I got abuse from the crowd. They would call me black bastard, coon, nigger. Certain people would call me names. But it never worried me.'

It helped that from the beginning Blissett was part of a group:

'In Willesden High I played in an all-black team bar one white player, John West, who was our skipper. He played in midfield but he had to earn our respect. When we played other schools there would be a hostile atmosphere. We would go to some schools where there were no black players and they would be shouting "coons, black bastards, niggers", the lot. But when you are in a group together you can take it. It is you, your group, against them. You go out and you want to show them. You think, I will stick the ball in the net – that will show them. When you are in a group you are there to do a job and if you have done that you feel you have answered the people who are abusing you.'

This was the advice Graham Taylor, his manager at Watford, later gave him: 'Concentrate on your game, play your game and stick the ball into the net.'

Blissett clung to this advice and when I spoke to him he was reluctant to talk about the racial abuse he had suffered. Then finally I was able to draw out of him the night in Peterborough long before he became famous, a night he would rather not remember. Blissett, making his way at Watford, was playing in a reserve game. It was the 1976–77 season, an evening game:

'I was the only black player in the Watford team, the only one in the park, probably the only one in the entire stadium. There were about 1,000 people. The Peterborough players were calling me names. But name-calling had never bothered me. I was not perturbed by the atmosphere. In those days I was very single-minded. Anyway, I was used to abuse. But it was the crowd – it was just horrendous. They were shouting everywhere, in the stands, on the terraces, everywhere. But the abuse and the shouting was horrible. Monkey noises – "Ugh-ugh-ugh-ugh-ugh" every time I got the ball – and shouts of coon and everything else. They didn't throw things; it wasn't fashionable to throw things. Even the Peterborough players were calling me names. One of our players said to take no notice. They said the best way to shut these people up is stick the ball in the net.'

Blissett did not score that night but that game made Blissett determined to succeed. He also developed a code:

'If people spat at me, I ignored it. Players did spit on me, in isolated instances in the league, or supporters when I was going for a corner. As long as it was not against me in the face. But if anybody spat at me and it hit me in the face I would have turned on them. Then the gloves came off.'

It took Italy, where Blissett went in the late eighties, for him to realise that the game can generate passionate support but avoid the hate so endemic in English sport:

'Italy has fanatical support. I was very well treated. In Italy it is a national pastime. Everybody will have an opinion but there is no name-calling, no spitting. In Italy fanaticism is about football; it is not about hating the other team or their supporters. I think there is hate in English football, a lot of hate. I don't know the real reason for it. But something has changed. It has become far more organised.'

David Pleat had suggested that if I wanted to speak to an articulate black player, one aware of the political undertones, I should speak to Brian Stein. He had been part of Pleat's Luton team of the eighties and had been as much a hero of Kenilworth Road as Blissett had been at the same time at Vicarage Road. Both had also played for England about the same time. But although they share the same skin colour, Stein had come to this country from South Africa and the difference in outlook was immense:

'I was seven years old when I came here from South Africa. My father was politically active in South Africa – he suffered 24-hour house arrest. He was always at home, and couldn't read political material. We lived in Athlone, a coloured township, and the colour bar was a bit like a caste system. By the time I left South Africa I was aware. Edwin, my brother, was very aware. In England, when I met Ricky Hill and Paul Elliott, I realised they were aware. I had played football in Cape Town and I always wanted to be a footballer. My heroes were Pelé and George Best. In England we lived in Willesden and the first thing that struck me was that there were no black players. When I started playing I heard this myth about black players not having stamina. They couldn't run for 90 minutes. Players lack stamina, and when it is snowing they can't get going. This was in 1977. I was only 19 then.'

Stein went to school in Hampstead, a predominantly white but mixed school:

'We knew the difference between black and white but as kids you can adapt to anything. Kids live from day to day. Terry Dyson, the Tottenham double hero, was the sports teacher. He didn't particularly encourage me. My brother Edwin, former assistant manager at Birmingham, pushed me more. He got me motivated more than my schoolteachers. Edwin urged me to start playing. I went to college, got my A levels, but my parents weren't wealthy – we had eight kids – and I stopped playing football after 15. Then Sudbury Colts came in and paid me £5, Edwin having persuaded them. At Sudbury I played under Des Taylor for six or seven teams. Smith was the manager of the first team and there were no problems of colour. I played for Sudbury for half a season. A chap came from Edgware and said that if you go to Edgware you can earn more money, so Edwin and I went. After a month and a half we had a lot of scouts watching. One Wednesday, the chairman of Edgware said Luton were interested and they signed me. Pleaty was the reserve team manager.'

Pleat took over as first-team manager in 1979 and soon realised that Stein was different. The driver of the Luton coach could not be more right wing. His support for apartheid was vigorous and he often voiced his dismay over the ban imposed on white sporting South Africa. Pleat, aware Stein might get into a row with him, said, 'Whatever you do, do not argue with the coach driver. It is a waste of time.' Stein avoided any major rows but there was always the crowd:

'You would get mostly supporters shouting "Ugh-ugh-ugh-ugh-ugh," – monkey noises whenever you had the ball – or throwing bananas. Cup game against a team from the Third Division. Wigan or Hartlepool. Got a lot of stick. We played a game in the eighties. Cup match. One of the players called me black something. I did not let that go. I gave him a bit of stick. In the early eighties Chelsea crowds gave a lot of stick to Paul Canoville, terrible abuse, much more than either Ricky Hill or I received. They destroyed him. It was particularly nasty – Phil Walker and Trevor Lee had a terrible time.'

But there are two abiding, horrific memories for Stein, both from the supposedly friendly, warm north – Blackburn and Burnley:

6

'Early in my career, the north was much worse. Past Birmingham the black explosion of players did not develop. Blackburn was one of the worst. Burnley, they spat at me. At Blackburn I was a sub and I was walking through the tunnel. It was just before the match and the crowd were throwing things. Coins, bananas. By the tunnel at Blackburn the crowd were close. I was spat at. I was very upset. I nearly spat back. I felt like Cantona did when he was abused but I did not react like him, although then and later I had a lot more abuse.'

Then there was the night before a game at Burnley when he and Ricky Hill decided to go for a walk around the town:

'It was a Friday night. This was about six in the evening. Not very dark. Just went for a walk to stretch our legs before dinner. Ricky and I were sharing a room as well. As we walked we became aware of a couple of kids with their parents. The kids pointed at us and said, 'Look, there's a darkie', and they were laughing as if they had never seen people like us. It was like the Dark Ages.'

Stein felt his South African experiences had equipped him to handle things:

'I could handle it better because of this awareness. I had seen a lot of it in South Africa. But there it was defined. It is not defined here; it is much worse as there is no set thing. Here you can do everything but you don't know where they will stop you.'

This heightened awareness may explain why, unlike Blissett, Stein was intensely aware that he played in a Luton team with brilliant black players watched by all-white crowds:

'At most we would have about 50 black supporters, mostly friends of players. A lot of my friends used to come to watch, but some would end up in fights. Everybody is unconsciously a racist. Some of them pretend. We had a new coach one year. We had a little chat, Ricky, me and maybe three or four black players. He had been at Derby. He said, "Brian, nice working with you. I am not a racist." For me that remark told me everything. I just couldn't get on with the man.'

By this time Stein had learned that:

'Most footballers are not aware. Footballers are not particularly bright. Most of them felt I was from some part of the West Indies. Later on in the eighties a lot of the sports stars became more aware of the racial problem. When a rebel tour to South Africa was organised by Jimmy Hill I was approached. Pleaty asked me one year to go and coach black kids in South Africa. I did not, could not.'

In 1988 Stein, like Blissett, left England to play football on the Continent, his destination being Caen in France, for whom he played for three years from 1988 to 1991:

'The crowds watching us were predominantly white, but it was different. To be honest, more African players were involved. Different sort of atmosphere. I was more easily accepted. Ugh-ugh-ugh-ugh-ugh monkey chants? None of that in France. True, France being a big country, you do not get a lot of away support, but whichever opposition supporters were there, they did not get at me. The teams had a lot of black players and a lot of them were French black players. The French crowds did not exhibit the racism the way English crowds can.'

Stein's charge that footballers were not very aware could hardly be made against Garth Crooks, perhaps the most articulate footballer of his generation, regardless of colour, and one who turned all the stereotypes, both about footballers in general and black footballers in particular, on their heads. Here was a working-class boy for whom football had provided a way to fame, but who disdained the gold bracelets and the fancy trappings thought mandatory. More, here was one able to assess himself and his contemporaries with a steely but sympathetic eye.

Crooks had always been a favourite of mine. I had admired his play at Tottenham and always held him in special regard for that moment at Anfield on 16 March 1985 when, after a Micky Hazard shot had been saved by Grobbelaar, he had put in the rebound to provide Tottenham with their first victory at Liverpool since the sinking of the *Titanic*. As a Tottenham fan that moment for me was magic. And we had barely settled in the cafe opposite BBC London radio, where Crooks then presented his weekly programme, when he began to speak with the sort of disarming frankness rare amongst professional sportsmen:

'Professional sport has given me access to an entirely new world. But I am very ordinary working class. My father came from Jamaica in 1956, mother from rural Jamaica in 1957, and I was born in Stoke-on-Trent in 1958. Father was a manual labourer who worked in a tyre factory for 25 years. He returned to Jamaica three years ago, and my mother still lives in London. I went to comprehensive schools, in reality secondary modern, and the only thing different was that teachers made me interested in English and said if I applied myself I could do very well. I graduated in political science but I knew from early on that

8

sport was to be taken seriously. I always felt that I had to be 15 per cent better than the white person to get the same chance.'

And he was quick to pick up anyone who sought to categorise him:

'Whenever I go to one of the football dos, I gravitate towards black players. Once Ray Wilkins said, "What is it with you guys, always with the brothers?" I said, "Ray, when you come you always congregate with Bryan Robson. Should I read anything into that?" Ray went quiet after that.'

While Blissett had to be reluctantly drawn on his problems with white crowds, it required little for Crooks to relive that terrible day when he made his debut for Stoke at St James' Park. It was a December night in 1978:

'I was the only black player on the park. Terry Hibbitt, Jimmy Greenhoff, Alan Hudson, Peter Shilton, Denis Smith, John Mahoney and Terry Conroy were playing. I was 18 years old, and I was the butt of the most cruel racism – jokes, chanting, the whole Gallowgate Kop in unison singing racist songs and shouts. Every time I touched the ball there would be deafening monkey noises – ugh, ugh, ugh, ugh, ugh, ugh – and just abuse. I have never felt so alone, so vulnerable, so stripped of my being. Denis Smith, John Mahoney and Terry Conroy wanted to protect me. They tried to protect me. They couldn't as the whole crowd was on me all the time. At half-time Tony Waddington, the Stoke manager, took me off. I did not want to come off. "Never mind, you are coming off," he said. My purpose was to perform to the best of my ability, to show them on my debut. I couldn't. I was in tears as he took me off.'

His move to Spurs, which made his career, brought another dimension. Here was a fashionable, rich North London club, whose predominant support was Jewish but whose boardroom at that time had no Jews:

'In racial terms my presence was very important. Chris Hughton was already there, very quiet, very unassuming. At Spurs I had to put up with the images of the stereotype black. I perceived certain people at Tottenham saw me as a bit of a rogue, not really capable of mixing with the middle classes very well, unable to conduct myself very well.'

In many ways some of his best duels were with his own defenders, Graham Roberts and Paul Miller, in particular Miller:

'Miller was a deep thinker. Typical Essex man. Wanted to be socially mobile. Very ambitious, always keen to maximise his attributes. He had married the daughter of Morris Keston [a legendary Spurs supporter]. Paul could sound very bigoted but very funny. Some of the things he said were outrageous but they made me laugh and I could not take offence. I remember sneezing and covering my face with my hands as I did so [as he tells the story he repeats the action, cupping his hands over his nose and mouth]. Miller said, "What is it with you people? Do you only come out with a handkerchief when you are playing cricket?" '

Crooks is aware that he carries a double burden, that of the articulate footballer in a game where a meaningful sentence is like a novel, and that of an articulate black footballer, but pays generous tribute to others. 'Many black players have played their part. Laurie Cunningham was a gem. He had a shyness which was mistaken for aloofness.' He reserved judgement on only one black player. Dropping his voice he said, 'Viv Anderson is the most successful black player. He has done very little to promote the cause of the black sportsman.' It is the only time in our conversation he had a bad word to say about anyone black or white. For a man who enjoyed his football and finds it 'difficult to become angry', that was very eloquent.

So far the black footballers I had spoken to all fitted the stereotype: players of pace, playing up front, dazzling with goals. But there was another player who demonstrated that you could make it to the top even if you had no pace. In fact, the position he played in was the only one where pace played no part. So, I was keen to talk to Alex Williams, the former Manchester City goalkeeper.

Williams fascinated me. I had a memory of a Friday live television match on the BBC – in the days when BBC and ITV shared league soccer – and of Williams keeping goal for City against Chelsea. The memory is of the dazzle of lights and of Williams, probably the only black man on the field, being cruelly baited by Chelsea fans. The noise of 'ugh, ugh, ugh, ugh' every time he touched the ball reverberated in my ears.

My first sight of Williams increased my fascination. Just as on that night at Chelsea he was the lone black sentinel, so he was on the afternoon I first saw him in person. However, this was not amidst baying white hordes but an audience that presented the face of English decency, good humour, kindness and generosity that I had long ago accepted as the essence of this country. A warm, caring but robust image of English football.

This face of soccer was displayed at the Littlewoods presentation ceremony at the Institution of Mechanical Engineers in Birdcage Walk where Williams had come to accept an award on behalf of Manchester City,

Littlewoods then being the sponsor of the League Cup. Williams is tall, over six feet four inches, and he would stand out anywhere, but in that English crowd – particularly at the buffet of delicious savouries on bread and stick, washed down by wine – he stood out as the only shiny black face in a sea of pale pink. A couple of weeks later I was sitting in the Manchester City reception and Williams told me how his family came from Moss Side where City then had its ground. He 'was born in Moss Side, born and bred there', and would come and watch Manchester City. He added, 'I used to be quite small so when they used to pick the team, they would put me in goal as being the last player to be picked.' He made his first-team debut in 1981 against West Brom, aged 19:

'Nineteen was quite young really, especially for a goalkeeper, and obviously it was quite unique to see a black goalkeeper. But I never, ever thought of myself as being a black goalkeeper. I just thought of myself as a goalkeeper. I didn't really have any problems being a black goalkeeper. When I played as a youngster it wasn't looked upon as a big thing to be a black goalkeeper. I would play schoolboy football which at the time wasn't really that serious. Obviously, when I actually joined Manchester City and I was playing in the second and third teams, then it started to become more apparent to me that it was quite a unique thing, generally because of the reception I got at most away grounds. It wasn't particularly a race thing at all, it was really, "Oh, there's a black goalkeeper."

'I never experienced anything serious playing youth and reserve team football. The only time I really had a bad experience was when we played in the Youth Cup final at Millwall in about 1979. It was played over two legs. We played the first leg here (at Maine Road) and we drew the game 0-0. They brought quite a few supporters up here and it was actually quite bad. The shouting consisted of black this and black that, the usual sort of things. It was bad enough here but certainly when I played down there it was much worse. I can't remember anything in particular but there were plenty of the usual monkey jibes – ugh, ugh, ugh, ugh, ugh – things like that. Leeds wasn't as bad as people made out.

'One of the worst experiences was West Ham. I remember I played there once in particular and we actually got beaten 5-0. At the start of the game I was getting all sorts of race criticism but I actually played a brilliant game and at the end they did actually clap me off the pitch – or perhaps it was because I let five in! Chelsea again wasn't too bad because I think there's a large running area around the pitch.

So even though the abuse you got was quite bad, the fact that they were quite some way away actually did help. I remember I always played quite well at Chelsea. I do remember one incident though where we were actually in the hotel before one of the Chelsea games, and somebody sent a parcel. When I opened it up, it turned out to be a razor blade or something inside.

'I remember playing at Everton one year. I was running up to the Everton end and somebody had screwed up a programme and burnt it, reminiscent of the Ku Klux Klan thing. I found at Liverpool that the racism there was a comical racism.'

These experiences made Williams distinguish between different kinds of racism:

'There are two kinds, the comical mickey-taking kind, and then there's the genuine race hate of West Ham and Millwall. Liverpool was always a mickey-taking place. They would start and everybody would start laughing and it's not meant with intent, it's more of a joke. That particular instance with the programme was more mickey-taking than race hatred. Millwall and West Ham are quite bad but you've got to expect that from the dock areas of London.'

As for many players of that generation his white colleagues let him suffer as if this did not concern them:

'Sometimes they would just say, "Oh, just get on with things," but more often than not they didn't really comment as such about the stick I was getting. When I was playing they were bad places to go to, but I think that now most clubs have cleaned up their act. They've got a lot better now, so I certainly wouldn't like it to be taken in the wrong context. Most places are now quite accustomed to black faces. Now with so many black players in the Premier League it has changed. Black players are more common, more accepted.'

Williams left City in 1985 with a back injury and went to Port Vale, hoping he could get fully fit and return to the glory days. 'But it never happened. I had about 18 glorious months at Port Vale but they never really saw me at my best.' He cannot shake off the feeling that he did not quite achieve what he could have. 'I made the England youth squad and I was in the Under-21 squad on numerous occasions but didn't actually play. I managed to obtain a European Youth Championship medal and an England Under-21 championship medal, and my aim was to go on to the full squad and do the same again, but it wasn't to be. I have always had a sense of not fulfilling my potential. I've played at the top and I've enjoyed it and I thoroughly enjoy the job I do now.'

Interestingly, Williams – whose father came from Jamaica, and was a good fast bowler – confessed that when he was 'a kid growing up in cricket I actually supported the West Indies, probably, because they had the best team then. I wanted to support the winning team under the great Clive Lloyd.'

The job that Williams was doing was with City's community scheme, which aimed to get young people involved first and foremost with the football club, play together and play football. The Moss Side community was then 200,000 people. The majority, 60 per cent, were ethnics: Asians, blacks, Caribbean, Chinese. 'In fact,' said Williams, 'in some of the schools, 95 per cent of the kids are ethnic-orientated. We had a school recently, Royce Primary School, and I think every child bar one was Asian.' And just as Luton parents do not flock to Kenilworth Road, so Moss Side ethnic parents did not come to Maine Road – but their kids did come to the Platt Lane complex.

As Williams drove me back to the ground we saw an Asian couple walking past the front entrance. The man was in salwar kameez, like the one sported by Imran Khan at his wedding, the woman covered from head to foot in a long salwar and along with them was a little child. They walked on the forecourt of Manchester City, past the crowd that had gathered in front of the ticket office queuing for their season tickets. They were not only completely oblivious of the crowd but even of the club. They did not even look at the crowd, let alone share their knowledge or enthusiasm for City.

'You will have to attract them, won't you?' I asked Williams.

Williams looked at the couple and said, 'Yes. The younger generation will come. But it will take time.'

A quarter of a century later changes have come about that could not have been imagined when I met Williams. Manchester City is one of the best clubs in the land and have moved from Moss Side. The club play at the Etihad, a wonderful new stadium built for the 2002 Manchester Commonwealth Games, and is owned by a Middle Eastern royal family.

Williams, now 60, is Ambassador for City in the community and is talking to me via Zoom from the Etihad stadium and is well aware of how things have changed. 'When I was playing football in the '80s if somebody wanted to give me physical abuse they would have had to come to the match. Today they can sit on the other side of the world and pick up a computer or laptop and on social media give abuse.' Yet he insists:

'There are a lot of positives. The biggest change is everybody is much more aware of racism and not just in football. In life. In yesteryears it[racism] would have been [treated as] a laugh and a joke. But now because a lot of black and ethnic players are in top flight football it is taken seriously by the players who want to do their best to stamp it out. That has been the biggest change of all. Footballers today are all seen as role models. When they have something to say football is such a dominant sport now, it does give them a platform to support things.'

The area round the Etihad is not full of Asians but has many migrants from Poland whose colour means, as Williams admits, 'sometimes it is harder to distinguish when they are white what their origin is'. So, the question of Asians living round the ground flocking to see City, which we discussed 25 years ago, does not arise. The Asians who come to watch City are the well-off and do not live round the Etihad. 'For whatever reason there seems to be quite a high proportion of wealthy Asian business people in Manchester, male and female, and we do have facilities for corporates to come along and in that sense I have seen a large increase in Asian people coming to football matches.'

Williams has not given any thought to questions about white privilege and institutional racism, 'I go about my business to promote racial equality and social inclusion. Yes I am sure there are things that are happening in teams and organisations.'

This may help explain why Williams, who does not have children – he has nephews and nieces – is happy to spread his message of hope to the some 20,000 school kids he sees a year:

'One of the things I do when I visit schools is tell young people you could have a different colour skin, you could have a different sexuality, nationality, religion and everybody at some stage will get a knock-back in life. It is how you deal with that knock-back and persevere. You just got to be a strong person to get through that. If you are good enough at certain skill or level, irrespective whether it is sport or industry, you will come through. If you can get to the top of your profession you will get an opportunity to change the world. And that is the way this thing [racism] is going to change.'

But how are things at Luton, another club which is surrounded by Asians living round it? Luton had always fascinated me and in the months leading up to Euro 96 I had also spoken to many people at the club.

TWO

BLACKS DON'T SWIM, DO THEY?

I had read about such sentiments regarding blacks but that was in faded old newspaper cuttings and they came from what looked like the prehistory of sports. In 1968, when apartheid South Africa was still looking to hold on to its position in international sport, Frank Braun, then head of the white-only South African Boxing Association, told *Sports Illustrated*, 'Some sports the African is not suited for. In swimming, water closes their pores and they cannot get rid of carbon dioxide, so they tire quickly.'

Then in 1995 two men in Luton told me their feelings about blacks in sport which, in essence, was not all that different from what Braun had said. Yet they were a million miles from the white supremacist ideas that prompted Braun. The Luton men's sentiments were expressed in the context of an effort to understand why certain races play certain sports rather than to justify the exclusion of a race from sporting activity or assert that one race was superior to the other. They were hardly alone in harbouring such thoughts.

We were in a room at the back of the main stand at Luton, yet another Luton room with a bar. I had often been in that room for post-match conferences when the room had been packed with journalists. Now there were just three of us – Colwyn Rowe, the Luton community officer, Terry Westley, then the Luton youth team coach, and me. We were speaking three months after Eric Cantona had displayed his knowledge of kung fu and while he was serving his community service sentence. We discussed why young Asian players were not flooding into Luton's youth team, the children being from the houses where you only have to open the door to almost smell the jockstraps of Luton's players. We were now talking of the attributes of black players.

Both Rowe and Westley were from Ipswich. They arrived at Portman Road in the days when Bobby Robson was manager of a fine Ipswich side in the early 1980s, challenging for the championship, weaving in the Dutch influence of Mühren and Thijssen with the traditional British strengths. Terry Westley, the same age as his namesake Terry Butcher, joined as an associate schoolboy player and is of a generation when there weren't any black players in school, in football teams or anywhere else for that matter. Rowe says, 'Black players had not yet broken in. There was one I remember in my whole school.'

But although they knew no blacks, nor had hardly ever seen them, tales of their power and speed had reached them. 'I had always known them as quick,' says Westley. 'I remember going to Portman Road and the quickest players in the school had to go for a 100-metre race straight down the pitch.'

'If there was a black in the race,' Rowe cut in, 'you thought he was going to win.'

'That's right,' confirmed Westley. 'I used to look up and down the line at the start of the race and if I saw a black face I thought, well, he is going to win it. They are the quickest players, aren't they?'

That is when Rowe said, 'They don't swim, do they? You don't see a black swimmer, do you?'

I looked at Rowe and then across to Terry Westley and the two faces could not be more earnest, more eager to establish that all this was part of a genuine desire to make sense of the whole question of people of different colour in sport. It was clear Rowe had spoken about the lack of black swimmers as if he felt this balanced his praise of blacks as quick on their feet. What he seemed to be saying was that they may be quick on the ground, but in water it does not work – there the fast twitch muscle is no good.

'Black players are explosive,' nodded Colwyn. 'Ron Atkinson has a lot of coloured players and they are very fast. They have great power. It is just their athleticism. Are they an asset because of their pace? I would say they are.' So black players, in contrast to what the romantics thought they would do when they came into the English game, had not added fantasy – they had made a fast game even faster.

Colwyn's reference to Ron Atkinson was significant because he shared their views about what made a black athlete genetically different. Two years after I published my book, *The Sporting Alien*, Atkinson, in his 1998 memoir, *Big Ron, A Different Ball Game*, wrote:

'Compared with white players, the black footballer is certainly blessed with a different muscle development that is of great benefit in most sporting activities. That's fact, not fiction, or even football fantasy. In most cases, it makes the individual more agile and flexible, athletic and very pacy. Sometimes they do struggle with stamina, but they have speed to burn. Also, and this might be something to do with their roots, there is an innate grace and flair about their game. Think of the Caribbean cricketers, for instance. That same easy-going, "this is a doddle, man" approach is part of the make-up of the black footballer.'

What makes what Atkinson said even more interesting is that for him this genetic advantage made them 'a decidedly valuable asset in any side'.

David Pleat had told me this was the major effect of black players coming to the game, and now in my conversation with Rowe and Westley I had confirmation. Westley said, 'Power, pace and strength; that is what the majority of coloured players have brought.'

Just before my conversation with Rowe and Westley I had been asking Dwight Marshall, a black player who then played for Luton, why most of the blacks in football play as forwards. Now Westley took up the argument:

'You asked Dwight why most coloured players play up front. Their nature is very explosive, a powerful type of player. That is the front player. That is an asset for forward players, exceptional power. Gilkes at Reading is quick. I can't name any white player that quick. Why? How do black players become that quick?'

Rowe provided the answer. 'They have this fast twitch muscle that gives them speed. And they are bulky, aren't they?'

'So naturally,' said Westley, 'you start to mould that player as a front player. We have one coming through next year in my youth team. Afro-Caribbean. Luton boy. He is very, very quick. We are trying to mould him into a wide player. He has real pace. Like [Les] Ferdinand. Real powerful lad. He will bench youth team players next year because he is so powerful. That is his make-up. He isn't a midfield type, a neat, tidy, little passer like David Preece. I think generally they are powerful players and that is why they play up front. I look for a player to have an outstanding asset, any asset. One asset – maybe pace. Trevor Peake, he has reliability, week in week out. You must channel a player in a particular way. But that is not just a coloured player, you would do that with a white player.'

It would be easy to condemn them as racist. Both Rowe and Westley came over as very sincere men who may be naïve but did not seem to have any malice. And they were in a way reflecting views that back in 1995 were quite commonly held. Views that would be articulated and written about in books many decades after I spoke to them. What was significant was that by the time I spoke to these two men in 1995, the black presence in football was taken for granted and there were many white players and managers who played and fraternised with black players and who counted blacks as their friends: yet even now for some of them meeting blacks was still a fairly new experience.

Westley had revealed this to me when we discussed how Dwight Marshall had been received at his first club, Plymouth. Marshall had been a hero there and Westley said, 'Dwight Marshall told you how well he had done in the first few games. If he had been a white player and he had got to Plymouth and not done very well in the first five games, the crowd would have been on his back. If you go there and do well it does not matter what your colour is, you will be liked. That is the way supporters are. If the black player is the best player he will be idolised.'

The implication was clear. As far as fans are concerned Marshall was no different from anyone else. He may have been black, and he had a fast twitch muscle which made him an ideal front player, but from Plymouth to Carlisle he would be acclaimed if he scored goals, but reviled if he failed, irrespective of colour. But is that how Marshall saw himself – having some characteristic black attributes, but his blackness playing no overall part?

Marshall had come to football late – 24 when he got his first professional club – and when I had spoken to Pleat he had told me he would be an interesting study. He had also told me a story about Marshall that seemed to bring out all the contradictions.

Marshall came from London and should have been glad to move to Luton. It meant he could be near his family and since he had told Pleat he planned to marry his girlfriend, who already had two of his children, Pleat thought this would have a good, settling effect. Sometime after Marshall had moved to Luton, Pleat asked about his marriage plans. Marshall said he had decided not to marry. 'Why?' asked Pleat, fearful that he might have broken up with his girlfriend. 'She is pregnant again,' replied Marshall. There was no hint of irony in his tone or awareness that as a reason for reversing a decision to marry someone it sounded crazy.

Pleat had shaken his head, just as he had shaken his head when another black player had revealed that he had never heard of Wilf Mannion. 'Not heard of Wilf Mannion?' reflected Pleat. 'I used to go to Notts County as a boy just to smell the liniments. And I can still smell the abattoir. And not know who Mannion was? These players, they go to football grounds, but they do not even see where they are going. When we went to Middlesbrough for their last game at Ayresome Park, one of my black players did not even know it was the last game or that the club was moving to a new stadium. He had a ghetto blaster stuck to his ear and he was in another world.'

Again, it would be simple to see it as black versus white. But it was the lament of the educated, cultured voice of football, mourning the passing of the age of reason and knowledge. The civilised Roman railing against the approach of the barbarians, aware they would win and destroy everything he held dear.

Despite all this, I was hoping Marshall would help me explore the contrasts the black player provided in English football. Marshall, born in Jamaica, arriving here at the age of five or six, his early hero being Pelé, could be expected to have a very different football apprenticeship to, say, Kerry Dixon, his then strike partner at Luton. Marshall's answer began promisingly: 'Quite a lot different.' But just as I thought he might open up on the racial and social differences, I realised he was treating the question in a very narrow footballing sense. For Marshall the difference was that Dixon, although turned down by his home club Luton, had worked his way via Tottenham's youth team to first-team football at clubs such as Dunstable Town, Reading and Chelsea before arriving at Luton. Marshall was different because he had to wait until so long before a club would even have him.

I had to tease out Marshall's story of working in the outside world until his early 20s before entering football. 'I had been involved in football in junior school. I had trials when I was at school but I failed to get in anywhere. I did a couple of O levels and I did a B.Tech diploma in Public Administration at the North East London College near Tottenham. From 18 onwards I was working nine to five, Monday to Friday, so I could only play football midweek evenings and Saturdays.'

Then, suddenly, he received a call from Plymouth Argyle, but here again, as Marshall told the story, it was not so much the man of colour going to a part of the world where there are few people of colour, more the city boy who had never been to the country and never taken a long train journey:

'When I was on the train I thought, "The train is never going to stop. Where the hell are you going? I am never going to get to this place. This is so far away there is no way I am signing for these people." It felt strange because I had never been that far in the country by myself. I had been on school trips, had been to Spain but not that far in England. It was not city. It was country.'

As he said this he laughed loudly. 'I was there for three seasons. I was made to feel welcome. To be fair to Plymouth, it is a cosmopolitan place, and people come and go; it is quite a friendly place.'

At 24 he knew Plymouth was his last chance to make the grade and, as luck would have it, his feet did the talking and broke whatever barriers there might have been. 'Luckily for me I went down there and in the pre-season I scored in every game and the crowd was behind me from then. A week before we signed there was a testimonial and Aston Villa came down. We lost 2-1 but I scored again. And the season started well for me. I scored quite a lot early on and the fans were all behind me. I had the best season I ever had. Fans will always remember me for that season.'

'Does it bother you that there are no black faces in the crowd?'

'It does not bother me. I don't go out there thinking we should be getting a few more black faces into the stands. My job is to play football; that is what I want to do. Not worry about which particular faces are in the crowd. It does not really come into my mind.'

It was not far removed from what Colwyn Rowe had said: 'I have never been to a football match and thought that the black players make up 20 per cent of the teams and the crowd is white. Now that you are telling me, I am beginning to think about it.'

Marshall could barely recall suffering any racist abuse. 'I have been a professional for four years now and I heard very few taunts.'

'What is the worst you have ever heard?'

'They said the normal things really. Just coon and nigger. But that, as I said, very rarely happened to me. Once you get on the pitch your whole concentration is on the game. Although you can hear the crowd in the background it is very hard to hear anything specific, unless you go right to the touchline and somebody directly abuses you. You very rarely hear anything specific.'

By now, with Marshall sounding just the sort of black player of whom Terry Westley or Colwyn Rowe would approve, I expected him to echo that yes, it is a twitch muscle in his thigh that explained his pace, his position as a forward. But his explanation was:

'Maybe one of the reasons why we like playing in the glory positions, up front, is we seek glory. You don't get much of that if you are being a keeper. That is one of the reasons why you don't get too many black keepers. There are no black keepers, no role models for young black kids to become a keeper. You would want to be Ian Wright. Peter Shilton is not a choice black kids have.'

And while Pleat had said the problem with Marshall was that, unlike a Wright, he did not throw his shoulders out as he walked on the field, like a strutting cock, Marshall did not quite fit the sporting stereotype. True, he loved films like *Pulp Fiction*, *Alien*, *The Terminator*, Eddie Murphy and action movies, but he shunned the traditional sportsman's pursuit of golf. His game was chess. 'It is a very good tactical game. It is not boring. Football and chess are two different things. Chess is a very time-consuming game. I could fit in a couple of football games in the time it takes me to play one game of chess.'

Sometime after that I spoke to Peter Hart, then acting head of Beech Hill Community School, just down the road from Kenilworth Road and there was again a reference to blacks and swimming. 'I am told Afro-Caribbeans do not float easily. Whether it is true or not, it is much more difficult for them to learn to swim than it is for Asians and others.'

Hart did not have many Afro-Caribbeans in his school. They were mostly Asians and we were talking about why Asians were not emerging into football. 'They have come,' said Hart, 'from village communities. The parents may not even speak English. In the eight years I have been here I have seen communications get easier but it is still not ideal.'

The area around Kenilworth Road had always been a natural magnet for such newcomers. 'We tend to get the new communities. The housing is cheap and there is a great community feel.' Twenty years ago, when Hart first came to Luton, the area around Kenilworth Road had no Asians. 'I suppose there must have originally been what we may call white English. But when I came it was mainly Afro-Caribbean. Then they moved out and now it is mainly Asian.' Even here there has been change. 'Asians of Indian origin have moved out as they have made more money. Now it is Asians from Kashmir in Pakistan and Sylhet in Bangladesh in this area.'

Beech Hill was nearly 100 per cent Asian, with the Bangladeshis dominant – 65 per cent of the students were of Bangladeshi origin, which was hardly surprising, given that Luton has the second highest Bengali population in the country. And over the years it had retained its classical image of a poor community. 'There is', said Hart, 'a high proportion of the unemployed. In the eight years I have been here the majority of parents have been unemployed. The houses date from the 1900s, terraced housing, and it is a poor community.' So poor that most of the parents of the Asian children who went to Denbigh, another school near the ground, were unemployed.

Hart was keen to emphasise, 'They do love football. A lot show interest.' The problem was Beech Hill did not have the sports facilities of Dallow Road, another school. 'Unlike Dallow we haven't got a field,' said Hart. 'We are a typical inner-town school. That is our major difficulty. So, we play games on our playground but have to adapt the rules or play a different type of game.' The situation had worsened since Luton tore up its plastic pitch and went back to grass. 'The school and the club', said Hart, 'were much closer when they had a plastic pitch, as we could go down there and play. When the plastic was torn up they said we couldn't go. Our children play in the car park and there is not much sport at our school.'

The Beech Hill staff member who ran the football club for older boys on Friday was aware that he must finish in time to allow the Muslim children to go for their religious education. 'All our clubs', said Hart, 'finish at 4.15. With school finishing at 3.30, they can only play for half an hour. We have to finish by 4.15 because mosque classes start at 4.30. So, while other students who are not Muslims might play games or practise sports between five and seven, we can't. This would, obviously, not apply if mosque classes were not there.'

Contrary to what many had told me, Hart denied there was parental pressure on them not to play. 'As long as it does not interfere with other things that are considered more important, religious studies for instance.' However, he had noticed that on open days, parents were less interested in how their children were doing in sporting activities than in Maths, English and Science.

THREE

CHOCOLATE DROPS
AND GOLLIWOGS

'S adly, I used to fight.' The words are those of Brendon Batson, describing his early days as a black footballer. The way he spoke the words, and how he reflected on those events, shows there have been two Brendon Batsons. They also tell the story of how far English football has come since the seventies and how much further it still needs to go.

The first Brendon Batson I watched from the press box when he played for West Bromwich Albion, along with Laurie Cunningham and Cyrille Regis – the 'Three Degrees' as their manager Ron Atkinson dubbed them after the American pop trio of that name. They were making history because West Bromwich Albion were the first British club to field three black players. The club played some magical football in the 1978–79 season which, but for some of the worst winter weather Britain has seen, might have pipped Liverpool to the title.

The second Brendon Batson I met many years later. He was now not in shorts but in a suit. He was Brendon Batson the administrator under whose chairmanship I served on the board of Sporting Equals, the quango that promotes sport and physical activity among ethnic minorities. I got to know him well and call him Brendon. If the first Brendon was a rock-solid defender who made sure the gains made at the other end of the field by the brilliant attacking skills of Cunningham and Regis were not squandered, then this Brendon, asked to take over the chairmanship of Sporting Equals in a difficult period, was quite the best chairman I have ever served under in any committee – and I have served under a few in various committees. By this time he had been awarded an MBE, which he received in the 2000 New

Year's Honours List for services to football, to which was added the OBE in 2015, but he never once flaunted these awards. I would never have guessed he had been so honoured and only discovered that much later. And this is somebody who signed schoolboy forms with Arsenal at the age of 15, stayed on at school for an extra year 'not to any great extent', and left school without any qualifications.

I am talking to Batson in the middle of Covid, we cannot meet, and I am speaking to him in his home in Spain after he has just come back from walking his dog. We start with familiar banter about our football rivalry, his support for Arsenal and mine for Tottenham. But while our banter avoids the tribalism which so often marks the game now, when both sets of supporters call each other scum, when Brendon first started kicking a ball in England he would have considered 'scum' almost a polite word. And not just on the football field but wherever he went.

Batson's arrival in England is part of the Windrush generation story, the people from the Caribbean colonies coming to Britain expecting to find the motherland, only to discover that reality mocked what they had been told Britain would be like. This was not a welcoming mother longing for her child to return. This was more like the classic Hans Christian Andersen fairy tale of a wicked stepmother who did not even know she had a child and had no time for it.

Batson was born in Grenada in February 1953 and moved to Trinidad when he was six. Although that was his father's home, he says, 'I saw my father only twice in my life.' It was his mother who was his guiding star – 'my mum was fantastic' – and it was his mother who completely changed his life when he was nine years old:

> 'My mum sent my brother and me to England to live with my uncle and aunt. She joined us with my sister after two years. Trinidad was so cosmopolitan. We had mixed bloodlines in our family – Indian, Chinese. Then I came to a country where my colour stood out and I suddenly attracted abuse, and that required a mental adjustment. It was a shock.'

Batson's first port of call was Tilbury where he, his brother Godfrey, his Aunt Sybil, who was a midwife, uncle and their three kids were the only black family. In the streets they were the only black boys and easily identified. In the school, St Mary's, a Catholic school, there was racist abuse from the moment he stepped into the schoolyard:

> 'My first encounter of racism was as a nine-year-old in the junior school in a lab when I was called "the chocolate drop" by another boy.

I didn't quite understand why I would be called that. I remember it so clearly, but then I realised what it meant and don't forget, those days there were TV shows like *The Black and White Minstrel Show* [the BBC's long-running variety show (1958–78) in which white actors blacked up], and Robertson's jam with a golliwog [a caricatural image of a black man] on the label. So, all those names were being thrown at me and Godfrey.'

Many young white kids growing up then would have seen no racism in using such terms – some as grown-ups even now don't – and they would love to collect golliwog badges that Robertson's Jam, a staple at British breakfast tables and teatime meals, distributed. But for Batson it meant he was the outsider marked by his colour in a way he could not escape. Two years later his mother and his sister, Diane, who is the eldest of the siblings (Brendon is the youngest), arrived and the family moved to Walthamstow:

'Godfrey and I went to the same school in Walthamstow, McEntee Tech. He was four years older than me and nobody dared touch me when he was there, but once he left it was open season. It was hell. I used to fight from the first time because I just couldn't cope with being called names. That's when I had to defend myself. That was my default method in reaction to being called names. I fought well into my teens. It certainly taught me how to grow up.'

Before coming to England, Brendon had never seen football. 'I had no idea about football.' The only position he knew was goalkeeper. Despite this, even when he was at primary school, he took to the game. Dennis Sheridan, a fellow pupil, encouraged him, and Mr Fitzgerald, a Maths and English teacher, after suggesting he would be better suited to cricket, lent him football boots. Batson soon became an excellent defender. On the playing fields in the sixties it was lonely being a black player. 'I played in the Regent's Park League for my Sunday team. I think I was 14 before I played against another black lad on the opposition side, a mixed-race player.' But while 'the white players in my team did not call me names, the opposition players did. I was called a "nigger" or a "black whatever". I had plenty of that in particular at schoolboy level. There was no support mechanism. None whatsoever. I fought back.' He also responded with his fists when he played league football.

In 1971 Batson got a full contract and became the first black player to play for Arsenal in a league match, in a 2-0 defeat at Newcastle in 1972.

'I came on as sub for Charlie George because he was being sick at half-time. I did not play in my normal position. I played in midfield as a nuisance value. Malcolm Macdonald was playing for Newcastle. That was my first taste of the North East, and I took "dog's abuse" as we called it when I came on.'

Batson made nine appearances for the first team, but with Pat Rice in the team he knew he would never be a regular. In 1974 as a 21-year-old he transferred to Cambridge in the Third Division and that is when his response to racism showed what football was like in this country at that time. It was not the racist who was sanctioned but the man who was racially abused:

'Playing for Cambridge United I was sent off twice – against the same guy in actual fact. I never named him until Ron Atkinson put him in his book. Tony Coleman. [Atkinson says Coleman was making monkey-like gestures at Brendon.] We were playing Stockport County. When I was sent off the first time, I just lashed out and the referee was right next to me. I caught the player on the jaw, knocking him to the turf. I then walked off. We appealed against my sending off. In those days, you could have a personal hearing. Interestingly, the chairman of the disciplinary committee was Bert Millichip [then chairman of West Bromwich Albion]. He was only plain Bert. He didn't have his knighthood yet. The referee actually came up and spoke in my defence. He spoke about the provocation and I didn't get any sanction, but Bert Millichip warned me not to come back in front of them again. In the return fixture I was sent off again against the same player. We didn't bother appealing then. I got sent off a third time against a lad called Robin Friday. He played for Reading. A bit of a character. A cult hero at Reading, he passed away many, many years ago. A sad case.'

That Batson feels such sympathy for his tormentor shows his great generosity of spirit:

'Ron Atkinson turned me round a bit. This was Ron's first season as a manager in professional games, and his first season at Cambridge. I had had a bit of a reaction to another player in my own team in train-ing and he sent me off the training pitch and pulled me into his office in the afternoon. Ron had given me the nickname Batman. His famous words to me were, "Well, Batman, you'll always be black. What are you going to do, keep fighting?"'

This did make Batson cool down on the field of play, but Atkinson's words and Bert Millichip's warnings to Batson provide a revealing insight into how white people who ran football in this country saw race in the seventies. It could be argued that there had been tremendous progress on the race front since the sixties. Then Stanley Rous, chairman of FIFA, who is still revered as the great leader of English football, did not conceal his racism. After FIFA suspended South Africa in 1963, Rous headed a commission that went to South Africa and concluded that it was not FIFA business to change South African 'internal sports policy' and felt that facilities were widely available to all races to play the sport. He recommended the ban on apartheid South Africa be lifted, which was hailed by Vivian Granger, the manager of the white National Football League, as a 'defeat for communism'. Rous also played a huge part in the African boycott of the 1966 World Cup as FIFA decided that the continent could only get one place in the competition, and to get even that it would have to fight two other continents, Asia and Oceania.

Millichip, in accepting the referee's explanation of how Batson was provoked, showed we had moved from Rous's openly declared belief in white supremacy to one of white men prepared to give the black man a chance. Yet Millichip was still telling Batson that he must accept the white football world and its racism, and not want to change it. That was going too far.

In addition to being racially abused by opposition players, Batson had to put up with abuse from the fans. 'I would have the monkey chants. I had the N-word. Black bastard. The whole range. Nothing original. And I used to react.' Once, during a game at Bradford, when provoked by a fan who had thrown the ball back at him, he wanted to jump into the crowd to confront the fan but was stopped by John Docherty, Atkinson's assistant. 'There was', recalls Batson, 'actually also a National Front march up there that day. I was getting it full blast.'

He signed for West Bromwich Albion in January 1978 and his debut at Birmingham City saw him encounter his first banana on a football field:

> 'I had a horrendous debut against Birmingham City away. You had to come down the steps on to the pitch from the dressing room. It was a really horrible evening with a damp, greasy pitch. I stepped onto the pitch and I slipped. I looked down and I had stepped on a banana. I couldn't believe it. So those Birmingham supporters had come to greet me with a handful of bananas. That was their mentality.'

Although West Brom won 2-1, Batson had a terrible debut and what makes this match interesting is how the reporters and fans who were at the game reacted. Rob Downing of the *Express & Star* would tell Paul Rees for his book *The Three Degrees*:

'I think the debut was probably the worst I ever saw. All of us report-ers went up to Ron's office the next day and asked him for his thoughts on Brendon. He told us he'd come good. I shot back that he hadn't been good last night, because you could talk to Ron like that. He said, "Brendon will be all right, he'll prove himself." And he did.'

The Albion supporter John Holmer told Rees, 'Brendon was terrible that night. His positional sense seemed to be all over the place, and he couldn't control a ball for love nor money. He had come out of the Third Division and he looked lost.'

Neither man mentions the banana and it is not clear whether they did not know about it or did not think it worth mentioning. Batson slipping on a banana on his debut was a world totally foreign to Downing and Holmer and one not worth exploring. To be fair to Downing and Holmer, they were reflecting the age. When racist incidents occurred, the policy adopted by the crowd and the media, who were almost uniformly white, was to ignore it. As Batson puts it, 'It was quite a regular occurrence.'

There were exceptions to this cosy, collective amnesia, and Batson gives Gerald Sinstadt credit for being the first person to mention the abuse. But, as Gerald Sinstadt told Rees, it was not easy to talk about it on television. In 1978–79, the season after Batson's debut, Albion were playing some of the best football seen in the country and challenging Liverpool for the title. In December they played at Old Trafford in what was an epic match. Then, league matches were not televised, and the only live matches were the FA Cup final and England internationals. Edited highlights of league and cup games were broadcast. Sinstadt, hearing the booing of Regis by Manchester United fans, said in his commentary, 'Once again there is unsavoury booing of the black players, which says nothing for their sportsmanship at all.' Sinstadt was the only one to talk about it and, as he told Rees, 'There was this almost laissez-faire attitude to the abuse of black players. It was sort of accepted, which worried me greatly. I was determined to have a go about it at some point.' But because only edited highlights were being shown, it meant:

'Even with a great game like that one, you were lucky to get 30 min-utes on air. So, if you intended to have a go about something you had to judge when there was the most reasonable chance of making the edit . . . In a way it disappoints me I wasn't able to make a stronger point. But I got no comeback from what I said, either from ITV or the viewers.'

As Rees points out, 'It was then a taboo to report the racist abuse that was being regularly meted out to black players in the British game.'

Batson, after his retirement, did try and get the television companies to report such abuse:

'I was watching a game on television and heard the racist abuse directed at the players. I was so conscious of hearing through the television screens that I decided to have a word about it. I was told by the BBC it was not possible to make out what was being shouted. I had heard it and I thought their response was a joke.'

And, of course, this was a time when people referred to black players as 'coloured players', as Atkinson did after the Old Trafford match when selecting Regis as his man of the match and calling him 'one of the coloured front people'.

Atkinson, with his sharp eye for publicity, could also make them look like exotics, even if fitting a stereotype about blacks. When The Three Degrees group – three black women: Helen Scott, Valerie Holiday and Sheila Ferguson – were on their tour of Britain and visiting Birmingham, Atkinson persuaded them to visit the Hawthorns [the West Bromwich Albion ground]. He arranged a photocall with Batson, Regis and Cunningham. Batson recalls:

'The girls were wearing Albion strips and we wore fur coats. We were then paired off and wrapped in the fur coats with them. I was paired with Valerie. It was contrived.'

The photo was published in the *Evening Mail* and the *Express & Sta*r. The caption read, 'West Bromwich Albion's Three Degrees meet the three sizzling singers'. There were then 50 or so black players in the entire Football League and Atkinson's publicity stunt seemed ideal. Yet even as this stunt was making the headlines, what passed unnoticed was the hell these players were subjected to by the fans every time they took the field. Not at the Hawthorns where, Batson says, 'The West Brom supporters were absolutely fantastic. They helped me settle in really well.' But it was very different at away grounds up and down the country. However, he and his fellow Three Degrees, Cyrille Regis and Laurie Cunningham, never worried about going to away grounds:

'Oh, we never dreaded it. None of us, Laurie, Cyrille, me. I don't know many black players of my era dreaded going to away games because, don't forget, we grew up with racial abuse being hurled at us on a regular basis as schoolboys and young men. We had grown up with it, people driving past us in the street racially abusing us. I remember walking down the streets in Walthamstow, where I grew up, and cars with white lads would drive past, put their window down and shout, "Black 'this', go home. Why don't you go back to your country?" and all that sort of stuff. We were hardened to it. I knew some of my brother's friends who could all handle themselves as well. At Cambridge I was getting a lot of abuse, and I remember going to places like Bradford and Leeds and getting abuse. But what changed when I joined West Brom and began playing in the top flight was the volume of abuse we received. I thought there will be safety in numbers. And the three of us would win people over. We didn't. It seemed to incite them. And don't forget, this was not long after the "Rivers of Blood" speech at Wolverhampton of Enoch Powell.

'The National Front were recruiting at football grounds. We saw them as we came up in our coach to the ground. In their bovver boots and their Union Jack. And as we were getting off the coach, they would hurl abuse at us. There would be spit on our jackets. There was no protection. The authorities did nothing. It is ironic. Many years later, Manchester United players arriving at Liverpool had their coach sprayed with something and that is when they started having secure entrances for the players. They don't have to run the gauntlet of home supporters. In those days you were stepping out of the coach on to a pavement most of the time and walking into the players' lounge. I remember at Chelsea the National Front handing out leaflets. Leeds was a very hostile place as well. I thought sometimes, they don't have any black people up there. But we weren't afraid; we weren't intimidated in any way. Cyrille famously said he would just be angry and he would bang them in the back of the net and take the points. It's great credit to the black players of my era that despite all the abuse that kept on coming in ever-increasing numbers, they kept going.

'It's hard to differentiate between any of them, but I think the biggest shock I had was actually playing West Ham in the 1979–80 season – Laurie by then had gone to Real Madrid. It was a Saturday afternoon at Upton Park. We ran out for the warm-up. I tended to just run across the pitch and have a little bit of a sprint. On this occasion, I did this without realising I'm running into a bank of West Ham supporters. As I ran across, I saw a whole lot of bananas coming towards me. Cyrille was not far behind me. I just stopped and looked, and they were landing all around me, so I picked one up and started peeling it. I threw one to Cyrille, and Cyrille [Brendon laughs as he says this] tucked it in the waistband of his shorts. Because we didn't know what to do.'

When other black players got together, they did not discuss their racist experiences: 'Sometimes when we got together for a meal and we had received a racist letter, we'd read it out and have a laugh about it. But it wasn't a big topic of conversation.'

Batson is full of praise for Ron Atkinson and his white teammates for being supportive. But it is a measure of what black players of the '80s expected that Batson calls his 'teammates fantastic. And they were really supportive', despite the fact that they said no words to reassure Batson or the other black players. 'We didn't need them to be saying, "Oh, don't worry about this or that", to reassure us, because we were strong characters.' Given all this it came as a complete shock to Batson when on the evening of 21 April 2004, while commentating on the first leg of Chelsea's European Champions League semi-final against Monaco in France (which Chelsea lost 3-1) Atkinson used the N-word. Thinking he was off air, he referred to Chelsea's Marcel Desailly, a French international defender of Ghanaian origin, as a 'lazy fucking nigger'. Actually, the ITV broadcast was still being carried in the Middle East and soon the world knew:

> 'Cyrille and I could not believe what we had heard. I had just flown in from Barbados that morning. I didn't see the game, only the result. I just got home when I got called from the press and I rang Ron. We didn't have a really long conversation because he just never explained anything. He just had no explanation. I think he thought the mic was off, which makes it even worse. He never apologised. I can't explain why he used that word because all his actions previously never gave any indication that he held those sorts of views. I remember going to functions celebrating ten years of Kick It Out and Ron would be one of the few managers there in support of that campaign. I'm not calling him a racist because I think things are said. Sometimes people get carried away with themselves. But I have no idea why those words came out of his mouth.'

Atkinson in *Big Ron, A Different Ball Game* gave an insight into how he saw race. In a chapter entitled 'The Three Degrees' – for some reason he spells Brendon's name 'Brendan' – Atkinson wrote that 'the race card has, in my view, been dealt too often on the sporting table. It is an issue that should be approached with mellowed understanding and humour, not political correctness and the prejudice of personal agendas', and that 'as a committed champion of black footballers, banter and humour were the weapons to fight back with. Aggro causes lasting grief all round; it is not the formula for understanding or reaching common agreement.' How curious that Atkinson on race was taking Gandhi's non-violent attitude to hate and violence. He also said Batson was 'carrying a chip on his shoulder and forever smouldering about the colour question'. Atkinson described how, when he was at West Bromwich Albion, an Everton supporter would write to him saying, 'Atkinson, are you bringing those monkeys to play against us again? We don't want them here – they should be sent back to the jungle.' Atkinson's response, which he narrates with some pride, was:

> 'Deliberately, I used to call Cyrille, Laurie and Brendan [sic] across to read it. They treated it as a joke but, amazingly, we usually finished up with very good results on our trips to Goodison Park. Wonder why? I didn't need to motivate anybody.'

Atkinson was so certain that his view of how to deal with racism was right that he wrote that 'the vast majority of black players would subscribe to that philosophy'. By the time Atkinson wrote his memoir a new generation of black players had emerged, and Atkinson was not happy with the way they reacted to racism:

> 'Seriously, no matter how much I genuinely admire that early, pioneering generation of black footballers, I have never been too happy with what came later. There was an alarming period, created by a more resentful, openly hostile element, when the race issue threatened to become very volatile. This second wave of black players – not all but dangerously enough of them – seemed to be hell-bent on stirring up the whole unsavoury atmosphere once more. I saw it as reverse racism and a worrying tendency that might destroy so much encouraging progress. This minority came into the game, brash and swaggering and full of arrogance, with an attitude that the world owed them a living, simply because they were born black. They certainly didn't do their race any particular favours and, absolutely no question, didn't behave anything like as well as the great black personalities who paved the way in earlier years . . . These latter-day stars weren't like the earlier generation, who were mostly happy guys, squaring up to the world's daily demands with a smile. Now all we had were growing [sic] men with a chip on their shoulder, so morose and sullen, and apparently reluctant to build relationships with their white team-mates. Maybe they had been brainwashed. Maybe they were innocents being exploited for racist purposes by more sinister forces who saw some mileage in their public fame. Ask me if there was a secret agenda, and I just don't know the answer.'

Atkinson also mentions that there were some players, 'senior pros, mostly' who were 'quite anti the Three Degrees.' He says he hasn't forgotten the names 'but I'll protect their anonymity, even though they may not have earned or deserved it'. The logic is interesting. White racists he would not name. But black players racially abused should learn to take it on the chin. But even as Atkinson published his book in 1998, a whole generation of black players were born, like Raheem Sterling (born 1994) and Marcus Rashford (born 1997) who, as they grew up, made it clear that by keeping silent on racism you do not deal with the scourge.

Batson is well aware that people of this generation, including his son, cannot understand how he dealt with the racism. We are speaking a day after his son's birthday:

> 'He is 42, living in still a very white country, Slovenia. He has got a fantastic circle of friends and it is lovely to see the way he has integrated into that society. He wouldn't put up with some of the stuff I put up with. He says, "Dad, how did you put up with it?" I say, "Listen, Jason, it was different. When we grew up, we had to make our way within the environment we were in at the time." The present generation are living in a different way. They have got a much higher profile and a bigger platform than we had, and they use it to great effect.'

However, Batson does not agree that players should walk off the pitch when faced with abuse:

> 'We've come too far to let them drive us off the pitch, because that's where we want to carry on our sport and our profession. I don't think it should be left to the players to do that, anyway, it should be up to the clubs, to the managers, to the board of directors. But I will support any player who felt he's had enough and wants to walk off.'

Yet for all the racist abuse and bananas he had to cope with, Batson never once thought of leaving the game:

> 'No. My mum bought us up in a very strong way in terms of "stand up straight and look the world in the eye". We didn't look for a support mechanism. We handled it ourselves. I think I had an easy ride in football because when I hear what my brother had to go through, it was much worse. He was an apprentice electrician. A lot of lads I knew were working on production lines for the Ford company and places like that. The names they were called and the abuse they took day in, day out was horrendous. So, luckily, I had an easy ride. I did

not feel like wanting to give up the game. I was fortunate, Mihir; the game was very good to me. Take away all the abuse I had to take from the spectators, the game helped me being involved and meeting people on the way.'

This praise for the game may seem strange. Batson wanted to become a manager and only ever got one interview when he applied for a job:

'I got my A licence in 1983. I would have liked to have had a crack at becoming a manager. I was only 31 when I retired because of a knee injury and I just thought I knew the game reasonably well and would like to throw my hat in the ring, just to see. I was one of the first to try and become a manager. But I never really got a chance. I cannot remember now how many clubs I wrote to. It was not many because I was casting my net very small and low down, so to speak. I did not write to any of the old First Division clubs. I felt I had no chance. I did not get many replies. The only interview I got was from my previous club, Cambridge United. Our generation was too early for becoming managers. But you have to look now at the modern game and how many black managers are there? We are still having this conversation that we were having back in the early eighties.'

Unable to become a manager, Batson became the rare black man in a suit in the committee rooms of organisations that run English football:

'I was approached by Gordon Taylor [then Chief Executive] to join the management committee of the PFA [Professional Footballers Association]. The PFA when I went in was still a white man's club. But I did not find any racism in the PFA. The PFA was a welcoming world, and it was a joy to be on the committee.'

Batson was the first black member of the management committee and in the spring of 1984 accepted Taylor's offer of a full-time job at the PFA. He remained there for 18 years, latterly becoming Taylor's deputy. He is now the chairman of the PFA Charity. We are speaking about Taylor, the highest paid trade unionist in the country with earnings of £2 million a year, having left the PFA with many ex-players critical of his leadership and how the PFA is run. But Batson will not hear any criticism of him, which may reflect the fact that here was a white man giving a black man a chance when other white men shunned him. Batson also feels very strongly that football has not acknowledged how the PFA led the way in tackling racism:

'Kick It Out was the initiative of Herman Ouseley and the PFA. The FA and other organisations said we didn't need it. It was David

Davies [then head of FA communications] in the end who dragged them into it.'

Batson thought taking the knee was 'excellent'. But:

'At the moment I don't see anything on the horizon that suggests there's going to be significant change to what we are already experiencing. When we started Kick It Out in 1993, we had to encourage clubs to get rid of the graffiti. Stadiums are much more welcoming places than when I first started playing. We should applaud how far we've come in the battle against racism, but at times I think we've hardly made any progress on the way.'

The reason for his pessimism is what he saw when, following the murder of George Floyd in May 2020, Batson went to a couple of the Black Lives Matter protests in Birmingham.

'It was very uplifting. It was fantastic to see so many young kids, black, white, all different colours supporting that. But in the Black Lives Matter protest I saw a student interviewed in his early 20s and he was saying things that I said in a similar fashion about what I was experiencing then. I've been retired since 1983, 1984. I started playing in 1969. I talk about my experience when I came here in 1962 and I hear the same things being spoken about now. So, you tell me how much progress we've made. Things have improved, but how much have they improved and where are we going to go from here?'

Listening to Batson it is hard to avoid the conclusion that while we may have moved on from the days of the chocolate drop and golliwogs, fundamental change is still some distance away.

FOUR

THE BEST-KEPT SECRET

The best-kept secret is almost the first thing Ricky Hill tells me when I talk to him. It refers to his race and shows how complicated the race story can be. Even settled narratives, like that of the Windrush generation, do not tell the whole story.

I have in front of me Hill's book *Love of the Game: The Man Who Brought the Rooney Rule to the UK*, which was published in March 2021. In it he mentions he is the first player of South Asian heritage to play for England. The words have jumped out at me. During my years covering football I had seen Hill play often for Luton, part of the glittering array of black stars David Pleat had put together there, but I had never imagined he was South Asian. Now it turns out his ancestors lived not far from mine in India.

'Yes,' Hill says, 'that's probably been the best-kept secret throughout my whole career.'

The story he tells me has echoes of the story of the family of V.S. Naipaul, the Nobel laureate. Like the Naipauls, Hill's ancestors were indentured, or bonded, labourers. While the slave trade was abolished in 1807, the British Empire still required cheap labour and, starting in 1830, malnourished Indians were exported to the Caribbean, in what the historian Hugh Tinker in his seminal book called *A New System of Slavery*. Like Naipaul, Hill's great-grandfather came from Uttar Pradesh, and Hill pronounces the name of India's biggest state perfectly, just as an Indian would. Naipaul's ancestors went to Trinidad, as most Indian indentured labourers did; Hill's great-grandfather and great-grandmother went to Jamaica. This would have meant 26 weeks at sea from Calcutta, then the capital of British India, to Jamaica in what was called a 'coolie ship', with Hill's great-grandfather berthed separately from his great-grandmother in long, gloomy decks lit by coconut-oil lamps. They would have worn regulation clothes and had an identity disc to mark them as coolies; they would have had to put up with the sharp language of the recruiter. The journey was not as dreadful as the one endured by blacks transported as slaves from Africa, but much longer and grim enough even so. In Jamaica, the barracks Hill's great-grandfather and great-grandmother occupied were called 'Nigger Yard', denoting the slaves who were once housed there.

'To a degree,' says Hill, 'it was a form of slavery. They worked the land of a J.W. Hill. And when my grandfather was born, they registered my grandfather in his name.' But while they may have acquired the name of their master, they retained their Indian, Hindu traditions, as much of the family still does, except for Ricky's father. He went outside the Indian circle to find a black bride:

> 'My parents knew each other from back in Jamaica. They had grown up in the same region in Kingston, went to the same Sunday school and church, but they never got together romantically in Jamaica. It wasn't until they came to the UK that they actually met again, reconnected and decided they were going to get married. I know it was difficult for my mother at times because she was predominantly the only black woman. She often said they would have liked my dad to have married someone from an Indian background.'

But why did Ricky Hill deliberately keep his Asian origin quiet?

> 'As far as I was concerned, I was a black Caribbean. My dad was born in Jamaica, my grandad was born in Jamaica. If you looked at me, my family, my sister and my brother, there are traits; we are not totally black African. My eyes or my hair, the texture of it and my skin tone look slightly different.'

There is a picture in Hill's book of a family photo showing Ricky as a small boy with his father's hand across his shoulder. Ricky does look a bit different from his cousins, but it is still very much an Indian family photograph that I would identify with: 'That is an Indian family. This is Indian in every respect apart from the fact that we were born in Jamaica.'

It could be argued that in keeping his racial origins secret, Hill was keeping in step with the traditions of English football of his era. Hill's club, Luton, was managed by David Pleat, who for many years tried to keep his own Jewish origins secret. Pleat is the anglicised version of Plotz, which was the family surname of Pleat's Lithuanian ancestors. Pleat was initially reluctant to talk to Anthony Clavane for his book *Does Your Rabbi Know*

You're Here?, the classic study of Jews in English football. Clavane's chapter on Pleat is entitled 'The Invisible Jew' and Pleat, whose football career began as a 17-year-old with his home club Nottingham Forest, told Clavane, 'When I first started in football something always used to crop up, like a moronic centre-half in a dressing room saying, "He is a Jew, you know."' Hill says, 'Initially, we didn't know Pleat was Jewish. It came to light, possibly when I was 20, 21 and had been at Luton for four years.'

But while Hill with his anglicised name could pass off as an Afro-Caribbean, he could not, unlike Pleat, hide his skin colour while growing up in Cricklewood in the sixties:

'You go up Cricklewood to a youth club over in Kilburn, and it's predominantly white, and then you get the: "What are you doing here? You are not really welcome here." You would stay and stand your ground. But there was always that tension, where you felt it could kick off at any given time. And we were in a couple of fist fights when we were about 14, 15. But that was no big thing. It was just part of the journey. We were always told by our parents, "You have to never give up, whatever you want to do. Be ambitious. Commit yourself, throw yourself into everything that you possibly can educationally. And if sport is your thing, do it to the best of your ability, but always recognise that you have to be at least twice as good as someone who is white, to even be noticed. And even then, it may not be enough. Because that's just the way it is." So, we were always guided that we can never be complacent. We can never take things for granted; we always have to be the best that we can possibly be every day of our life if we want to achieve our ambition. But it never made me say that I wasn't equal to someone white.'

Not being seen as Asian meant he avoided the then stereotypical thinking that Asians could not play football at all. 'I was saved by that.' However, he did carry the black footballer's burden:

'The doubts that they [the white coaches and managers] had were: Do they like the cold weather? Can they head the ball? Do they have the character? Can they take information and conduct themselves? Did they have a sound mind whereby they wouldn't freeze or bottle it? Now, when I look back and think of all those false stereotypical statements that were put out against black people, things that we had to go through, more so than our white contemporaries, if we weren't made of steely stuff, we would never [have] got past this space, speaking in baseball terms. And not only did we have to prove that we were good enough to play, we were also automatically recognis-able because we were different: one black man and 21 other white players on the field of play. Or when Brian Stein came to Luton, in 1977–78, two years after I made my first team debut for Luton, it was Brian and I and 20 other white players. So, anything that Brian and I did would be highlighted, spotlighted, projected, and if we were playing badly, everyone would know it is "them, they are playing badly". So, we had the whole package of obstacles that were denying us entry initially. And then to navigate a career for that longevity took some doing.'

Hill's uniqueness lies in that he became a midfield general at a time when it was generally thought blacks did not have the intelligence required to play in that vital position. The feeling in English football in the seventies was that black players may be good defenders and their pace would make them wingers, but they could not control the game from midfield. Yet Hill, who made his Luton debut in 1976, five months after joining the club, got into the first team as a right midfielder of a three-man midfield. The other two midfielders were the white players, Alan West and Pasquale Fuccillo, an Italian born and bred in Bedford who had been at Luton for many years. So, how did Hill break through this racial curtain?

'I decided to become a central midfielder because I thought if I was a striker, I was reliant on someone playing me the ball. If I was a defender, then I am nullifying what I believed were my creative gifts to the game. Even as a young child I saw myself as the guy that gets on the ball, has the most touches, has got the most ability. Whether it was naivety, or just conceit, I don't know. It just felt so natural to be able to go anywhere I wanted on the football field, to support the front, to help the back, to get the ball from knock-downs. I never looked and thought that there is no one of my colour playing in midfield.'

One white man, also an outsider, helped Hill break through the glass ceiling:

'I had been ignored by the system but was spotted playing for my school. David Pleat was one of the three who witnessed me playing away for my school in Hertfordshire and invited me for a trial at Luton. David was very instrumental in my career. I knew there were other managers who didn't think that way. In that era, from the late sixties into the seventies, there were managers who had come out and categorically stated they wouldn't sign a black player. David Pleat was someone who had the foresight and the courage to say, "Well, if they're good enough for my team, that's all I'm interested in. I don't care really, if they're black, white or green." So, from that perspective, I found a perfect environment.'

This extended to Hill's white Luton teammates:

'I was in and around the first team for the first couple of years on my own as a black person, and my teammates didn't treat me any differently. In fact, they embraced me all the way through. I never had another player in all the time that I played for Luton Town who called me a black so-and-so to my face. In the dressing room I never encountered one moment's problem at Luton in respect to colour. And I'm proud to stand here and applaud my fellow contemporaries and ex-teammates and opponents. Not one of the people that I competed against said anything to me with a racial connotation. I would be abused, but never regarding my colour. Pat Van Den Hauwe trod on me in the box when I was on the floor, on my face. I didn't know at the time, but Brian Stein was in the stand and he told me, "That player done you." That wasn't very nice, but Pat didn't say you black this and that. And people have obviously fouled me, and I have broken my leg from challenges, had eyes split open through elbows, but no one's ever used the racial slur at the same time.'

Nor did Hill face any racial abuse from the Luton fans. However, what Hill did not know was:

'There was a National Front presence when I got to the club, within the supporters in the Oak Road section. And unbeknown to me they were handing out leaflets urging fans to join the National Front. I had been at Luton maybe 18 months, and I wasn't playing on that Saturday for whatever reason, when Laurie Cunningham came down with Leyton Orient. I remember him playing on the right wing and giving our left back a really difficult time. And I vividly remember that when he was going down the right wing and doing what Laurie did best, he was getting the monkey noises "Ugh, Ugh, Ugh, Ugh." I came out later that week in the press and said, "Well, I'm disappointed to hear that because if our fans are doing that to Laurie, then they would do that to me. And Brian. And I don't think that's the right way to conduct yourself here. And if you are for me, you won't do that. If you do that to Laurie, then you can't be for me." So, from that moment, to be honest, I never had any opposing players who were black or Asian getting any of that kind of treatment at Kenilworth Road.'

Racists and 'Que Será, Será'

But if racists at Luton's Kenilworth Road home ground could be dealt with through one appeal in the press, it was a totally different story when Hill played away. Like many black players of his generation, the further north he travelled, the worse was the abuse:

'The first time I experienced real abuse was at Burnley in my first away match. It was terrible. They sang two songs about me by the time kick-off came. At 2.30 it was just "ugh, ugh, ugh, ugh" monkey chants, and the statements were "Go home! Go back to where you come from! You are a coon." By three o'clock, as I came out – and I was the only black player on the field, just 17 years old – they started singing a song. They used the Doris Day musical background of "Que Será, Será", singing, "He is a coon, a coon is blacker than you and me and it is plain for us to see. He is a coon, he is a coon." And this was three-quarters of the crowd. The Burnley crowd was entirely white. The team was entirely white. There was always verbal racial abuse at Burnley, Newcastle, Everton. At Newcastle, Brian Stein, me and the black players had on occasions to run in at half-time with our shirts over our heads, because father and son would be leaning over the side and spitting. Everton was always bad. In 1987 playing against Everton at Goodison, I broke my leg when tackled by Peter Reid. I sat there easing myself over the touchline waiting for Dave, our physio, to arrive from the other side of the field. I got terrible abuse while I was incapacitated, unable to move from the Everton fans. "Nigger! Fuck off, wog! Coon!" they shouted. And I'm sitting right against the touchline. And I looked into the crowd, waved and said, "I hope you have a good week in the factory next week." I said this to try to lighten the mood. When receiving abuse, I used to wave. It was one of my default positions. I used to hear the monkey chants frequently, because I used to take throw-ins and then I was right next against the crowd. At West Ham, which was volatile, racist and just aggressive in general, the fans were right on top of you, and you could hear every comment being made. You could hear the sounds and I would try to isolate where the projection of the voice was coming from. I would turn around and look in that direction. I'd have the ball in one hand and I'd lift my hand up in the front of me. And I'd wave that hand towards that area. And those around would start laughing. And the joke would have been turned on the person who was saying whatever they were saying.'

Hill had to devise his own way of dealing with it because he knew he could receive no support from his manager or his white teammates:

'In my whole career I never had one manager even mention the abuse that I or Brian or any other black player received. It was as if it wasn't taking place. Not even David Pleat said anything. My white teammates never said anything. When I was abused at Burnley as a 17-year-old, I looked at one of my white teammates and he had sadness in his eyes. There was this helplessness in their appearance as they heard the abuse. It was something weird. I don't know whether they didn't know what to say. Or they felt if they said something, it would highlight it and maybe expand it. I wouldn't say they were in denial. I would say they probably didn't know how to address it. They didn't know what words of comfort they could give.'

This is, of course, a world away from Raheem Sterling's generation, who are ready to walk out if abused and know their white teammates will join them:

'We couldn't have done that then. It is slightly different because there is a 30 per cent black labour force on the field of play. For me, or any of the black players, we couldn't say, "Okay, I'm going to walk off now." Or look at my teammates and say, "Are you going to back me up? Let's walk off." Or look at the manager. If we had done that, we wouldn't have progressed to where we are now. If I and my fellow black players from that generation – Cyrille Regis, Brendon Batson, Garth Crooks, Chris Hughton, Brian Stein, Mark Stein, Paul Canoville, John Fashanu, Justin Fashanu – had walked off, then the industry would have said, "They can't handle it. Yeah, they're not made of the right stuff. Don't bother with them. They are volatile. They've got a little bit of a character deficiency." And that would have been all they would have said. They wouldn't have had to justify why black players would have had to put up with this kind of abhorrent abuse that no one else has to put up with. One thing was certain, that we couldn't afford to show weakness of any sort, whether that was mentally or physically, because of the words that in those days were bandied about black players. "They won't come back for more. You know, they can't handle that." So that was always part of our journey.'

This journey would see Hill selected by Bobby Robson as part of his first England squad when he became England manager in 1982:

'Bobby had always admired me and had tried on occasions to get David Pleat to sell me, saying "When are you going to sell me your boy?" I got into the England squad and there were six black players: Viv Anderson, Mark Chamberlain, Cyrille Regis, Luther Blissett, John Barnes and me, and it was wonderful. I heard rumours that certain members of the FA had made comments to suggest that "Was it necessary to have so many black players in there at the same time?" Now, whether Bobby took any notice of that or not, I have no idea. He treated me fabulously – apart from not playing me when I believed I should have been playing.'

Hill's lament is understandable. He played only three times, a match against West Germany his only 90 minutes against a world-class team. Hill's cause was not helped by Alf Ramsey saying that Hill was somebody he wouldn't go to war with:

'I was deeply offended because if I didn't have a certain toughness within me, I wouldn't even have ascended to the level where I ascended to internationally. I would have crumbled at the first obstacle when I went away from home and someone shouted obscenities at me and made derogatory statements about my colour, and I'm on my own in a wholly white environment. So, for someone as successful as Sir Alf Ramsey and who didn't know me, who I'm not even sure had much interaction with black people, to come up with that was a slur against my character.'

Ramsey, of course, was reflecting the general white view of black players. In 1983, a year after Robson had called up Hill, *Shoot!*, the most popular football magazine of the time, when discussing how black players were emerging, had said:

'Twenty years ago the chances of Cyrille managing to bridge the gap between non-league football and the big time would have been strictly limited. Black men did not play league football in those days. The trouble with most black footballers hoping to make a career in the British game in those days was that they bore all the physical attributes necessary to play but had glaring weaknesses in technique and attitude. They often lacked commitment, they struggled to concentrate for a full 90 minutes and tended to wilt under pressure.'

Hill's generation proved Ramsey wrong, and Hill was an 'inspirational figure' for players like Ian Wright who recalls with gratitude Hill going to watch Wright play for Ten Em Bee, an all-black team in London. But if this first battle for equality was won, Hill's angst is that four decades after his generation broke through, a second battle for equality has to be fought to get the game to accept black coaches:

'It stems from the stereotypical statements that we started with, Mihir, that we did not have the brains, the acumen or the education or the ability to lead. This falsehood created by the industry was allowed to permeate throughout the industry. That black players were only good because they were quick, because they were strong. And they can defend, but we were never classed as being that person who had football running through his body. That his soccer IQ is on such a level that this person is now going to be a very good coach because he should be able to empower others with that intelligence and knowledge. Irrespective of how stylistically I played my game, and people would be eulogising me and be in awe of it, they never ever thought, "Well, if he does that as an individual, what would his team be like? How does he teach the game? How does he innovate within the game?" That conversation was never raised and is still never raised where black managers are concerned. The first battle for equality we were able to win just through visually being able to display our ability. The second one as a coach is impossible because without having an opportunity, we cannot show what we are capable of creating.'

Hill, who after getting his coaching badges went to the US to work as a coach, has tried to provide American ammunition to win this English battle. In 2004 he started a campaign to persuade English football to accept the NFL Rooney Rule established in 2003, which required the National Football League [NFL] to interview minority candidates for head coaching and football operation positions and increased black coaches in the NFL. But Hill feels the version accepted by English football is pointless as it has too many caveats. It means a black, Asian or minority ethnic candidate may be interviewed for an Under-18 coaching role, but for a senior role, white candidates are still preferred:

'When appointing a coach, someone from the same cultural background, someone who looks like the interviewer, someone who would be the so-called acceptable face of the club, will always prevail.'

Despite receiving three Coach of the Year Awards in the US, until 2019 Hill had received only one reply to 'countless applications for coaching roles' in England. This was from Alex Ferguson. He had a two-hour interview for a job coaching Manchester United reserves, and when Ferguson turned him down he rang to explain why he was not being selected: Manchester United were going in a different direction. Even Luton, having appointed him as manager, sacked him after four months.

So, is there white privilege in football?

'I don't know if you want to say it is white privilege. It is white dominance. There's a disproportionality in terms of black ex-players retiring and being able to continue having some form of employment and life within the game for the next 40 years of their life, as opposed to our fellow white ex-players who, if they so choose, can somehow find themselves being able to navigate a pathway into the game a lot easier than we can as black players. This disproportionality over the last 30 years is something that Britain should not be proud of. The football industry continues to harbour white personnel who can, within the industry, find a way to serve the game. Whereas black and Asian ex-players are deemed to be just labour. And what we have to offer, after our playing careers, is not really being embraced by the system.'

There is no mistaking the anguish in Hill's voice as he says:

'That first generation of black players, born and schooled in the UK, who in the mid seventies forced their way in is, most definitely, a lost generation. We only have Chris Hughton from that generation, who's a flag bearer and has managed to last the course within the industry. Outside of that, there's no one over the 60-year-old bracket who's working currently in professional football. Whilst we have great white older custodians of the game, like Sam Allardyce, who maintain a career and standing at the highest level of the game, the 60-plus-year-old black British first generation black players have not had a proper opportunity within the industry in the past 30 years.'

I spoke to Hill before Nottingham Forest's dreadful start to the 2021–22 season saw Hughton sacked in September 2021. Yet Hughton was still a black ex-player who has stood alone in the managerial world, a player I had often seen play for Tottenham and interviewed many times. He was indeed an exception.

FIVE

ALL ON HIS OWN

I am speaking to Chris Hughton as he is driving home and I have asked him of the problems faced by black players trying to become managers. Until now he has been speaking in his characteristic, gentle style, but now responding to my question, like a player suddenly showing an acceleration of speed, he begins to emphasise each word as if to make sure I do not miss the significance of any of them:

> 'There is no doubt that it is harder for an ex-black player to get a manager's job than an ex-white player. It is unconscious racism, but it's what we went through. We went through eras of stereotypical views of black players: they are fast, they are strong, but they're not really captain material, they're not really management material, they are not great organisers. That was a stigma that existed for years. And in some quarters, probably, it still exists.'

Hughton has the sort of managerial CV that no other black ex-player has: managing Newcastle, Birmingham, Norwich, taking Brighton to the Premier League and keeping them up, and then at Nottingham Forest. A career that has seen him become the first black manager to win the Premier League Manager of the Month award. An Irish international, he has also been assistant manager of the Republic of Ireland team.

In the past when I have interviewed Hughton he has not spoken much about race.

Now he opens up on race and his experiences going back to his childhood. The son of a Ghanaian father and an Irish mother, he was aware that when his mother came to England 'there was a lot of racism towards the Irish and, of course, towards blacks as well'. But:

'They never really spoke about the sort of racial experiences they would have had. All they tried to teach me was about working hard and trying to be as respectful as you can. Save your money. Try and get on in life. These are the values that they inculcated in us.'

His parents are still alive, and he says with a note of satisfaction in his voice, 'They have both had their jabs. They are proud of me. But I am very proud of them.'

Mixed-race couples were rare in the fifties. But while his parents may have not told him about their racial trauma, Hughton, who has always regarded himself as black 'because to me you were either white or black', knew from his youth that his colour made him a target:

'I was brought up in a very multicultural area, in Upton Park, about ten minutes from West Ham. Racism was something we were used to as a kid growing up. We didn't live in racial harmony. I knew places that were very racist in the East End. You couldn't go there. I remember on one occasion going out with my friends to a place in Leytonstone. This would have been probably in the late seventies. I was at Tottenham, but I wasn't in the first team. I remember what happened very well because I still have some of those black friends. The place we went to played soul music. As we came out of the place, we saw there was a huge group of white fellas outside armed with sticks and we had to do a runner.'

At Tottenham, where he had signed schoolboy's forms at the age of 13, he made his debut in the first team in 1979 and another reality based on his colour confronted him. He was part of one of the most talented and cosmopolitan dressing rooms in the country: Glenn Hoddle, the most gifted English midfield player of his generation, Ossie Ardiles, an Argentinian World Cup winner, and his fellow Argentinian Ricky Villa. Hughton stood out as the lone black player in the dressing room – and often on the field of play. Unlike other black players, Hughton never had a banana thrown at him, but:

'I was called racist names consistently in football. I had loads of arguments with players and supporters of opposition teams who would call me a black so-and-so all the time. Not Tottenham fans. In my era, you would go away from home and you would get racial abuse continually. There were two types of abuse: group ones and abuse from individuals. The monkey chants would be the group ones. Sometimes it would also be racial chants from a group of supporters. You heard it very clearly. The little bit more confrontational one was when the ball had gone into the crowd. You are trying to get the ball back and somebody is calling you an effing black so-and-so. Up north was bad. Probably the hardest places. It's very hard for a lot of people to comprehend what we went through. But we went through it, and you had to be mentally strong to get through it.'

Did he ever think of giving up football?

'No. Never. But for me, Mihir, racism in football was also a reflection of society. Football was no different from society. There were certain areas in society where you could go and certain areas where you knew you couldn't go. You knew that if you went into a pub there was every chance, depending on where it was, that the atmosphere in the place would be racist. Football was no different. The National Front would be outside distributing their literature saying, 'Get your colour supplement now.' Football accepted that racism was part of life. It was something in the game. Yes, it made me angry. And at times you reacted to the crowd, but you were very much your own. You did it by yourself. You did not turn to your parents or anybody else. Because it was always the attitude that you had to be better than them. You have to be stronger than that and you have to get on with it. I never had conversations with anybody at the club about the racial abuse I got.'

He never took up the racist abuse he received with his manager, Keith Burkinshaw, who fashioned a successful Tottenham team that in the eighties won the FA Cup twice and the UEFA Cup, the last time Tottenham won a European trophy:

'The reason was because you just got on with it. It wasn't a subject that we spoke about in the dressing room. I did not discuss it with Glenn or Ossie. It was something in the game. It was accepted. Remember, I was the only black player in the changing room.'

Things did change in the Tottenham dressing room when Garth Crooks, Mitchell Thomas and other black players came. 'Players started to realise that any type of racial banter you might have got away with before, you no longer could as there was a bit of a different attitude in the changing room.'

But when I ask him about any incidents from his early days, he sighs and says, 'I've never ever mentioned names before. I could do but I've never done. But there would have been numerous things that I would have heard even in our own changing room.'

As Hughton speaks he is pausing, searching for the right word to say, and I press him: 'Give me one incident.' Hughton sighs again. 'No, I can't. There would have been lots of references to black people. You would have heard some individual players on the football pitch, not Tottenham players, racially abusing other players from other teams.'

Hughton, a gentle man who hates confrontation, says:

'I'm encouraged by the fact that what we do have for players of today is a support mechanism. There's no doubt the changing room is completely different from what it used to be in the past. The younger players' starting positions are different from ours. Players have a platform. Through social media, through television. They are on the television far more than in my era. We had two football programmes: *Match of the Day* and *The Big Match*. We never got interviewed. It is different now. If a player gets racially abused now, then there is a support mechanism within that changing room. Not just black players but also white players as well. They [white players] are more aware, and something's done about it. It's not acceptable now. Where we are now to where I was [as a player] is chalk and cheese. When I played, you had to be strong, and your support network was really your friends.'

Yet for all the racist problems he suffered, and the fact that his generation of players earned nothing like what the present generation does, Hughton does not wish he was playing now:

'Irrespective of how racism was very prevalent in the game, I really enjoyed the era. We were able to enjoy life and have a bigger connection with supporters. After an away game we would have got a coach back to the training ground and then almost the whole team would have gone into the local pub for a couple of hours and talked about the game before we went home. Of course, if there were any supporters there, we would have spoken to them. Not every game. But a lot of the games.'

He regrets that that world has vanished.

What makes Hughton's managerial career very fascinating is that colour played no part in his becoming a manager. Indeed, he got on the first rung of the managerial ladder in the classic tradition of one mate helping another, the result of the bond formed in the Tottenham dressing room:

'The breakthrough for me was Ossie Ardiles getting the Tottenham job [in 1994]. Ossie rang me and said, "I'm just going to be offered the Spurs job and I'd like you to come in as my reserve team coach."

Strangely enough, I had taken my licence actually with Ossie. Ossie knew I wanted to coach. I stayed at Tottenham for another 14 and a half years as a coach, for a large majority of that time working with the first team and working with some seven different managers.'

How difficult has it been for Hughton to be a black manager in a sea of white faces?

'I was a coach for a long time. I was a coach at Newcastle and then I got the job at Newcastle. So, I think the pathway for a lot of black coaches was different and harder than mine. There is no doubt about that. Chris Ramsey said something to me once, and it's very much stuck with me. That we lost a generation of good black players, influential players, certainly the Cyrille Regis, Brendon Batson type of era, that never went into management, never went into coaching because of the unconscious racism that existed in life and existed in our game in that era.'

And on institutional racism his answer is unequivocal:

'When you look at the make-up of so many football boards and the FA board for so many years, then yes, I do think there was over a period of time. How can an FA structure exist that allowed black players to receive so much racial abuse? This was a system that turned a blind eye. The clubs did nothing about it. The football authorities did nothing about it until a later date and that was very much pushed by the various campaigns such as Kick It Out. If it happened now, then there would be people losing jobs because of how things have changed.'

But welcome as this is, there is no doubting the anger he feels about how the game has failed players of his generation:

'To me probably, Mihir, the biggest injustice, biggest shame is that it has taken this long from where I was and how it was in the late '70s. It has taken an incredibly awful incident to rush into where we are now. If people had said two years ago that the players would be taking a knee before games, I would say "certainly not". It took probably one horrible incident, the murder of George Floyd, for that to happen. So, if you had said to me in my era, would you have seen where we are now, I would have said no. This is to do with the modern-day media. So, if an incident like that happened many years ago, it would never have got the media time that this has. And it was seen throughout the world. And there had to be a reaction to it.'

As the most distinguished black manager in the game, does he feel he carries the burden of his entire race? That if he fails, people will say, 'Oh, black managers fail.'

'Burden is not the right word. I feel pressure as a black manager to do well. And that's more because I want to encourage more black players to coach and go into management. I have been told on many occasions, certainly in the community, that I'm seen as a role model for young aspiring black coaches. So, this is something that I'm very proud of. It is something that I accept. So, yes I do feel pressure in being a black manager because I want to be the best that I can. And I want to inspire as many young potential black coaches and managers as I can.'

The day we were speaking there had been a two-page article in the *Guardian* with the headline 'English football is consumed by racism and hatred':

'Racism will always be there. What will change are the legal parameters around it. We are now seeing more diversity on television, on Sky television, on adverts. We are seeing mixed-race couples in adverts, which was unthinkable a few years ago. And I do think that there will be changes in our game. Even though we haven't even seen the number of black managers that we would like, but certainly in the game there are far more black coaches at grassroots, academy level and Under-23 levels. If you look at what the FA are doing as regards diversity, the diversity code that has come out, I do see changes. Racism will always be there because it is emotional. And it will take a long time for perceptions and how people see diversity and see black people to change. But what will change is what is acceptable and what is not acceptable.'

Nobody can predict what will or will not be acceptable in the future. All we can be certain of is that it will surprise us. But then looking back at how the football world has changed it seems astonishing that such a world existed for quite so long.

A CHANGING WORLD

SIX

FROM NO BLACKS TO BLACK MAJORITY RULE IN SOUTH LONDON

'There is much more awareness of racism. It was something that was then brushed under the carpet.' The two eras being compared are that of Ian Wright and the modern era of Raheem Sterling and Marcus Rashford. The man doing the comparison is Alan Smith, who managed various football teams in South London, including Wimbledon and Crystal Palace. Smith's time in management would see the game there go on a journey from when there were no black players, even in non-league football – and this in South London, which had a large and growing black community – to a Palace team dominated by players like Ian Wright and Mark Bright. It also saw the emergence of one of Smith's protégés, Gareth Southgate, now rated as the most successful England manager since Alf Ramsey, heading a coaching team whose solitary black face is a black coach who had developed as a player in the youth teams of Palace when Smith was in charge there. And was a teammate of Southgate.

During the pandemic, after being with Alan Smith on a Zoom conference about sport, I rang to interview him. He began by telling me what he had told Gareth Southgate. Smith had made Southgate his captain at Palace. The two speak every other day and Smith watched the final of Euro 2021 in the company of Southgate's family. On this occasion, Smith told Southgate:

'I did something with Mihir Bose on Zoom, something about ice baths. Gareth said, "Alan don't make me laugh. When we were at Mitcham there was no hot water, and the bloody shower was freezing. So, there were ice baths long before our time." I said that is what I told Mihir we had. Gareth sends you his best.'

But if there was no need for ice baths in Mitcham in the 1980s, then the decade before that there were no black players – not just at Palace but in all the clubs in that area:

'When I went to coaching courses there weren't any black guys on it. The proportion of black players was quite small. At Dulwich Hamlet when I was manager, I brought the first black player to the club, John Cumberbatch. A defender, a very good player. I had brought John Cumberbatch to Wimbledon and when I moved to Dulwich from Wimbledon, I took him with me. That famous team that won the Southern League championship, under Allen Batsford, under whom I worked, certainly didn't have a black player. To be in a club in South London like Dulwich Hamlet, where I spent about four years, and not have a black player is just ridiculous. If you actually go and watch today's Dulwich Hamlet team, every player is a black player, and the manager is black and so is the coaching staff. That's a complete turnaround. Even when I first went to Wimbledon, which was in 1975–76, we didn't have a black player there at all. Those two clubs were both based in South London, and when you think South London, containing Brixton, Streatham and Norwood, is made up of quite large black communities, it was ridiculous not to have black players.'

It was still a very white world at Crystal Palace where Smith was appointed youth team coach by Alan Mullery in the 1983–84 season:

'At that time, the only black player we had was Vince Hilaire. Wonderful player, but he left pretty soon after I got there to go to Portsmouth. Vince Hilaire faced an incredible amount of racism. He was a winger, so he was always on the touchline and got the brunt of that abuse. That dreadful thing where people would throw bananas. Not from Palace fans. He was actually quite legendary at Palace. And it was clear, not for any political reasons but being based in South London, we had to bring black players in.'

The first stirrings of change came when Steve Coppell took over as manager in 1984. With Ron Noades, who had owned Southall and Wimbledon before buying Palace, Smith now formed part of a trio that began to hunt for players further afield than Palace had ever done before. The change, to a certain extent, was forced by the fact that Palace did not have a lot of money to spend.

'Andy Gray was one of our first black players. He came from Dulwich Hamlet, and so did Tony Finnigan. Ian Wright came from Greenwich Borough. And then coming up in the youth team we had Chris Powell. He went on to play for England. So, for the first time there was a breakthrough for black players.'

The result was that this historically dominant club of South London was transformed from a white enclave in the midst of one of the most concentrated black communities in the country to something more representative of the world around it. 'Most weeks there were probably more black players in our dressing room than there were white players.'

Did these black players who came to Palace face problems in the dressing room? 'Never. They were a bunch of the most powerful of the group. Andy was very outspoken. He worked in the market in Brixton while he was playing. They ran the changing room not because they were black, but because they were good players.'

The power of black players surfaced, most dramatically, at Anfield one Saturday:

'We were due to play Liverpool in an away game in the league. The club [Palace] had just got a sponsorship from one of the blue-chip manufacturers on some new tracksuits. The black players – Andy Gray, Mark Bright and Ian Wright – all said they didn't like the tracksuits. The black players always used to be smart. They had a way, and they had a style of their own. And I must admit it did look a bit cheap and nasty. So I went and saw Steve and said look, "We've got a bit of a rebellion. The lads won't wear the tracksuits." He said, "Alan, I couldn't care less. We've got enough problems beating Liverpool on Saturday, so don't let's digress. They can turn up in what they like." So, we turned up at Liverpool, and they all had different tracksuits. It pulled the team together in a way because they thought they'd sort of beaten the management. And this was led by the black players. We beat Liverpool 2-1. It really was a magnificent performance. After the match, the kit man, Spike, came along and I asked where all the tracksuits were that were in the corner in their plastic bags. He said, "Andy Gray has put them in his car. He is going to sell them down Brixton Market." So, on the Monday I said to Steve Coppell, "Look, Steve, we have got to really stop this. This is player power gone too far." He said, "Alan, on Friday what would we have given to beat Liverpool?

£500, £5,000, £10,000? Listen, let Andy Gray have his tracksuits. Let him win the day. We got the three points." Steve was very good at handling those sorts of things. Our basic white players would have been Nigel Martyn in goal, Alan Pardew, Geoff Thomas and John Humphrey. But pretty much outside of that the team was predominantly a black team.'

But while Gray sounds like the leader of the 'black power' revolt, Smith says:

'All the black players were leaders in this revolt. Mark Bright, although he was quiet, was a leader. He was very specific on what he wanted, how he wanted to train, how he wanted to look. He was the first player that I knew who did stretching even back in those days.'

However, black players did not arrive at Palace as fully formed leaders ready to take on the world:

'Ian Wright was not the person that you're seeing on the television. It is unbelievable how confident he has become. When he came to Palace, he was insecure because he had just been on trial at Brighton. They didn't take him. We couldn't understand it because the moment he came on our training pitch he was electric. I think he played one game in our reserves and he was straight in our first team. He was our talisman. He did everything. He led from the front. He gave us a vibration. Ian Wright was probably the best player I ever had in my group. He was superb. Ian Wright's exuberance, his enthusiasm, his passion for winning was so intense. He had a spring in his jump when he headed it. He had a spring when he chased after the ball. And again, to quote Steve Coppell, Steve would say to me, "Alan, Ian Wright needs a certain controlling. Alan, he keeps us in the job. We've got to temper these things and make sure he plays all right." '

Wright's insecurity given his traumatic upbringing was not a surprise but he was not the only player who needed special handling:

'We had a very insecure squad at Palace. We realised that they had to be handled differently. Andy Gray needed a completely different style of management to Gareth. Andy Gray still had his insecurities, still had worries. And you had to spend a lot of time, putting your arms round him. We realised Mark Bright had to be treated differently to Andy Gray. Andy Gray, Gareth, John Salako, Richard Shaw, would come back to my house. Sometimes they would stay overnight because we never got back in the coach from a match till two o'clock in the morning. Now, with the horrible things that have happened to young boys, going back to bloody Jimmy Savile, you couldn't do that sort of thing, but then the mums and the dads and the players trusted us.'

Unlike the racism Vince Hilaire had to endure in the seventies and early eighties, Smith says:

'I can't remember having too much racial abuse with that group of players. The Palace black players did not get problems at other grounds, not at all. They were respected. They were so powerful and so good. Gray, Wright went on to play for England. We were such a tight unit. The black players were very protective of one another. If I hadn't joined their gang, I wouldn't have succeeded as the coach or assistant manager. That was the power that they had in the changing room. But it wasn't the power of being black, it was the power that they were really very good players. I still have a great relationship with Andy Gray. He texts me once a week. Ian Wright, Mark Bright were very demanding in what they expected from the team, and if you didn't do your job, they would shout. Eddie McGoldrick and John Salako, wide players, would get an enormous amount of stick from Ian and Mark if they didn't do their job. Wright and Bright behaved that way not because they were black, but they just had that mentality, "You give me the ball and I'll score." '

Smith, despite not having seen any black players in Dulwich Hamlet, had no problems dealing with so many black players at Palace:

'No, I didn't actually need to adjust. I never had a problem with players of colour. I took the view that if the player was good enough, his colour didn't matter. Even very early on we realised that everybody was different. We didn't try and treat everybody the same. As a team we were a little bit rebellious in our approach. We were very much the poor man's crazy gang [Wimbledon advertised themselves as the original crazy gang]. I like to think we were a bit more sophisticated. They [Wimbledon] would scrawl things in the changing rooms at away grounds and played very loud music. We never did that. We didn't antagonise the opposition in that way, but we were very much free-spirited.'

What makes Alan Smith's role in bringing black players to Palace particularly noteworthy is that he had not grown up with black people in his schooldays or worked with black players early in his career: 'No, I didn't. Every coaching course I went on there were no black players. It must have been about 2001 before I went on a coaching course and saw another black guy on it. It was Chris Hughton.'

In many ways, the most interesting aspect of the Smith story and black players at Palace is that at the same time Smith himself was making a very English journey of class, from a football world of forelock-tugging to being considered very much the equal of his bosses. This was vividly highlighted when he worked for the then owner of Wimbledon:

'I was doing a variety of coaching jobs. I had broken my leg and Sydney Black, who was the chairman of Wimbledon FC, offered me a job so I could continue my coaching badge. Sydney was a multi-millionaire in property. He was the brother of Sir Cyril Black, who was the MP for Wimbledon for 20 years. In those days, if you were a Wimbledon player you got employed in that firm, Black and Co. An enormous firm owned by the Black family it had properties in Bermuda, the Bahamas and South Africa. They were rich. They never knew my name as Alan. I was just Smith to them. And I called them "Sir" and "Mister". The class system then was ridiculous.'

Things did change. 'At Palace I always called Ron, "Ron", and I never called Simon Jordan "Chairman".'

It is interesting that Smith in that respect was different from Sir Alex Ferguson, also very much from the working class, albeit from Glasgow. In his time at Manchester United, despite all the honours he won at the club, Ferguson always referred to Martin Edwards, the chairman, as 'Chairman' and not 'Martin'.

Cantona: xenophobia or racism?

Smith and Ferguson were in opposing dugouts during the now infamous match against Manchester United at Selhurst Park on 25 January 1995 when Eric Cantona, having been sent off, did something that had never been done before. As the linesman's official report put it, 'Following his dismissal, I saw Cantona walk along the touchline, stop and then jump two-footed over the advertising hoarding into a spectator.' This became known as Cantona's kung-fu kick. 'Alex', Smith recalls, 'said to me, "What the fucking hell was that all about?" I said, "It is an everyday occurrence in Putney High Street." '

The 'everyday' occurrence had been triggered by the fact that a spectator, Matthew Simmons, had abused Cantona calling him, as Cantona told his lawyer Maurice Watkins, a fucking cheating French cunt, bastard and wanker. Smith recalls:

'Richard Shaw was a young black guy from a one-parent family. He was probably the best man-marker that I ever knew. Richard Shaw had the job of man-marking Cantona. He gave Cantona quite a tough time. Cantona rebelled against that and stamped on Shaw. That was why he was sent off.'

In effect what had happened was that a white referee had sent off a white man for what he had done to a black man. Then another white man, supporting the team the black man played for, abused the white man. And while Simmons's abuse of Cantona was xenophobic, was it racist? Simmons had referred to Cantona's nationality not his race as a Frenchman could be black as well. The whole incident showed how the divide between xenophobia and racism was getting blurred.

Smith's time at Palace would see Southgate, released by Southampton when he was 13, mature into a player who would go on to play for England. Euro 2020 would see the further development of Southgate as manager of England, identifying and leading the most multiracial team in the nation's history. Yet, as Smith admits, before he came to Palace, Southgate had had very little contact with black players. Southgate, who is from Watford and was brought up in the south of England, did not grow up in an ethnic minority background mixed community. Unlike Alan Pardew, whom he played with at Palace, Southgate did not mix with children of people from the Windrush generation in his school. It was at Palace he first played with players of different colours.
Smith appointed Southgate captain:

'In football the position does not carry the same status or responsibility that it has in cricket. The captain in football doesn't have to do anything tactically. He needs to be sometimes a middleman between the manager and the players. I would call Gareth Southgate in and ask him what he thought, and he would put it to the players. I chose Gareth because when he said something, he meant it. He was very determined. I thought he was a winner. He had an enthusiasm, a passion and an honesty. And I knew he could communicate with the more senior players. Gareth was not particularly noisy. He did not do a lot of shouting and was outshouted by other players in the team. He was always immaculately turned out. He had everything that I thought represented Crystal Palace. Gareth conducted himself incredibly well, being quite statesmanlike in what he did.'

Yet Southgate's first venture into captaincy ended in tears in Smith's room:

'We had had a reserve team game against the British Army at Aldershot in a military stadium. We had a very good team out. We lost the game, and I was not happy with the performance, to say the least. After the match I got the players and I sat them down. I went through what I felt about the way we had performed. I noticed Gareth was not in the room. And when I looked out of the window of the changing room, I saw he was shaking hands with the Army guys. He came in and he sat down. He was 16, captaining people in the team who were 22, 23. I just said to Gareth, "Where have you been?" He said, "Look, they have invited us down here. I thought I should go around and shake their hands and say, "Thank you for the invitation." They had invited us into their mess for a drink and something to eat. That is the way that the Army or the Navy perform. I said to him, "I'll make sure we're all in there afterwards." The next day I called Gareth into my office. I just said, "Look, Gareth, six of those guys are in the SAS. They don't go round shooting people and picking them up after. Gareth you've got to start toughening up; you've got to be a bit more selfish, more single-minded. You're trying to be all things to all men; you'll become a travel agent not a footballer." He got a bit tearful. He left the room.'

Smith is keen to emphasise that the leadership qualities Southgate demonstrated owe a lot to Southgate's parents:

'His mother and father, Barbara and Clive, have got to take major credit. They are sensible. Clive is an athletics coach. I watched every game with Clive and the family during the Euros, which was an incredible honour. I am not surprised by how well Gareth has done. He has always shown those qualities. I am not surprised he has become a national figure, how he shut out the media during the Euros. He is quite single-minded in what he wants. Even as a player he could communicate at different levels. I don't see anything different in Gareth from the person I saw when he was 16 and when he was 22.'

The Euros were also to see another former Palace player, a black player, play a part in the England team as part of Southgate's England coaching team. This was Chris Powell:

'Chris Powell coming together with Gareth is a wonderful coincidence. They both played together in the youth team. Chris is the other boy who has never changed. He's a Tottenham fan and is the director of their youth academy. Lovely, lovely boy. I just spoke to him yesterday. He sent me a text yesterday. What I would say about Chris and

Gareth is that neither of them have had it easy. Both Chris and Gareth had to prove themselves. They weren't given anything. Gareth played 100 games in the reserve team before he ever played in our first team.'

But it meant he was playing with black players, something that would not have been possible had he arrived at Crystal Palace a decade earlier. And this change meant Southgate formed a bond with Powell which explains why Powell can so easily fit in with Southgate's England set-up. Powell's journey has, not surprisingly, been very different from that of Southgate but it is very much part of the story of how football has changed.

Over the years I had spoken to Chris Powell often. What was striking was that while he measured words carefully, he was never afraid to talk about how the game had handled racism, which was in stark contrast to other black players and managers in the game.

This emerged very powerfully when in February 2012 I interviewed Powell, then Charlton manager. He had accepted the Manager of the Month award for the second time in the season, testimony to his success at keeping the League One club on course for promotion. In the weeks leading up to the interview, racism in football had made all the headlines. Two weeks previously John Terry, the England and Chelsea defender, had been stripped by the FA of the England captaincy. This had come after he faced criminal charges for allegedly racially abusing Anton Ferdinand during a QPR v. Chelsea Premier League match in October 2011. The FA decision so outraged Fabio Capello that the Italian walked away from his £6 million-a-year job managing the England team.

I knew the Terry affair had badly split the PFA along racial lines with many black players very upset that the situation was not dealt with soon after the incident took place. Gordon Taylor, the PFA chief executive, had been trying to hold his union together on the issue and had tried hard to persuade John Terry to withdraw voluntarily from the England captaincy. It was after these efforts were rebuffed that the Football Association decided to step in and strip the Chelsea player of his England armband.

Off the record, several black players I had spoken to were scathing about how the FA had mishandled the Terry affair but they wouldn't come on the record. I was speaking to Powell in his office at Charlton's training ground and I knew I had to ask him about the Terry affair. Powell was then one of only two black managers in all the four divisions and it would have been understandable had he sidestepped the issue, or asked me to switch off my tape recorder. But much to my surprise, and delight, he did not. His reply was prompt: 'It should have happened straightaway back in October. They shouldn't have waited this long. It should have been dealt with straightaway between England, Chelsea, John Terry and the Premier League. It's just carried on and it's going to carry on now well into the summer. It's affected what's happened to our national team and it's affected one or two things that are happening in the Premier League.'

This was a reference to the Luis Suárez affair. I had met Powell the weekend after Suárez, then a Liverpool player, having been punished by the FA for racially abusing Patrice Evra, had refused to shake Evra's hand when Liverpool played Manchester United. This had caused more problems for the PFA with Taylor telling me, 'Saturday [when the match was played] was a terrible day for the image of the game. I don't want any of my black members to feel reluctant to complain if they are at the receiving end of racial abuse because they fear the backlash. It is important the game protects them. We have a duty to protect them.'

Powell was right about the Terry affair which lasted not only well into the summer but until the end of the year. In July 2012 Terry was cleared by Westminster Magistrates' Court of racially abusing Ferdinand. In September 2012, nearly a year after the incident and seven months after I had spoken to Powell, the FA, after a four-day hearing, found Terry guilty of racially abusing Ferdinand and banned him for four matches and fined him £220,000.

Before the Terry affair the general perception in the football world and the media was that racism in the game was no longer a problem. I asked Powell, 'Has it not surprised you? We thought English football had dealt with it, it was all gone. We don't have the monkey chants, the sort of things you guys went through – that was hell.'

Powell replied:

'That's the mistake in what you've just said, Mihir. We thought we'd finished with it, and you can't ever think that you have. It is not strictly just football's problem. We do know it has been part of football in the bad old days but it's a problem that emanates in society. I look at football as a game, and it should be available to anyone regardless of where they're from. You should be free to go and sit in a stadium and watch the game, support your team regardless of people thinking you shouldn't be here because of the colour of your skin. I'm loath to talk about it. I shouldn't be talking about it in 2012, I should be talking about football.'

But, surely, I asked, back in his playing days (Powell had made his debut with Palace in 1987) it was a more a case of fans' abuse of black players rather than players' abuse of each other as had been the case that season.

'Oh, there was,' sighed Powell, 'don't be fooled by that, without a doubt there was. We all knew it was happening, both from the terraces and between the players. Nothing was done. So don't kid yourself it didn't happen. What I'm saying is back in the seventies, eighties, nineties, nothing was reported because nothing was happening with the authorities. So, player to player abuse was almost, sadly, accepted in those days. You got on with it but the players fought their corner.'

So, was he racially abused by other players? He looked at me in some surprise and said, 'Come on, what do you think?' But like a lot of players of that generation he said, 'I don't want to talk about then. I want to talk about now. I want players to feel comfortable playing and feel free to report if things happen. That's what we're seeing. People won't accept it these days. It's being dealt with now regardless of how long it's taken. In days gone by we wouldn't even be talking about it.'

A decade later the generation that has succeeded Powell is certainly talking about it. But while that is a major and welcome change, the fact that they have to, and there are still some who claim racism is not a problem, shows that despite the long road we have travelled since South London football was all white in the seventies and eighties, we are still far from anywhere near a truly non-racial sports world.

SEVEN

WHITE V. BLACK MATCHES

British rule in India and South London in the 1980s might appear to have nothing in common – except that in both parts of the world, sports matches were played along racial lines.

The British in India introduced cricket using very distinct racial and religious demarcations. The British in India called themselves 'Europeans', to emphasise that they were the master race ruling over, as Winston Churchill put it, 'primitive people' who needed to be civilised. Their cricket team was called 'The Europeans' and only those of pure European blood could play for the team. They played Indian teams organised along religious lines, meaning separate teams for Parsees, Hindus and Muslims in what was called the 'Quadrangular Tournament'. This, the Indian Premier League [IPL] of its time, was one of Indian cricket's greatest tournaments and it lasted for more than four decades, nourished Indian cricket and made it into a national Indian game. But while the British were Christians, race meant they could not have Indian Christians in their team, and it was only in the late 1930s that a Rest team which comprised Indian Christians, the mixed-race Anglo-Indians and Jews was formed and the tournament was renamed 'The Pentangular'.

Fast forward and it is the 1980s. The empire is history. The game we are talking about is football. We are in South London on a winter Friday afternoon and during training at a London club, teams based along racial lines have reappeared. Let one of the participants tell us what happened:

'We used to have black v. white on a Friday as a fun game. Five or six black players in one team against five or six white players in another team. A proper five-a-side. We played on a half-size pitch. There would be big goals. It was mainly the first-team players. Normally the black players would name themselves "Brazil", or something like that, and we would be "England" or "Great Britain", because there were some Irish players in there. I can remember those games and they were fierce games. Trust me, it was competitive. The rivalry came through, actually. We would say, "We're gonna get you," and all that. I tackled hard. But I can't remember the language being bad, of course. When I look back now it's just bizarre really that we did that, but at that time it didn't feel abnormal.'

There was a crucial difference between cricket in India during British rule and South London football. In India then, race was integral to cricket. In South London the Friday afternoon matches 'weren't a racist thing. It was just a bit of fun. There was great camaraderie about that.'

The man telling me this story is Alan Pardew. It is 4 p.m. on a February afternoon in 2021. London is gloomy in the middle of the third lockdown, but over in Bulgaria, Pardew, now Technical Director of CSKA Sofia, is basking in the sunshine as his team get ready to train.

Pardew's memory of his playing career is part of that crucial period when the first black players started making their way into the league teams in significant numbers. Pardew, who grew up in Wandsworth, went to the first of the comprehensives in the seventies and thinks he was:

'The first generation that went to school where the children were 30 to 40 per cent of mixed races. They were from the Windrush generation, probably the first children that were born in England. So for me, personally, it was always just a natural thing to mix with Afro-Caribbean and Indian people. That was just part of school normally. The generation before me didn't experience so much of that. I wouldn't say there was racism, but it was definitely "them and us" thinking. And the terminologies used by the older generation, not my school friends, of course, would be so inappropriate now. Because there was a lot of mixed-race kids – the word that was mostly used was "half-caste". That was a name that was just normal. That wasn't a naughty term when I was at school. You would openly say you are "half-caste" or you are "black", blah, blah, blah. You would often hear on a football pitch, even at my school, "You black bastard", if someone fouled you or was really aggressive. There would be "white bastards" as well. It would certainly be "black bastards". There wasn't a stigma to the words.'

Pardew played for a number of non-league teams round London starting in 1980–81 with Whyteleafe, then Epsom & Ewell, Corinthian-Casuals and Dulwich Hamlet. His early football experience matched that of his school:

> 'In non-league I was brought up on multi-race teams. I always played with Afro-Caribbean players or African players. You had the odd Asian boy, but Indian and Pakistani players never seemed to break through in district or non-league teams. In my experience we treated the black players equally, as peers – some of them, of course, were better footballers.'

It was different when he went to Yeovil:

> 'That was the West Country. I don't think they had the kind of take on race that I had. Not a lot of the players I played with in Yeovil had black kids, or kids of different races, at their school, so there was a little bit of racism there if I am honest in the group, particularly when we played away. We did have two or three black players at Yeovil that we bought from London, but when we played away there were not too many other teams with black players. Some of the places down in the West Country, these players suffered [what was then] normal terminology that you would now associate as a racial term.'

But what is significant is that the media said nothing about the racial problems black or other non-whites faced in football in the West Country. When Yeovil was mentioned, which was quite often during the FA Cup, what was talked about was its famous slope. 'It ran across the pitch,' says Pardew with a laugh. 'So, I always used to like to play at the high end of the pitch, not the bottom end.' As a defender his problem was more the weather, because 'the dynamics of the weather at Yeovil were quite extreme.'

Spotted by Crystal Palace chairman Ron Noades and manager Steve Coppell, Pardew coming to Palace 'was almost back to my roots'. Mitcham, where Crystal Palace trained, was not far from where he had grown up. And this was a Palace team with black players.

'Steve Coppell assembled a very cheap team, really non-league players who had been released, but he brought in some great players. When I was first introduced to the team, I struggled a little bit. I didn't really have the confidence to play with Ian Wright, Mark Bright, Jim Cannon – Geoff Thomas came a bit later.'

At Crystal Palace there was no problem getting black players. 'I actually played for Crystal Palace in a League Cup game against Chelsea. And I think the only white players were me, Geoff Thomas and Nigel Martyn. I used to actually go to Chelsea games and some of the [racial] language there was not the best.'

Talking of the black players he played with at Palace, who included Chris Powell, Pardew recalls:

'They were big personalities. Mark Bright and Ian Wright were great players. They were very defensive of anything racial even then. I see Ian on TV now expressing his views strongly, and even then he was very vocal. If anyone said anything out of turn, or a race term was mentioned in the game, we would be discussing that. For the senior group of Palace players this was new to them.'

So, within the Palace dressing room would there be white players who would call the black players names? 'Well I think when tensions got aroused,' says Pardew, 'it would get mentioned,' but he quickly adds a bit defensively, 'but this does sound really weird in today's age.'

Pardew did hear black players being advised to ignore the racist abuse they were getting from the fans. 'I've heard that said in the changing room. "Don't rise to it, let it go, be bigger than that." That was the way that the senior management and the club wanted to deal with it at that time.'

Palace having black players did not cause problems for the home fans:

'Particularly because it was South London and a lot of fans would be working with African people, and they were all around us. They had had coloured players before at Crystal Palace. Vince Hilaire springs to mind. Brilliant player. I don't ever really remember fans being racist in any way. You would get the odd shout, but it was certainly nothing that I can recall where Ian Wright, Mark Bright mainly and Andy Gray would be overtly complaining about our own fans, that the language was inexcusable or something like that.'

Pardew's managerial career saw him build up quite a portfolio of managerial jobs. He managed at Reading, West Ham, Charlton, Southampton, Newcastle – where in the 2011–12 season, he did the rare double of winning both the Barclays and the League Managers Association's Manager of the Season – Crystal Palace, West Bromwich Albion and ADO Den Haag. By this time every team had black players. It was the era when clubs had a very cosmopolitan dressing room:

'It became a learning experience for me. At Newcastle I saw Muslim players going into the shower to pray and I didn't think that was right that they had to go into the shower. So, we talked about getting a prayer room and we had to have a multi-ethnic prayer room at Newcastle. And we had a lot of African players, mainly French-speaking. And they were a different kind of black player to the Afro-Caribbean players that I had grown up with. Mostly the players I played with were born in England, of course. We had Cheick Tioté who has now died of a heart defect. He was a great player for us at Newcastle. He came from the Ivory Coast. He was very African, very cold. I found it difficult to communicate with these guys because I was actually more natural with Afro-Caribbean players. There was a language problem with them speaking French. Football, of course, is a universal language. If you can't get over your message with your facial expressions, with a sort of pidgin language, then you are in trouble in football, so I never really had a problem communicating. I think players always knew exactly what I wanted them to do. But there were also one or two cultural issues. Everything was new to these guys. For example, one of the African players left and we found out that he'd never paid a parking fine because we didn't have things in place to look after him, like we do right now. These guys had no one around them to advise them.'

During Pardew's managerial career he has been able to chart how black and white players have reacted to racism:

'A lot of the black players we had were starting to get very savvy about race. It was definitely coming more and more on the agenda. They would react to some of the chanting, some of the individual insults coming from the fans and there would be little verbal exchanges between a fan or maybe a substitute. Because the substitutes could hear them. When you are on a football pitch, you are so engrossed in a game you don't hear the abuse. As a substitute when you're not that focused on the game, you can hear the fans more, and you can react. I wouldn't call it racist chanting but a racial sort of statement to one of our players.'

But what has changed since he was a player is: 'It would not necessarily be a black player reacting. It might be a white player saying, "You can't say things like that. Who do you think you are?" What was said would definitely be something along the lines of "you black something".'

Pardew, who is very much working-class, had the sort of work experiences which most footballers don't, and makes the interesting point that racism in football is not as bad as in the world outside football:

'My building site experience was from 17 to 23. Before Yeovil. And I experienced more racism in a building site than I did on a football field. There will be all sorts of terminology used on a building site because people are just not educated, so they say stupid, racist things to black people. There were a lot of black people on the building sites. The Windrush first wave of immigration. My experience on the building site was worse than my experience in football.'

Pardew is aware that football in its ownership structure has completely changed since the days when he started playing, with many of the clubs now being owned by non-whites, which fans are prepared to accept and even welcome if it brings success.

But, he admits, the absence of black and ethnic minority coaches is an issue in the game:

'There is no doubt about it. It has not carried through. I have no idea why. In my first period of coaching, speaking to some Afro-Caribbean friends, I found they felt that in coaching they weren't going to get an even break so that they didn't go in for coaching. So, that was kind of self-defeating, in a way. I think that period has now passed, thank goodness. I think Afro-Caribbean or Arab players, or any kind of ethnic group now think they can go into coaching.'

The day before we spoke, Pardew's friend and ex-colleague, a black coach at Kilmarnock, had got sacked.

'I was really disappointed. That is one less. They do need to see a pathway and it would be nice to have a figure, a Frank Lampard figure, a Steven Gerrard figure, who is black doing very well in the Premier League. That would really help. That is what we really need.'

Pardew's managerial career has seen players who are racially abused walking off the field, something Ian Wright could never do, and Pardew says: 'I think if a coach or the players decide after consultation with the coach that that's what they want to do, then depending on the incident, of course, you will have to agree that they should do.'

Social media has made a difference in how modern black footballers can respond to race in the way black players of Pardew's generation could not:

'I am proud of what players like Raheem Sterling and Marcus Rashford are doing because they are highlighting not just race. Like the problem with school meals that Rashford is very much part of highlighting because, obviously, it was very personal to him. This is something that some of the great protagonists of sport in the NFL and the NBA [in the US] have done for years. Now we have two Afro-Caribbean background players highlighting the issues and it's been great to see. I couldn't be more impressed with those two guys.'

Is this something that Ian Wright or Mark Bright could or would have done?

'I don't think they had the platform because of social media. Maybe they could have done something in the South London press about it. They are very much the same kind of people as Rashford and Sterling. But they didn't have the power these two guys have. I can't imagine what Ian Wright would have tweeted after a game in 1993. Sterling can say something after the game that is back-page news. Ian Wright and Mark Bright could never have done that in their careers.'

It is, perhaps, not surprising that in many ways having been a white player, who was one of the first to play with black players, Pardew is optimistic that society can tackle racism:

'I think about growing up and how [attitudes to] racism have changed. People are more educated on what to say, what to do, what not to say. We had a doctor at Crystal Palace, Dr Zach, he's still there by the way. There would be a joke made at the dinner table, and we would say, "You like rice." He would say, "Why do I like rice? Because I am an Indian." Actually, when I go back 25 years, there was closet racism. Wow, there was a lot of that going on. All these things that you don't really understand unless you have been in the position of an ethnic player.'

EIGHT

THE HILL AT LUTON

B ack in 1995 I had just picked up the phone, asked to speak to Peter Hart, and arranged to see him. In 2021, even allowing for the fact that we were in the middle of the Covid pandemic, I just could not get through to Beech Hill Primary school. My only route was via somebody whose post would have been inconceivable in 1996, showing that when it comes to diversity, at least one box has been ticked.

This was Beverley Knight-Davis, an assistant head, whose remit was Inclusion and Intervention, a post that was set up in 2009. She is very friendly, and when I leave a message for Chris Davidson, the head, he rings back. He is very keen to talk, but then I encounter another problem I did not face in 1995. I have first to get authorisation from the press office. The idea that the school has a press officer emphasises how much the world has changed in the last 25 years. Davidson tells me I have to contact another Chris, Chris Hutchings. I fear I may be turned down, fears that grow when a similar request to Denbigh High does not even merit an answer. But after a chat with Hutchings on the phone, followed by an email, when I ring Davidson again, he agrees I can interview him once half-term is over.

When the interview is arranged, it is not only Davidson, a Watford fan, I am talking to but Natalie Carson, deputy head, Abdul Azad, governor of the school and Faisal Khan, the sports coach. But this being the pandemic they are in Davidson's room in Luton and I am in my loft in Shepherd's Bush, a world removed from the face-to-face meeting I had with Hart all those years ago.

The school, says Davidson, which has 820 children from reception to year 6 with a separate nursery for 100 children, 'has not changed in terms of the ethnic breakdown much since that time [in 1996]. The breakdown between boys and girls is roughly 50-50 and the language of the vast majority of our children is Bengali.'

But if the ethnic origin of the school is unchanged since I spoke to Hart, what has changed, in an almost revolutionary fashion, is not only the availability of sports facilities but also the attitude of the parents. The school, says Davidson, has had funding for 'a 3G sports all-purpose football pitch, as well as a basketball court. It's called a MUGA pitch, a multi-use games area, but basically it's a basketball court with a rubber-leaf surface. That is all outdoors. Also, we have facilities inside the school that are used for various sporting activities as well.' And despite the school not having a cricket pitch, 'Cricket is still our strongest sport.'

Beech Hill's strength in cricket is no surprise because Faisal Khan is an English Cricket Board [ECB]-qualified coach and he proudly tells me how the school has 'won about seven to eight titles in cricket. They would be both boys and girls from Year 3, Year 4, Year 5 and Year 6. They have won interschool and county championships as well. In 2016 the girls' team won the county championship. And we have seen various students in the recent past who have made it to a minor county side.'

'Can you', I ask, 'see one of your cricketers playing for England?'

I can hear a woman's laughter in the background, which I suspect is Natalie, but it is not mocking, more that mixture of surprise and pleasure a question like that may provoke. Khan's voice rings out clear, 'Definitely!' He has already identified a child who could play for England: 'I regularly speak to the child's mother.'

Indeed, parents often talk to Khan about how, if their children do well in sport, they could become professional in it. 'I have never had an issue with parents being hesitant. They have been dropping their children off in time and they've been amazing.' But what about the complaint Hart had made in 1996, that Muslim families' requirement for their children to go to the madrasa was a barrier to children taking part in sports?

The problem, says Davidson, has been overcome by the timetable:

'We start earlier, we finish earlier. We finish at 3 p.m. So therefore children are able to partake in after-school clubs. And when we have our sporting activities, that will often be till four. For any club and tournament we let parents know in advance if there is going to be a late night. There have not been any problems at all.'

But with the majority of children being Muslim, I ask, 'Do parents come to you and say that their daughter will not take part because it offends them in some way?'

Davidson's voice could not be more emphatic, 'No, not so.'

As we have seen, Hart had told me that black people don't swim. Before Davidson can respond, for the first time I hear a female voice. It is the lady who had laughed, Natalie:

'Can I interject? I've worked across several London schools and addressed various barriers to children learning to swim, etc. At Beech Hill we have boys and girls swimming separately, and certainly since I've been at the school, which is four years now, we've never really had issues around girls not being allowed to go swimming, boys not being allowed to go swimming. We are very inclusive in terms of what we allow the children to wear for swimming, and we promote and encourage the girls and boys to swim. We also currently have a sports coach at school who is actually a Paralympian swimmer. And he, with the children and members of the staff, has engaged in joining the children in the pool as well. And that's really promoted the importance of learning to swim. This has certainly not been a barrier. There is a waterproof hijab available for the girls to wear and swimming caps as well, but it's certainly not something that has come up as a barrier. Our parents are happy that the children learn to swim in same-sex groups. The way that we work is that the boys go for a swim and then the girls go for a swim, and they take it in turn to switch.'

With many of the girls of Islamic faith, would there be problems in what sort of swimming costumes they wear? It is Chris's turn to come in: 'All I can say is we haven't had an issue with that. All our children swim, whether they are boys or girls. We provide some information each year about children who can swim.' The school does not have a pool but provides transport to a place called Inspire, but he says, 'It doesn't take us long to walk.'

During our conversation Davidson had said, 'I don't see colour or race being an issue.' But if these were sentiments that I have heard many white people express whenever the subject of race is discussed who then go on to deny there is any racism, it was clear talking to Davidson and his colleague that was not the situation at Beech Hill. Here steps were being taken to make the school inclusive. It was more than a box-ticking exercise.

But how much has Luton Town FC changed and how has it fared in its search for an Asian footballing Imran Khan which would make the Asian community truly part of the club?

NINE

TAKING CHARGE OF THE STORY

I t is Christmas 2019. A 42-year-old man is driving in Norwich, his home town, after doing his Christmas shopping. Suddenly he is stopped by the police:

'I was in a traffic jam. A police car drove past me going in the opposite direction. He looked at me and couldn't turn round quickly enough. He then followed me, and I remember doing the research, for 4.8 miles. After 4.8 miles he then pulled me over. I asked why he'd pulled me over. He said, "I noticed that your number plates were illegal." I said, "OK, so my number plates are illegal. I bought them from Halfords, so they're not illegal; next question? And by the way, officer, when you decided to pull me over, I was in a traffic jam and you went past me in the other direction at 30 miles per hour, so you would not have been able to see my number plate in bumper-to-bumper traffic. So can you really explain to me why you pulled me over when all you saw was my face?" The officer said, "I pulled you over because of your number plate." "Yes, but you couldn't have." We had a bit of to and fro. I got breathalysed etc. on the roadside and then I went off about my business.'

This is not the first time he was stopped by the police when he was driving around going about his business: 'I can remember being pulled over to be told, "Your vehicle's showing as untaxed." In those days, there were tax discs in the car. I said, "Well, the tax disc is in there, help yourself, have a look."'

The man telling me these stories is Adrian Forbes, the academy manager of Luton, an Afro-Caribbean, whose family come from St Kitts. He had told me these two tales when I had asked him whether he had been stopped and searched by the police. 'Oh, in my car, yes, countless times.' Could it have been the car he was driving that attracted the police officer to pull up this black man?

'That's what it boils down to, isn't it? I was in the fortunate position where I have a nice car, it draws attention. In Norwich I was driving a Jaguar XF. The one with the tax disc was a BMW X5. Every time I've been pulled over there's been no reason to be pulled over. It is just demoralising.'

He is determined that his children should not be made to feel they are different, and that is why he reacted strongly when he was stopped by the police officer:

'When I got pulled over by the police in Norwich, I dug my heels in and I did make a complaint. My thing was, I'm in my 40s, I've got three mixed-race boys, one 20, one 16, and one 11. I do not want my boys to have to be in a society where they are singled out just because they don't look like the white police officer who's driving the car. I do not want my boys to be singled out because there's a belief "How did they afford that car?" When I complained, they were just fobbing me off. It took me a long time to track down the people who could actually deal with it. To the credit of the Norfolk Constabulary, I did get an apology.'

Growing up in north-west London 'where we were multicultural', race had not mattered to Forbes:

'It's probably the older I've got, and the wiser I've got, I've become more knowledgeable and see more things visually, and am more aware of what I have to deal with. Because there'll always be one situation where you will feel uncomfortable, and you'll wonder why. I think also sometimes, as well, you probably get a little bit of paranoia. "Is that person looking at me because they might recognise me? Or is that person looking at me because they're wondering what I might be doing?"'

Like many, in early July 2020 Forbes listened to Michael Holding talking about race before the start of the first England–West Indies Test match. We shall talk about the Holding intervention on race later, but here it is interesting to note that Forbes says, 'I got emotional listening to him. I'm surprised that it has taken so long and that there's a necessity and a need for it in this day and age. It is disappointing for me.'

But despite this, Forbes weighs his words carefully when I ask him if he feels there is white privilege:

'That's a tough one. And the reason I say it's a tough one is because if I look at my own personal background, where I married a white girl and was surrounded by her family that was all white, and they welcomed me with open arms. And now my new partner, she's white, and her family have welcomed me with open arms. But do I see scenarios and situations where a white person would be treated differently or be given better opportunities than a black person? Yes. Do I see scenarios where, going back to the car, I could be driving my car and a white person driving the same car, do I feel more uncomfortable than the white person that it's going to be me that gets pulled over? One hundred per cent. I don't know if I would classify that as white privilege, but yes, there's definitely a differentiation between how a white person is treated to how a black person or an Asian is treated. One hundred per cent.'

And as for this country being institutionally racist, he says:

'That's a difficult one. Do you call it unintentional racism? Do you call it racism if people don't ever realise they are racist? I would probably say it's more unconscious racism; that people will say and do things and not realise how that might come across to the black person. As an example, going into shops you know 100 per cent that the security guard's going to be within your eyeline. My partner is white, and she's really conscious of it now because she's noticing things.'

He is aware that there is a huge gap between how blacks and whites see the world:

'My new partner, she's been brilliant in wanting me to help her understand: "Walk in your shoes for a day; help me understand how certain situations make you feel; help me understand how your parents felt when they came over here." Because she wants to know me, she wants to know my life. Me educating her on my life, and on my background and the cultural differences, I think has made us so much stronger and it's actually a real blessing. But it's getting that education for the masses, so people understand how certain situations, certain comments, how certain behaviour might make a black or Asian person feel. I don't think certain people get that. I can relate to the cultural differences between my West Indian upbringing and the upbringing of a white family, because when I came to Norwich I moved in with a white family when I was 16. I then married a white lady, so I was part of that. And so now I can understand those cultural differences because they've been a huge part of my life.'

Forbes describes himself as 'a winger by trade and I played a little bit up front. Left foot was good for standing and for balance, but 100 per cent a right-footer.' In his playing career he did the football circuit just below the Premier League: Norwich, Luton, Swansea, Blackpool, Millwall, and two years ago, after becoming a coach at Norwich, came back to Luton to take over the academy.

Forbes, born in this country, would be classified as a second-generation immigrant. And in footballing terms he is also part of the second generation who followed in the footsteps of the pioneers and who, growing up in the eighties and nineties, had role models like John Barnes, Ian Wright and Paul Ince to look up to. 'My ideal was a mix of John Barnes and Ian Wright with a little bit of Paul Ince.' His move from north-west London to Norwich in 1995 after he finished his GCSEs did present the 16-year-old with an enormous cultural and racial problem:

'Growing up in north-west London, I saw lots of people who looked like me, so I didn't really think anything of it. I had white friends, black friends, Asian friends. In Norwich there was no one who looked like me out in the street. There was, probably, me and two or three other black players in the youth team at Norwich. So, then how do you manage the situation?'

Yet:

'While living in Norwich and playing for the club, I faced no racial problems. In Norwich I never faced any monkey chants or had bananas thrown at me. I have always wondered, would I have faced something if I wasn't Adrian Forbes the black footballer in Norwich, where people knew what I was doing? I don't know. I chose to go back to Norwich after I finished playing because I felt that was the best place to bring up my three mixed-race kids. Now, while I work for Luton, I still live in Norwich. I commute every day between Norwich and Luton, two hours each way.'

He quickly qualifies this acceptance by Norwich fans:

'Don't get me wrong, there have been other clubs I've been to where I've faced it. I played for Millwall for two years. I can remember one scenario where we were playing against Nottingham Forest, and a Forest player, another black player, went into a little bit of a 50-50 tackle with me, and we ended up just in front of the fans. Then one of the Millwall fans basically said, "Oi, you black you know what, eff off." And I've gone to the fan, "What are you going on about, you

79

can't say that?" And the fan actually turned round to me and said, "No, no, no, you're all right, Forbesy, because you're one of us, but that black b . . . needs to eff off." And I am going, "How can I be all right because I'm wearing your shirt? He's the same colour as me, but he is wearing a different shirt, so he's not all right?" It didn't resonate in my brain; it didn't make sense to me. But I didn't personally face any of those scenarios where players had abused me due to the colour of my skin. Certainly nothing where my colour was taken into account by any other players that I played with or played against. There were no problems in the dressing room. Even Millwall. In Millwall there were black players in the team. Between us as a group of black players and the white players that were in our squad, it was absolutely outstanding, absolutely brilliant. I'm still in contact now with a lot of those players who were in that Millwall team with me.'

He agrees that his generation of players would not have dreamt of walking off had they faced abuse. 'I don't think it would have been something that would have crossed anyone's mind.'

It is late evening as I speak to Forbes on the phone and I am keen to explore how far things have moved in the near quarter century since I spoke to Terry Westley about the lack of Asian players and Asian spectators at Kenilworth Road. Forbes has happy memories of his three years at Luton and, having grown up not far from Southall with its large Asian population, 'Luton resonated from my youth in London.'

Yet after two years in the job, he is no better placed than Westley was when I spoke to him a quarter of a century ago. Luton recruits players from the age of nine all the way up to 16, 18 and beyond for their academy. But despite there being nearly 180 academy players, black and white, none are Asian. 'There must be Asian players out there playing grassroots football on a Sunday. My mission: to help change the narrative.' Where the narrative has changed in the quarter century is that the football authorities are no longer in denial on this issue. Now they recognise there is a problem and are willing to put in money to try and solve it. Their starting point is to have funding programmes to hire black, Asian, minority ethnic or female coaches. It is as if they are saying, 'Hire ethnic coaches, players will follow.' At the start of the 2020–21 season, Forbes was able to employ two Asian coaches at Luton, Taff Rahman and Nadim Akhtar, one funded by the FA, the other by the scheme run by the Premier League, the Football League and the PFA. Both have become part of Luton's football family with Forbes always calling Nadim 'George' because Nadim's father was a devoted

Manchester United fan whose favourite player was George Best. Their task, says Forbes, is clear: 'How, as a club, if we do happen to find that Asian player that we believe has the technical ability, the passion, the desire, the work ethic, to come into our academy, can we help him thrive in this environment?'

Forbes is not worried about the familiar Asian stereotypes of parents pushing their children to books rather than sports, or Muslim boys expected to be at prayer, just as other boys are playing keepy-uppy with the ball:

'I had a similar stereotype when I was growing up in a West Indian background, that education comes first. It's trying to find the happy medium where we understand the cultural differences that an Asian player coming into this world will face, but also making sure we can accommodate them, give them the opportunity to practise their faith but also hopefully realise their dream of becoming a professional footballer. It is disappointing that I've not been able to make as big an impact as I wanted to, yet. But it's not something that I intend giving up on. I'm still at the training ground, I've just walked onto the pitch and I'm looking across; you can probably hear the noise in the background now.'

For all Forbes's steely determination he pleads for time to change the Asian football narrative:

'Do I know 100 per cent that the talent is out there to allow that shift to happen? I don't know. It's going to take time, 100 per cent. Hopefully, five, ten years from now we – me and you – don't need to have this conversation because there will be Asian players playing and there will be Asian coaches coaching.'

TEN

FROM ENOCH POWELL TO THE PUNJABI WOLVES

Wolverhampton Wanderers and its relationship with ethnic minorities has a particular resonance in British society. In the fifties, following England's seminal defeat by Hungary at Wembley, the club, led by Billy Wright, widely considered one of England's all-time great players and the David Beckham of his time who married one of the Beverley sisters – the original Posh and Becks – pioneered European football. It was Wolves' victories over European clubs in the fifties, leading to claims it was the best team in Europe, that prompted two French journalists to propose that there be a European Cup, which would then be reincarnated as the present-day Champions League, the greatest club competition in the world.

But even as Billy Wright and his teammates were making history on the football field, the political world in Wolverhampton was changing. In 1950 the town elected as its MP Enoch Powell, who would represent Wolverhampton for the next two decades. In the city's Midland Hotel, one Saturday in April 1968, Powell made his infamous 'Rivers of Blood' speech where he chose a bloodthirsty Latin poetical reference about 'the River Tiber foaming with blood' to melodramatise his predictions of the result of large-scale migration of 'coloured people', as blacks and browns were then called. 'Hence the urgency of implementing now the second element of the Conservative Party's policy: the encouragement of re-emigration.' Against such a background, it was impossible for the town's ethnic community to fondly imagine that going to Molineux on a Saturday afternoon would stop them being booted out of the country.

But here I am in 2021 talking to a child of one of those immigrants, whose parents had migrated to this country from the Punjab in the sixties and had had an arranged marriage here – just the sort of migrants, in fact, whom Powell wanted to send packing to their homeland – declaring with great pride that Punjabi Wolves, the supporters' group he and his friends had founded, had been proclaimed by Kick It Out as 'officially the largest organised Asian supporters' group in Europe, if not the world'.

The man I am taking to is Pete Bassi, although Pete is not his real name. Pete is the anglicised version of what he calls 'my proper name', Perminder, a Sikh director of Punjabi Wolves. Asians supporting Wolves was not entirely a new story. However, in 1995 when I had spoken to Jas Bains it did not seem to be going anywhere. Bains and his friends were among the first to go to Wolves and pointed out to me how Asians should be natural Wolves supporters. The ground was surrounded by Asians: Muslims lived next door to their Molineux ground and in adjacent Whitmore Road lived a large Sikh community. But, Bains had said, 'The management of the club has no concept of Asians or how to channel it or even give a monkey's about it. Ultimately we need to take ownership and our case has to be made more powerfully.'

Now a quarter of a century later Pete Bassi could claim that the Asian supporters had taken ownership. And while the name may suggest only people of Punjabi origin belong, and that is how Punjabi Wolves started, Bassi says: 'We have people of Asian origins and also whites, blacks. We are absolutely mixed. We have got quite a few women supporters, white females, black females and they come on our coaches as well.'

Pete, born four years after Powell's speech, was well aware that Powell's views had cast a shadow over the club. 'That's why there weren't many Asians going to football matches. They didn't think they should be there. They were apprehensive. Hooliganism was also rife then.'

Pete, though, loved football and played the game at his comprehensive, which had a good mix of white kids and a lot of Asians: 'I used to watch Wolves whenever I could on the TV. I played football for my school, starting as a right-winger then moved to a holding midfielder role and then into defence, obviously when the pace wasn't there but I could read the game well.'

He then adds with great pride, 'I was quicker than Raheem Sterling.'

That claim may be very debatable but his description of how he went to his first match is a vivid insight into an Asian supporter finally able to declare his allegiance to his club:

'I remember going to my first match in 1987 when I was 15. My mum and dad had said, "There's no way you are going to a football match." I actually sneaked out on the Saturday, saying, "Look, I'm going to play with my friends." I was defying my parents. But I was too scared to go on my own. I went with five guys from my class, as they supported Wolves as well. I was the only Asian there. The others were all white. We decided to go on a Saturday, so we all got together and caught the bus. We went in there together, then came out together as well. I felt okay. I wasn't called a Paki or anything like that. I felt comfortable because I was with five of my mates at the time, rather than just going on my own, or just with one other Asian guy who would have been looking different. I also had somebody to talk to. [During the match] I just had tunnel vision. I was just looking at the match. I wasn't looking either side of me. Then I started going every now and then. I kept it hidden from my parents for a little while.'

In the nineties things changed, a mixture of acquiring more self-confidence and a sense of belonging:

'When I was in my 20s, I didn't feel intimidated going to football. Because one, we could handle ourselves. Two, we spoke the Queen's English so we could communicate with people and we could clearly make friends with a lot of people around us. Three, we were born and bred in this country. We felt we had the right to be there. When you are sitting with them on a regular basis, season in and season out in your seats, you get to know the people around you. And you make friends that way. And that obviously helped.'

A few years after Pete had felt confident enough to go, the idea of Punjabi Wolves was born:

'Twenty-five years ago there was no organised supporter Asian group who could actually contact Wolverhampton Wanderers. We were one of the original ones. There were six of us. We met at the gurdwara. We were all Sikhs. We wanted a voice within Wolverhampton Wanderers. The club responded very slowly at first.'

When Punjabi Wolves first started, says Bassi, 'There were about 15 supporters' groups, all white. Today there's definitely more of a mix. And you can see that on the terraces as well.'

But as Punjabi Wolves have risen, the area around Molineux has changed. Bains had described how in 1998 there was a mosque on the same road as the ground and a lot of Asians lived around the ground. Now Bassi says, 'The Asians have moved to more affluent areas. A lot of other immigrants have moved in, some Polish, more Eastern European.'

*

84

For Bassi and his Punjabi Wolves, the colour issue came up in a way that shows how fans who make racist chants distinguish between members of the same race, classifying some as friendly and welcome and others as not:

'We didn't encounter much racism. There were little chants here and there, depending on who we were playing. The one I remember, obviously, was when we played Leicester City at Molineux. We were all sitting in the South Bank, six of us again, and about ten rows behind us some fans started singing to the Leicester fans, "You're a town full of Pakis." When you go to away grounds, they can single out Asians, in chants and stuff like that. They start calling you "Raghead" and stuff like that because of the turban. I don't wear a turban. We've got a few fans who do wear the turban and go with us to away games. If we go away to Leicester, for example, and we've beaten Leicester 3-0, their fans are irate anyway, so they're just going to find something to vent their anger on. If it's not their players, it'll be the away fans they'll single out. Obviously, we have had that over the years. I hear racist chanting at Molineux, now and then, sometimes from away fans, sometimes from my own fans. Ten, 15 years ago, if you saw some racism or you were subject to racism, you didn't know what to do. Now you do know. Now they put [what you can do] across the tannoy system and on the website. It's in the programme as well.'

And then in a tone which suggests he wants to understand why such racist chanting may take place he says:

'The thing with football is they go there for 90 minutes and they vent their frustration. If they've had a bad week, they'll go to a football match and take it out on a player. Maybe a black, an Asian player, some other player. Unfortunately, it's become the norm. But it's just a bunch of drunken lads. It's not blatant racism. I don't think it's as big a problem as sometimes people want to make out. Sometimes papers just want a story.'

As I listen to Pete Bassi, I think this is just the sort of thing I often hear from white supporters who, while asserting they are not racist, cannot accept there is racism. Pete's tone may also reflect that he is now very much an insider, on a steering group within the FA. But despite this, much to my surprise, he agrees that there is institutional racism and white privilege:

'I haven't seen it first hand but I know it's there. I do still think there is institutional racism prevalent now. In the way that they've still got that stigma about Asians can't play football, or Asians like their curries too much, or they haven't got a proper diet or they haven't got the physique. I think it's throughout institutions. It's the coaches, it's the players, the managers.'

For Wolves supporters, this anti-Asian bias is ironic as the club is owned by a Chinese:

'The Chinese owner at Wolverhampton is very much liked. They have turned Wolverhampton around. A number of years ago there were times where I didn't want to go to a match and my son didn't want to go to a game as well because we were playing so poorly, so there was nothing there to cheer on or get behind. Then you roll on, fast forward ten, 15 years, and we've got these owners come in and they've turned the club on its head. They got us promoted, got a fantastic manager, some world-class players.'

The manager has since gone, but Wolves' status as a Premier League club is not now in dispute. Owners delivering success also highlights an aspect of racism. 'If you deliver success to the club, the white fans won't care what your colour is. They'll just want that success.'

Pete, who has been working since he was 19 – has not faced discrimination because of his colour:

'My upbringing was "turn the other cheek". The school that I went to, from infants' school right the way through was predominantly white, but there were a lot of Asians and black people. I had the confidence to assert myself. I never felt inferior, or was never made to feel inferior. [If there was racism] I could handle myself. I've had a fair few fights because of being called a 'Paki' or [subjected to] a racist chant. This was at school and the outside of school as well.'

He then tells me a story of what happened when his family moved to an estate which was predominantly white:

'There was a park there and my brother and my cousins and I, about five of us, went to the park. I was about 12 years old and I was the eldest. As we were walking along the footpath, five white lads came across us on their BMXs and stopped us. They were standing there just before the entrance. They went, "Where do you think you're going?" I said, "I'm just going to a park over there." And they went, "No, no Pakis allowed." "You what?" I said. And he said, "Yeah, no Pakis allowed." Because there were five of them, I said to my cousins and my brother, "Look, don't worry, come on, we'll walk back." So, we walked back to my house, got my older cousins, and came back up the same way, and we saw some of them. And I went, "That's them there." And they went off because my cousins were big lads. And then a few days later, we met them again and I had a fight with one of them. It was fists. I floored him and then after that, obviously, we shook hands. It was okay to go to the park after that. It was like, "All right, Pete, how you doing? Carry on." We could go to the park, do what we wanted.'

How will things be in another 20 years? 'I'm very hopeful and you can tell the differences already because the school that my son Prabveer has gone to, the people that he's friends with; he has got more white friends than Asian friends, and they don't see the colour, which is brilliant.'

Would it bother him if Prabveer married a white girl? 'No, not really, no. As long as the girl's right for him and he's right for her, then no.'

It is doubtful, for all his much-advertised scholarly prowess, that Powell, were he alive, would have understood, let alone welcomed, the changes that have come over the town and its football club.

THE OTHER MANAGERS

ELEVEN

BRENDAN RODGERS
AND THE FIRST ASIAN

Back in 1995 Terry Westley had told me there had been an Asian player called Bashir at Reading but in 2021 I was not finding it easy to locate him. I was led down several cul-de-sacs as I contacted a number of non-league clubs. The Aylesbury United website offered some hope. But then I found that its 'Player Profiles' started by describing Bashir as 'Unknown Club' and, after fairly sparse information, ended by saying, 'No profile of this player has been written yet.' In the end, I located him. His first words to me were, 'I'm still around.' Then, with unmistakable pride he added, 'The first Asian non-white manager in English football.'

The story Naseem ('Nas') Bashir tells me is not just a story of the first Asian manager but also the story of one of Britain's most successful and much sought-after managers, Brendan Rodgers, and the light it throws on the wider British family of nations made up of many races which is struggling to deal with children from different backgrounds:

'My mum, Iris, is English from London. My dad, Mohammed Bashir, is Pakistani. Dad came to England when he was 19. It was quite brave coming to a country with no relatives, no job. He was not really educated, although he is quite skilled in engineering. He met my mum while they were working in a factory; it was love at first sight for them and that was it.

'On my mother's side they accepted the marriage. But on my father's side, no. He was a Shia Muslim. He was due to have an arranged marriage. And after he met my mum he went back home and told his family that he was, obviously, going to stay in England. The family back home didn't like what he was doing. He did not sever his links, but he came back [to England]. I was not brought up as a Muslim or as a Christian. Not baptised. I think at the time maybe my mum was unsure what to do, because Dad obviously is Muslim, and it would be unfair for us to be Christian. So, nothing really happened. My mum didn't become a Muslim.'

But Nas, born in September 1969, was given a Pakistani name, as was his brother, Tarik, and his sister, Ramona. 'Because my mother wanted to be part of Dad's culture. Dad took my mum and us to see his family. My mum wore a sari. She tried to adapt. She was in love with my dad. My parents are still together after 50 years, still in love.'

Nas, like his father, fell in love with a white girl when young – he was 17, she was 18 – but gave his children very English names: daughter, Alice, son, Frankie. I am speaking to Nas Bashir soon after the television programme where Prince Harry and Meghan revealed how a member of the Royal Family had asked about what the skin colour of their child might be. Nas says:

'You know what I've always said in my life? Everybody wants to go on holiday and have the same skin colour as me. I was naturally born with a fantastic skin colour. And I've not had to pay for it. I look at people and say, "Oh, on holiday and getting a tan and I was born with one, so I must be very lucky." I have got a permanent suntan. And that's what I say to my kids. My kids have got a lovely little glow when they go on holiday. My children are whiter than me. In my marriage colour was never a problem with the families.'

He laughs again, clearly amused by discussing the skin colour of mixed-race children.

The racism he encountered while growing up on the council estate in High Wycombe, a decade before the Thatcherite revolution, did not affect him:

'Just a general thing like being called a Paki which I didn't find offensive. When I played football, if people were calling me names it was actually because I was better than them. That was the only way they could get to me. My mum always taught me when I was young, "Sticks and stones will break bones, but names will never hurt you." I've got to be a bigger person to ignore it and just crack on with what I'm doing. I have been very thick-skinned. Some individuals when people call them names may fight. I've never seen the reason to do that. If someone wants to call you a name, or whatever, that's up to them.'

If a white person has been preferred to him he has not seen it as racism, as happened when, having had a trial at Arsenal, he was denied a scholarship with a white kid chosen. For him it was a football problem. A midfielder who was 'unusual, both a right-footer and left-footer', he had emerged in an age when hoisting the ball and bypassing the midfield, patented by Wimbledon, flourished:

'Probably, looking back, I came a little bit too early. Those were the days of long-ball football. I was very technical. I wanted the ball to my feet. I could provide a through pass. At the time a lot of clubs were not looking for players like me. They were looking for somebody who was big, strong and powerful. I was not very tall, five foot seven inches. I weighed ten stone six pounds. I was very technical and I was very quick.'

But helped by a friend, he got a two-year Youth Training Scheme [YTS] apprenticeship at Reading. When he had first walked into the Reading dressing room, there was an initial feeling from the senior players that as the lone Asian in the dressing room he might have wandered onto the wrong sports ground and should have been at a cricket ground:

'There were first-team players who were like, "Who is he?" It wasn't until they saw me on the pitch that I gained respect. I had joined Reading when I was 16 – this would have been 1986 – and within five weeks I was training with the first team, because I could cope. I was so clever in terms of my awareness – if anybody tried to tackle me, I could get out of trouble. I could embarrass people if they came too close. I could just go around them. So, I gained the respect of the senior players straightaway because they thought, well, he has got a bit of whatever you want to call it. It was just bad luck that I did not make it as a footballer in terms of going to the highest level. I was 21. I got 'Player of the Year' for the youth team in 1988. I was on the verge of playing in the first team because I was training with the first team all the time. And then I broke my metatarsal while training. I just put my weight on my metatarsal and it cracked. It was my left foot I cracked. I came out for a period of time to try and get it to heal and cracked it again, came back and cracked it again. So, literally, within a year and a half of me being on the verge of playing first-team games, I was in the wilderness.'

The wilderness was non-league football and with it came the changes non-league football imposes on all players: 'Football was part-time, like two evenings a week training. I had to find a job. What I did between playing football was window cleaning. It allowed me to finish early, going to sleep before a game and stuff like that.' Finally, after spells at Slough Town, Chesham United, Aylesbury, Maidenhead and Hendon, he decided he had had enough.

Even while window cleaning he had got his A licence, and through a friend, whom he had played with at Reading, became the youth team coach at his local club, Wycombe Wanderers. That job meant he no longer had to be a window cleaner. Then another friend, Martin Allen, who was assistant manager at Reading to Alan Pardew, recommended him for a job at Reading as assistant academy manager and Under-17 coach.

'They were in League One and the academy was not great; it was a lot of hard work. I was quite lucky to be around a lot of good people, the likes of Alan Pardew and Steve Coppell. Steve Coppell was very influential when I went to Reading.'

In 2010 Bashir was sacked by Reading shortly after Coppell had left, and he managed a non-league team, Hayes & Yeading United. However, even as he managed Hayes & Yeading, he had started another venture which now takes up all his time. Using part of the money Reading gave him he set up the FAB Academy at Bisham Abbey National Sports Centre, a junior academy where young players come and get coached professionally by professional coaches. 'The academy is going well. It is 11 years old now and a lot of people have copied the idea.'

Compared to his own upbringing, he can see:

'Asian parents encouraging their kids to play football. Certainly, when I was younger, there wasn't enough encouragement from parents. When I was playing, I was pretty much the only Asian player around. We have got Asian players who are coming through. And the quality of the players has improved. Since I grew up there is a lot more respect for Asian people. Twenty to thirty years ago people would look at someone who's brown or black in a certain, prejudiced way. Certainly, people now have been more educated to say, "It's not just the colour of their skin."'

But, he sighs when I ask about when we can see black or Asian coaches in league clubs. 'I don't know. I'm probably one of the only pro licence coaches with an Asian name.' However, what makes Nas's story so interesting is how it throws light on the complex story of race in Britain. To appreciate that, we need to look at the career of the most successful British-born manager in the Premier League.

Who is British?

This manager is not a son of an immigrant from a faraway land, but he is also something of an outsider. He is white. He is Brendan Rodgers, a Catholic, born in Carnlough, Northern Ireland. Bashir's story is intertwined with that of Rodgers: 'Brendan and I were both at Reading together as apprentices, although I was a year older, so I knew him quite well as we grew up together.'

What is uncanny is that Rodgers' playing career matched that of Bashir. A genetic knee condition forced him to retire aged 20 and he, like Bashir, drifted into non-league football. If Bashir played in clubs based round London, Rodgers travelled round the country playing at various clubs: Ballymena United in Northern Ireland, Newport Town on the Isle of Wight and Witney Town, Oxfordshire. Bashir's and Rodgers' paths crossed again at Reading when Bashir took over as Under-17 coach, with Rodgers the Under-19 coach: 'In terms of coaching, he is very methodical, very structured and organised. He knows what he wants and has a good eye for a player. Brendan has done fantastic.'

Rodgers certainly has. He worked for Mourinho at Chelsea, then managed Watford and Reading before taking Swansea to the Premier League, making them the first Welsh side to play in that league. He also, but for a slip by Steven Gerrard in a match against Chelsea, might have secured Liverpool their first Premier League title. This was followed by great honours with Celtic. There he did not lose a single game in the 2016 season and won the league, the Scottish Cup and League Cup several times. Then, after suddenly leaving for Leicester in 2019, he guided Leicester to their first-ever FA Cup in the 2020–21 season.

In making the comparison I am not suggesting that Rodgers established himself as a successful manager because he is white and Nas Bashir is not. Yet tracing the story of these two people, who know each other well, illustrates how integration of people from different backgrounds works in this country. Rodgers' football journey saw him play as a teenager for Northern Ireland at schoolboy level, but he also represented the Republic of Ireland at schoolboy level. Rodgers' association with the Republic and Bashir's with Pakistan shows how the British Empire worked and the very different legacies it has left behind and its impact on sport. Ireland, unlike Pakistan, is not part of the Commonwealth. And unlike Pakistan, Ireland for several decades claimed a part of the United Kingdom, Northern Ireland. Rodgers, like all those in Northern Ireland, can get a passport of the Republic and in playing for the Republic could be said, at least on that occasion, to have declared his allegiance to a foreign country. But he would not be seen as having compromised his loyalty to the United Kingdom, indeed the question would not be raised. Bashir could not do that with Pakistan.

The fact is that Rodgers is part of the wider, white British family whose members' relationship with each other, while complicated, still means family ties remain. In sport it produces remarkable alliances cutting across national boundaries. In rugby Ireland fields a unified team representing the whole of the island of Ireland; Ireland also takes part with the United Kingdom in rugby tours overseas in a team that for many decades was known as the British Lions, although in recent years its name has been amended to the British and Irish Lions. And here sport has gone where politics cannot, as the problems of the Brexit deal for the province have illustrated.

In the English team that played in Euro 2020 there were three players who could have played for Ireland. The captain Harry Kane's father is from Galway in Ireland and, while there was never any question of Ireland tempting him or even trying to, the Football Association of Ireland tried hard to convince Declan Rice and Jack Grealish. Rice, born in this country but with grandparents from Ireland, was for a time torn between playing for Ireland and England. He played for Ireland in a friendly against Turkey and only pledged his allegiance to England in February 2019. Grealish, descended from Irish grandparents, played Gaelic football and for the Under-17, Under-18 and Under-21 Irish sides before choosing England.

There are, of course, no such links that Britain has with Pakistan or any member of what is called the 'New Commonwealth', meaning the black or brown nations this country once ruled. Nas Bashir feels British but the fact is that while Rodgers has always been part of the British family, Bashir belongs to a new, distinct group whose historic relationship with Britain is very different and whose welcome to the British family is still a work in progress. However it progresses it cannot reproduce the relationship that Rodgers' Northern Ireland has with Britain. It will have to be a very different relationship. And that will depend very much on how the children of Bashir and their generation relate to this country and the mainstream community.

TWELVE

THE 'PAKI' GREEK MANAGER

aringey Borough FC would always make a good pub quiz question. Which football team's ground is located on a street whose name is associated with a much more famous club that is not actually located there? The answer is Haringey Borough FC located on White Hart Lane, while Tottenham, the club historically associated with White Hart Lane, is a good ten or 15 minutes' walk away. And while Haringey Borough may be Isthmian League Premier Division in an area that reflects that London borough, a bit shabby, with public housing nearby, it has everything you would expect from a respected, established club: a decent, proper ground, stands with seating in the main stand, terracing, a main entrance and a clubhouse. It has car boot sales and its clubhouse has held weddings. However, little has happened at Haringey Borough FC over the years that has warranted much media interest outside of Haringey.

Then on an October Saturday in 2019, Haringey Borough made international news. They were playing Yeovil Town, in the fourth round of the FA Cup qualifying competition, with the victors assured a place in the first round of the cup. Yeovil have a reputation for being giant-killers in the cup, and 1,100 spectators gathered at Coles Park, Haringey's ground, to watch whether the club could do the same to Yeovil. The previous season Haringey had reached the first round of the FA Cup for the first time, losing 1-0 at home to AFC Wimbledon. For that match, 3,000 people had come to Coles Park, BBC cameras were present and the game passed off without any incident. But now in the 64th minute the match against Yeovil was abandoned amid accusations of racism, bottle throwing and spitting.

It could not have come at a more embarrassing moment for English football. Four days earlier, England's Euro 2020 qualifier in Bulgaria was halted twice as fans were warned about racist behaviour, including Nazi salutes and monkey chanting. That had been the occasion for much English moralising about how Eastern European fans could learn from the English who had long eradicated such racist problems in their game. Events at Haringey Borough showed this was yet another claim of English exceptionalism that could not be sustained.

Two years later the echoes of what happened that autumn night can still be heard as I discover when I talk to Tom Loizou, the 66-year-old Haringey manager, who had decided to take his players off the pitch.

Loizou, with his happy memories of the match against Wimbledon – 'not one incident' – and knowing how big a draw Yeovil would be, had spent days before the match working hard to welcome the Yeovil fans. Very aware that laws do not allow drinking in sight of the game, Loizou set about creating a beer garden for them to drink safely outside the boundaries of the stadium:

> 'We had gravel on the floor and for three days prior to the match I was putting shingle on the floor to make it more even and more comfortable for the Yeovil supporters. We bought a burger bar so we could segregate the fans because we were told we had to segregate so they could be in their own comfort zone. We put toilets on their side of the ground. It took us about ten days to organise all of this.'

But long before kick-off, Loizou kept hearing of problems these Yeovil fans were causing:

> 'Certain Yeovil supporters made a couple of the girls in the café bar cry. One Yeovil supporter asked, "Can I have a Coke, please?" and the girl at the café bar politely said, "Would you like a Diet Coke, sir, or a full fat Coke?" He turned round and said to her, "No, you keep the Diet Coke for yourself, you could do with it." And then a Yeovil fan asked one of the girls, "What do you serve here?" She said, "Burgers and hotdogs." He turned round and said, "Well, you can keep the hotdogs and shove it between your legs, darling. I'll have a burger."'

Loizou's team represents multicultural London: six blacks, three Greeks, two English. 'We have a Nigerian, a Jamaican, people from Dominica. There are Greeks from Greece and Greeks from Cyprus.' The team that day was aged between 20 and 30 with the goalkeeper, Valery Douglas Pajetat, who is on contract, a black Portuguese who speaks French, one of the oldest at 32. 'He is the nicest person you could ever meet. His wife is the one who went to work, and he plays football. Football is his work.'

At half-time Loizou felt everything was working fine. The score was 0-0 and the problems he had heard about in the burger bar seemed isolated incidents. The second half would prove very different:

'In the first half my goalkeeper had his back to our fans, about 700 of them. But as soon as we kicked off the second half and my goalkeeper's back was to the Yeovil fans, that's when the trouble started. There were about 300 of them. I kept hearing chants of 'Oo oo oo'. Like a monkey chant. When I questioned Yeovil supporters about these chants later one of their supporters said to me, "Well, it wasn't a monkey chant, it's our chant. We play in green and white hoops, so it was hoops, hoops, hoops." I said, "I heard something different." OK, if that's what they say it was let's say it was hoops, hoops, hoops.

'While the second half was on, I could see my goalkeeper touching the back of his head. I later learned some of these idiots had filled their pockets with this shingle stone I had put on the gravel to make the bar and started pelting my goalkeeper with it. I kept telling the fourth official, "I think they are throwing coins at my goalkeeper," and he said to me, "The referee will sort it out." It kept going on and on. The referee was getting a little bit frightened because the supporters were getting very vocal and very rude.

'Then I saw the first bottle come over. It was half filled with beer and at shoulder height. It narrowly missed the goalkeeper's head, hit him in the back and bounced off his shoulder by his neck. Luckily, I had the foresight to only serve beer in plastic bottles. I saw my goalkeeper pick the bottle up and some of my players said to the referee, "Look, this bottle has just been thrown." I said to the fourth official, "Did you see that?" What I learned later was these idiots had smuggled a few bottles of beer under their jackets onto pitch side. We never had a lot of security because we can't afford it. We're not like Spurs down the road.'

It soon got worse:

'The referee gave them a penalty. I don't think it was a penalty but let's not talk about the football side of it. My goalkeeper went over to the post to pick up a towel to dry his hands, because this is what goalkeepers do, and he was spat at. So, now he had phlegm dripping from the top of his head and his face, and on his shirt. I said to the fourth official, "Did you see that?" The fourth official said to me, "Sit down and be quiet, the referee will sort it out." Then I saw another bottle come over and my goalkeeper just managed to dodge this bottle.

'I said to the fourth official, "This is out of order." By then they were about to take the penalty. Really the game should have been abandoned there and then just for the hate and the abuse he had already received. They took the penalty and scored. And as they scored, my goalkeeper got hit with another bottle. I said to the fourth official, "That's it." Spitting is an assault and I decided to walk onto the pitch. He said, "You'd better not go on, mate, you'll get sent off, you'll get into trouble."

'I just said, "I don't give a fuck what happens now. I'm going on the pitch," and I walked over to the referee. As I was walking over to him, I heard the words "black cunt". I only heard it once, but I heard it. I said to my players, "What's going on?" and they said, "Some of us are getting racial abuse." I said, "Referee, what are you going to do about it?" He said to me, "Well, what can I do about it? Go and get the stewards." I saw the referee was frightened at this stage. He was a young man, must have been in his early 30s. He didn't know what to do.'

'"Right," I said to the referee, "it's not up to me to get the stewards. If you are not going to deal with it I'm taking my team off." It was not just a race incident, it was a hate crime. You've got to remember I've had some of these kids from the age of 17, and they're now 27, 28, 29. I've got them out of Sunday football. They're not used to this. We qualified for this round of the FA Cup on ability. I was brought up in Tottenham, Edmonton and I used to play in the Cypriot League, a local league. My teammate was Troy Townsend. He is black and was head of Kick It Out. We never had any incidents like that in that league in those days.'

This, interestingly, was not the most racist incident Loizou had ever encountered.

'No, I've had it before but not at our ground, at away grounds. In the FA Trophy a few years before we were playing Hitchin and it went to penalties, and my black players got racially abused as they came up to take a penalty. Then a girlfriend of one of the players, who was pregnant, was walking to her car after the game and they said, "I hope you have cancer, blah, blah, you black bitch, you and the baby inside of you fucking die." And the girl came back and was absolutely shaking. Shivering. The year before that my goalkeeper, another goalkeeper, was getting called a black cunt. They were giving him the monkey chant because he was black. I begged my goalkeeper to keep calm. "Keep calm and we'll deal with it."'

So why did Loizou not remain calm and decide to walk off when playing Yeovil?

'Because before, with my old side, we used to jump over the barriers and deal with it and it got us into a lot of trouble. This time I've educated my team, let's try it a different way, let's do it through the right way and it still hasn't worked. We still get racially abused. The media wanted to talk about me being the first manager to take his team off – I didn't want this. I didn't do that to put Haringey on the map. I didn't walk onto the pitch because my boys were getting racial abuse. I walked on because my players were getting hit by bottles. Then I heard the racial abuse. Then I took my team off. My captain didn't want to go back on the pitch.'

As a result of the incident Loizou had to take additional security measures for the replay which cost £7,000 and left the club out of pocket.

Loizou has been dealing with race since he was a child:

'I'm Greek Cypriot. My parents emigrated from Cyprus in the fifties, but I'm born and bred here. My mum used to go out to work and she used to leave me with the lodgers upstairs who were Irish. When I was beginning to speak, I was speaking English with an Irish accent. I have a dark tan. I had a lot of abuse in school, little comments from stupid kids. My nickname was Paki. They used to call me "Paki" and they would say, "Where's your Datsun?" or things like that. [There was a general belief that people of Asian origin drove Datsuns.] And then it got to, "Have you got a kebab shop?" When I first became a non-league manager a supporter thought it was funny to throw paper plates on the pitch. Smashing plates and stuff like that because the Greeks smash plates. When I managed Enfield I was told, "We don't want you, you Greek cunt." Back in the eighties my brother-in-law was playing for Chelsea and he got transferred to Millwall. I turned up at one game but I felt so threatened as I got singled out because of the colour of my skin. They were singing songs like, "Did you park your Nissan outside," or, "Your Datsun is outside." My brother-in-law played for them for three years. I never went to another Millwall game.'

Even as he qualified as a coach his looks made him feel he was the other one in a sea of white faces:

'They look at me and the feeling I get is they are looking at someone who looks Indian and who shouldn't be in the game. Many times I've been told by people I'm in the wrong sport, that I should be playing cricket. Even when I went to Lilleshall one of the coaches said to me, "You should be at Lord's or The Oval." I've never mentioned that before to anyone. When I took my UEFA A licence up at Lilleshall I was mentored by Les Reed who works for the FA. In my class I had Brian Kidd, David Moyes and Alan Pardew. They have all progressed to managing in the Premier League and I'm at Haringey Borough.'

So, is football in denial about racial abuse?

'Look, football rears a lot of ugly heads. Football is a vehicle for hate and racism. It has to be addressed. They sweep such issues under the carpet, and it gets forgotten, and nothing gets proven. If I drive my car down Tottenham High Road in excess of 30 mph I would have a picture on my doormat within a week, with a picture of my face and me breaking the speed limit with an endorsement.'

What really hurts is how the FA responded to the incident. In the aftermath of the walking off, the *Observer* ran a piece with a picture of Loizou. The world's media descended on Haringey Borough:

'CNN did. ITV did. BT did. Sky Sports did. The Vanessa Feltz show did. Everybody except the FA. We never even got a hello. I haven't had any contact with any FA member. It's a year and a half down the line and still no one has contacted me. Nobody at the FA said, "We should look into this." If they had looked into it, maybe half a dozen of the other incidents that happened may not have happened.

Loizou is now so disillusioned that he says, "I'm not reporting it [racism] any more. We should go back to the old days when we used to jump over the barriers and deal with it ourselves. Football authorities will never tackle this problem."

What encourages him is:

'Black people are now speaking out and highlighting it. I think they've got a voice now. I can't walk through Tottenham without a black person stopping and kissing me and thanking me.'

THIRTEEN

CHANGING THE NARRATIVE

There is one phrase Anwar Uddin uses with great frequency: the need to create a 'new narrative' about football, the game he fell in love with when he was a four-year-old:

'I've tried to do that my whole life. When I was 12, 13 because I was very, very good, people started to sort of ask me questions about my ethnicity, my faith and told me that I couldn't do it. I won't do it. I shouldn't do it. I was prepared for failure because of what all these adults around me would tell me. I've just been quite positive and quite narrow-minded about the whole thing, and what football has given me is amazing. I've had an unbelievable career, played in stadiums with 50,000 people watching me. I have played at every level of the game. I have finished the game and I now manage. I created my own campaigns with fans about diversity, which is now responsible for thousands of community members from the Asian, the black, the Jewish and the LGBTQ communities watching live football. I want people to understand that there's opportunity in sport. There are opportunities in everything in life, but you can't let these stereotypes, negativity, hold you back and misguide you.'

Uddin can lay claim to several firsts: the first person of Bangladeshi origin to play professional football in this country; the first British Asian to captain a football club in the top four divisions of English football; and now, assistant manager at Aldershot, a post he has held since 2019:

'I'm currently the highest ranking British Asian manager. How many Asian coaches are there? There are none. I was the first-ever assistant manager in the Football League with Barnet; I took over temporarily when I was a player and when Martin Allen, the ex-manager, left. I was the first British Asian to ever do that. I love it every single day. It is a fantastic opportunity. I'm privileged to be manager of a great club with a great fan base.'

He is speaking while driving to a match. 'Is it a Porsche?' I expect him to say, 'Don't be silly,' but much to my surprise he laughs and says, 'Yes, it is.' What makes it all the more interesting is that the Aldershot owner is also Asian. 'We have got a chairman from Pakistan, Shahid Azeem, and he's an unbelievable role model for the Asian community as well. It's not something that I could have imagined when I was young.' He could not have imagined it because of what he endured as a boy growing up in the East End of London in the early nineties:

'The word "Paki" was used all the time. That's how they described people who looked like me and you. It was just common practice. I thought it was in the dictionary. It was a dagger in the heart every single time I heard it and that is something I wanted to stop and challenge. During the time [I was growing up] it was like a circus.'

This circus turned into 'a freak show' when, between the ages of ten and 14, he played grassroots football in the East End and his dad, who is from Bangladesh, came to watch him play:

'When my dad used to come and watch me my teammates would say, "Who's that Paki guy?" They would not know it was my dad. I didn't want him to come because of the abuse. I thought to myself, "What a world we live in where you can't have your family, who want to support you, come to the match." My dad worked very hard six, seven days a week. But the one day he has off he wants to come and watch his son, but he can't because he had to deal with this nonsense. It was a big challenge to concentrate on being the best player, and now there was this additional barrier. I told my dad not to come. "You know what, Dad, let me bring you to a stadium when I have a professional contract and I'm being paid to play. Let me do this by myself. Leave this to me. And the minute I am able to play in stadiums and I have people singing my name, that's when you're going to come because that's when it's going to be okay." That happened the minute I started playing full time at West Ham. Then my dad would come. There would be thousands of people watching us. I played for Bristol Rovers, Dagenham, I played at Wembley, and my family would come to all these games. That was the moment I felt I had made my statement. It was not just for me. It was for a lot of young Asian people who would have experienced this sort of thing, and probably seen me. I wasn't going to allow some of the nonsensical behaviour during that period to stop me. But that behaviour has changed now.'

Anwar's father's story is a hopeful story of modern migration to Europe from the non-white world, one of trauma in his homeland and then finding fulfilment in his adopted country, England:

'My dad made a brave decision to come to this country, because he lost his family through illness. He was from Sylhet, and he came here in the early seventies. He saw an opportunity in this country, and he wanted to make sure that all these children realise how fortunate they were.'

In England he found love. 'He met my mother here. My mother, who is English, became a Muslim.'

But his pride in being a Bangladeshi and a Muslim never left him, and he was keen to instil that in his son:

'My dad felt quite strongly about our history and I'm so glad that he chose Anwar as my name. A lot of people I know in the second and third generations would like to change their names. I never wanted to change my name. When people in football come to me and I say I am Anwar they know who I am. So, when football fans say my name, they are embracing my name, celebrating it, and that's a Bangladeshi name.'

As he speaks, he emphasises the word 'Bangladeshi'. I ask in Bengali, 'Bangla bolen apni?' (Do you speak Bengali)? He says in Bengali, 'Balo na, balo na' (Not good, not good). 'My Bengali has never been great, but I understand it very well.'

But if his Bengali is not fluent, he quickly declares that 'I love hilsa fish', the great fish of Bengal. And there is no doubting his pride in his Bengali heritage:

'Oh my God, I am aware of my Bengali heritage. Because that's who I am. If it wasn't for my country, the trials and tribulations of my father and his ancestors, I wouldn't be where I am. I would not have had the life that I have had. I'm very much Bangladeshi. I am so proud of the country and everything it stands for. I miss everything about Bangladesh. I used to go back to my dad's village every year when I was at school. It kept me grounded. It was unbelievable. I've set up

academies in Bangladesh. I've done some work in the Rohingya refu-
gee camps [set up for people of Bengali origin who have been cruelly
driven out of their homes in Myanmar]. I have tried to do as much as
I can back in Bangladesh because I feel I can give something back. It
is important that no one should be divorced from their heritage. Everyone should know exactly where they're from and be proud of that.
I feel equally divided between Bangladesh and Britain, but my heart
is in Bangladesh because that's who I am. But I am also English.'

Anwar's story also explodes the myth that people from the subcontinent
know nothing about football: 'My dad loved football. He played on the rice
fields, and in the garden in his school in Sylhet. When he came to England
he had to stop. He always said to me that he felt he lived his dream for me
because I was able to.'

For Uddin, who played for a number of clubs including Bristol Rovers, the
highlight was playing in front of 50,000 at Upton Park:

'That is when we played in the FA Youth Cup final in 1999. Upton Park
was sold out. We won the Youth Cup 9-0, defeating Coventry, and
went to America. We played in exhibition matches all over Africa
and Asia. When I was at West Ham, we had the best youth team in
the world. This was from 1996 to 1999.'

The youth team had Joe Cole, Michael Carrick, Jermain Defoe, Glen
Johnson, all four of whom played for England, and three of them – Cole,
Carrick and Johnson – won Premier League titles and Carrick, the
Champions League. I am intrigued to know how they treated him, an Asian
kid, in a game with so few Asian players. There is no mistaking the pride
in his voice when he says: 'Listen, I was their captain. I treated them well. I
was a leader. It was about how I feel. I dictated things. You lead by example.
You look after them, they look after you. Being a captain at West Ham for
me was an honour. And for the club to say to me, "He's a young Asian boy
that we want to make captain to lead these fine and proper young players."
That was because I had the inner strength, and I wanted to get the best out
of everyone. I wanted them to get the best out of me. We were very successful
and very proud. Those memories never go away. They are forever.'

However, when he first went to the West Ham changing room, life was
very different:

'When I was in changing rooms, initially as a youngster, I felt very
isolated and lonely because everyone was either white or black. Some
of the terminology used I found offensive. And the older I became, I

thought, "I can't be my true self by sitting around the corner and listening, and every time I hear a word, or people make jokes, it hurts me." I had to assume this kind of leadership quality, to say "No" and challenge the terminology, challenge silly jokes and be a strong person. I didn't want to hide in changing rooms any more.'

The change from being the shy kid hiding in the dressing room to becoming a leader came when he was around 17:

'I became really serious. It was literally sink or swim. I know it sounds quite dramatic, but I was 17, 18 years old, and I was thrown into a changing room with the best players in the world at West Ham. When I joined, the first team had England internationals, superstars I had watched my whole life. Stuart Pearce, Rio Ferdinand, Frank Lampard. When you're in that environment, you have got to act like you belong there. Initially it was "He is the young Asian kid. Let's see what he's all about." It is about earning respect. And if you don't have that inner belief in yourself, don't even bother turning up. Everyone accepted me because they saw who I was first and the colour of the skin on my face was secondary.'

Yet for all his pride about his achievements with the West Ham youth team, there is one failure that haunts him:

'I didn't play for the first team. That hurts every single day. In life it is about timing. I was in the West Ham first-team squad for three years. In that period we finished fifth in the Premier League. We had players like Paolo Di Canio, Trevor Sinclair, Stuart Pearce, Rio Ferdinand and Frank Lampard. Five years later they got relegated. Had I been there a little bit longer, I'm confident I would have had appearances, I would have played more. But I was at West Ham at probably their most successful period ever.'

But there are firsts in his career which fill him with great pride:

'I was the captain of Dagenham for six years. I took that team from the National League to League One, playing against Sheffield Wednesday and Charlton. Dagenham is a very, very small club, and to do that is unheard of for a club of that size. And to lift two trophies as a Bangladeshi, South Asian player, and lift one at Wembley, and to win the National League Trophy as captain, as a champion. That's something that's never been done before and may never be repeated again for a long time.'

Yet even as he captained the West Ham youth team and his father could finally come to watch and not be worried about being called a 'Paki', the Asians who lived round West Ham's Upton Park ground were fearful of going to watch the match. 'That was because of the history of violence and racism; they did not feel comfortable, so they just didn't go. That is slowly changing.'

And what he has never forgotten is that for all the shouts of 'Paki' and racial abuse he suffered in this country, his experiences abroad were much worse: 'Every time we went abroad the language from fans and players and the way we were treated was a lot worse than it was in England. We played lots of tournaments and games in Europe. We played in games in France, Italy. It was hard.'

Anwar's views on whether there is institutional racism is much more nuanced than that of many other people of colour:

> 'It is very hard to say yes or no. In this country, being white and being English has its advantages, that's obvious. But to be honest with a lot of these things, personally, I don't really allow it to affect me or my life. I think sometimes when you read into all the issues, the problems, the concerns, it sometimes clouds your judgement about who you are. Ultimately, give people the benefit of the doubt and that should stand you in a good light.'

What he is keen about is that the Asian community 'needs to be more positive. We can't just be talking about the problems and issues constantly. Let us talk about some of our success stories. I don't think we do that enough.' But then, as Zulfi Ali and Imrul Gazi have discovered, finding success stories to talk about is not that easy.

WAITING FOR
THE ASIAN DAWN

FOURTEEN

HANDSHAKES, BROWNS, BLACKS, JEWS AND WOMEN

I t is November 2011 and Sepp Blatter, the president of FIFA, has said the way to handle racism in football is for players to shake hands after the match. I have come to Clapton to see how far this might work at the grassroots of football in London.

In some ways this is a walk down football's past. A Saturday afternoon with a match starting at 3 p.m. is what I remember from my student days and is now so rare in the Premier League. At first glance, the London APSA (All People's Sports Association) match against Bowers and Pitsea FC suggests that things at non-league level, the game's coalface, could not be better. You get to the ground, just up the road from Upton Park, which at the time was still the home of West Ham, through a car workshop owned by local Muslims. The match programme has a full-page advertisement: 'Let's kick racism out of football.' The two teams appear to be doing just that. London APSA, a largely Asian team, have a white goalkeeper. The visiting Basildon team have several black players and the referee is black.

The match itself, a classic game of two halves, sees London APSA take a comfortable 2-0 half-time lead, but they are lucky to hold on to a 2-2 draw. The game is full of that combination of skill, physical rigour and never-say-die spirit that makes English football so compelling.

Yet even before the match has kicked off, it has become clear that these surface impressions are very misleading. As the players warm up, Vince McBean, then chief executive of Clapton, tells me bluntly: 'It's not correct that English football has dealt with racism. There are major problems at the grassroots. From a strategic point of view, we have problems as black clubs and black players on and off the pitch.'

He agrees that racism has changed: 'The days of "nigger" bashing have gone. Whereas before somebody came up to and said, "You black bastard", they don't have to say that any more. It's subtly done now in terms of how the referee deals with us and how the league deals with us.'

The tall, imposing 55-year-old, who came here as a teenager from the Caribbean, served in the Green Jackets with tours of duty in Ireland, Germany and Canada. 'In the Army you can deal with racism by taking them round the back. The British Army has changed. Football hasn't, not really.'

While under McBean, the committee of the club and the players had moved from being uniformly white to all but three black, but of the 50 match officials in the Essex League, says McBean, only three are black, and he has no doubts his team cannot expect fair decisions. 'In our game here, we're frightened to tackle in the box because it's so simple to give away penalties. Some of the calls that we've had against us are not what I call reasonable.'

Insisting race plays a part in referees' decisions, McBean notes: 'We do not expect a white person to stand up for us against another white person. There's a certain relationship between the referees and white players. Our black players don't move in the same circles. We regard ourselves as the underclass.'

The divide between black and white is well illustrated when I later ring Robert Errington, the then president of the Essex Senior League, and ask him about the numbers of black and Asian officials in the league. He is outraged. 'I do not see the point of your question. I find it offensive.' When I put to him McBean's allegations that black players could not get fair treatment from white officials, he explodes, 'It is a disgraceful thing for him to say.'

Zulfi Ali, president of London APSA, has warmer memories of the Essex FA and Errington, both of whom, he said, were very supportive when he moved the club from the Asian League to the Essex Senior League in 2003. But the 38-year-old spoke sorrowfully of the racism his players had encountered:

> 'In our second season we were playing Barking, and Imran Khan, our goalkeeper, had his beard pulled by a white forward inside the box who shouted, "Shave it off you cunt, Paki bastard." Imran chased the player to the halfway line and was red-carded. When I complained to the referee he said, "It is nothing; he did not hurt him, punch or slap him." '

His most painful memories were of a match ten years earlier in the Essex Business Houses League:

'One of our players, Shabhas Khan, only 18, had his face smashed by an opposing player, and his tooth popped out. There was lots of racist abuse of the "You fucking Paki bastard" type. Fights broke out and I rang the police. The game was abandoned. It is not as bad now. But if any of our players has a beard, he will be called Bin Laden or a terrorist. To them now, it's water off a duck's back.'

Khalid Pervaiz, the 27-year-old assistant manager, who adored Ryan Giggs, certainly treated such remarks as jokes. 'I have a beard and I hear people say, "Go back to the mosque", "Why aren't you cooking curry?"'

A triallist with Aston Villa in his nearly eight years in the league, he had heard Asian players complain they have been called Bin Laden. 'You get them particularly when you are winning or going into a tackle. When we are playing five-a-side there is a lot of tugging of beards and our players get kicked left, right and centre. Then the same team would play other white teams and there would be no kicking.'

But unlike Pervaiz, not all players wanted to talk about their racist experience.

Sham Darr, a 26-year-old who worked in the public sector, only agreed to talk to me and have his picture taken if we did not mention his day job. The son of Pakistani immigrants from Kashmir, he had a trial for Leicester City. 'I think I did not make it due to racism. I was 19, a winger, and people who came to the trial felt I played an immaculate game. It was seen as a publicity stunt. Asian footballer from the East End being given a chance, rather than looking to sign me.'

While he agreed that the situation had improved since he first started playing, he insisted, 'There is still a problem, not so much on the field, but behind closed doors. People in charge of the game in the academies, coaches, managers are all white.'

Yet when I spoke to the white players and officials at the match, the divide between the races became very evident. For them these tales of racism seemed to be stories from another planet they know nothing about. Laurie Mallyon, the 58-year-old van driver who was an assistant in the match, was surprised there was any talk of racism.

'I have been officiating for 15 years in the Essex Senior League and I have seen no racism. In one game I was refereeing ten years ago, a person called a black guy "you black bugger". I called him over and said, "You cannot do that. You will be in serious trouble if you do." He said, "I am sorry, ref, I should have known better, I am half-caste." That was his word. We had no more problems from that.'

Then, in words that echoed Blatter, he added, 'If you approach the person who has said these things in the proper manner, then you can nip it in the bud. There is racism on both sides, from the white community and the black community. If you keep it in-house you can iron it out yourself.'

Lee Stevens, the white club secretary of Bowers & Pitsea, whose team was half black, not only was convinced there wasn't a problem but pointed out how his club helped ethnic minorities. 'A lot of the APSA players are Muslims. They pray to Mecca before a match. We set aside a piece of our ground for them to pray on their mats.'

London APSA's only white player, 34-year-old goalkeeper Ian Stanley, was surprised to hear there was any racism. 'If it goes on, I do not know. Being in goal what happens in the middle or the other end I would not know.'

Stanley, who was recently recruited to the team, did not mix with his teammates after the game: 'They socialise among themselves.' This may not be helped by the fact that many of the team, being Muslims, do not drink.

Zulfi Ali agrees that Muslims not drinking was a problem and this was also not helping his dream for the club to have its own home ground. 'To be financially safe, we need to sell alcohol. We cannot do that ethically.'

Another problem for Zulfi was that Asians did not turn up to support London APSA. Although this was a home game, the 20 or so spectators were almost all from the visiting team. Anjum Khan, the team manager, admitted, 'Asian parents do not want to use their weekend to watch.' And with tickets costing £5, 'they don't wish to pay.'

Worse still, they do not encourage their children to play football. 'Religion is more important to them. Kids need to go to the mosque every day. Asian parents do not see football as a career. They want to talk about their son as a doctor or a lawyer, not a football player.'

However, Zulfi could see changes in some of the younger generation of parents. He told me of a recent Under-9 match:

'The kids had been brought by their mums, many of them in hijabs. As the white parents started shouting and screaming, these mothers in hijabs shouted back. It was funny and wonderful to watch. As long as it is not racist, it is good for these kids to experience a certain amount of argy-bargy as it will make the kids stronger. It is a great way, especially for Muslims, to integrate. You won't party, you won't drink. How else do you integrate?'

A decade later, hope and despair

It is now a decade since I was at Clapton that Saturday afternoon in November 2011, and in the middle of the pandemic I can only talk on the phone with Zulfi Ali. He has been unemployed and has only just been able to get back into work. Both Brexit and the pandemic had hit him hard.

But if his work is looking up, London APSA no longer exists at the senior level.

The players from APSA now play for other clubs at the lower level. Zulfi runs teams at the youth level:

'Most of our team are Asian kids, from age five to 16. It is really, really good, a great environment. I can't say enough good things about this particular league. It has made immense progress in terms of integration, having players from all sorts of backgrounds. Asian, black, white, Chinese, you name it. I can't say that we've experienced any kind of racism. Some parents are rather aggressive, a lot of shouting, screaming, but generally towards their own team, or towards a referee, but not racially abusive. If there is racial abuse it's very minute, a small minority of teams, and I think normally it stems from the coaching staff and the managers.

'Remember that story I told you about turning up somewhere in Essex and getting abuse from opposition teams and the feeling of intimidation? Now across the board we feel safe wherever we go; we do not feel intimidated. Initially only the mums were there; the fathers were not. But as time has gone along, I've insisted that fathers, even though they may be working, find one week in a month to attend and watch their child play. They do and it's been brilliant. Mums and dads come along, and they bring younger siblings along. They love to come. It's a really nice, enjoyable place to come to. I actually believe that the game has changed and the people have changed. In fact a lot of professional clubs would dearly love to have an Asian player playing for them.'

So, has the old stereotype of Asian players not being strong enough and only fit to run shops vanished?

'I would believe that that is the case. Not for any other reason but for the financial reasons. If you get players born in this country but having Indian, Pakistani or Bangladeshi heritage, it will be huge, because it will bring in money from people in those countries. That market hasn't been tapped at all. And it can generate a lot of income for the FA.'

The unbridgeable colour divide

But despite Zulfi Ali's optimism, there is still a huge divide on race between whites and non-whites.

Imrul Gazi is almost the classic second-generation British Bangladeshi. The 46-year-old, who was born in Sylhet, came to this country when he was 18 months old. When I ask if he speaks Bengali, he says – in Bengali – '*Ektu bolte pari'* (I can speak a little.) 'I speak Sylheti. Sylheti is my mother tongue. I am proud of my Sylheti heritage.' He moved from Bradford to London about 11 years ago. He has 'been in pharmaceuticals for over 25 years. We promote a drug for stroke prevention. I have a background in chemistry, but my passion is grassroots football.' He manages Sporting Bengal United, working 'as a volunteer'.

But much as he loves doing it, things have not been the same since that evening in April 2018 when Sporting Bengal played in the Peter Butcher Memorial Cup at Aveley's ground in Romford. The tournament sees the 18 clubs in the first division of the Essex Senior League play the 18 clubs in the Reserve Division:

> 'It was a cup semi-final game. Ours was the first-team side and we were playing the Aveley reserve team. My team had white, black and Asian players. All throughout the game there was a lot of bias involved in the game and from the off the decisions were questionable, to say the least. Through the game there were comments being made by the referee to my players. It wasn't overt or in-your-face racism from the referee. It was the decisions and the smirks and the slight comments on the side that he was making. Just as we were walking off at half-time, with the score 1-1, the referee, who was a young lad, said to one of my white players, who most people know in this league is a big player in the league, "Don't be expecting any decisions here today." The player ran to me and said, just as I was walking off, "Come here, come here." He grabbed the referee and said, "Say that again. Tell what you just said to me, say it." The referee smirked and walked away. At half-time a lot of the players were upset. They didn't want to go out for the second half. We had black players saying, "Look, what is the point in us going out there? We don't have a chance."'

The referee had already sent off two Sporting Bengal players.

Sporting Bengal did take the field for the second half. But the match did not finish. In extra time with Aveley Reserves leading 3-2, the referee showed a red card to the third Sporting player. 'When the referee sent the third player off, we just walked off.' To make things worse as far as Sporting Bengal was concerned, the assistant referee, Eddie Andrews, who at 57 was much older than the referee, said to the Sporting Bengal players, 'Why do yous guys have to behave like this?' Andrews, Gazi alleges, was confrontational: 'He literally was head to head with my assistant in his face. This is an official. He shouldn't have been doing that in the first place. My assistant didn't move. The official walked maybe 30 yards to my assistant in our technical area to put their heads together.'

It is what happened afterwards that has scarred Gazi. So much so that when we talked in March 2021 he said, 'I'm a bit cautious about talking about these things because to this very day I'm feeling the effects.'

Andrews, having been charged by the FA, requested a personal hearing. Gazi recalled:

'My assistant and I went to the hearing. We had never been involved in anything like this so we weren't sure what was going to happen. We walked into the room and what do we see? Every member of the Essex Senior League was there. Michelle Dorling, the secretary, her husband Lee Dorling, the chairman, sitting there, which was a surprise to us. No one said anything, and they avoided eye contact. In my heart of hearts I knew why they were there. They were there to support the assistant referee. How do you think that makes us feel? We are a club, and we felt that we'd been wronged. But we don't have the backing of the league. They chose the official over the club, over us. A team that felt it was wronged.'

To Gazi and Sporting Bengal's relief, the FA ruled in favour of Sporting Bengal and found that the charge against Andrews was proven. The club in its statement after the verdict said: 'We are satisfied with the ruling and will continue to support football and society to help #KickItOut. There's no place for hate or discrimination.'

Immediately after the FA decision, Gazi said, 'I'm feeling relieved and vindicated as this was a long and tough process.' But he added, 'I've come away from this whole experience a bit bitter and resentful.' Three years later the scars have not healed:

'I have a huge bitter taste in my mouth. Since that evening, nothing has been the same really. Because of what we did on that evening it has had a net detrimental effect on the team. This is one of the big stigmas attached with reporting racism. You are then seen as that person who reported this incident. Sporting Bengal was the team that walked off that night. If you are a player who plays for Sporting Bengal it is not going to help you. Our relationship with the league has been stained. Of course we are still in the league, but if anything happens, if there is any opportunity, they will remove us from the league.

Michelle Dorling, who had been at another match, went to the Aveley ground when she heard there was trouble, and her version of what happened that April night could not be more different:

'What we had was really bad displays of discipline, on and off the pitch. The referee was telling the officials to go and sit back in the technical areas and get off the pitch. The assistant referee was telling them to do the same. He, unfortunately, was misinterpreted because he has a strong Irish accent. He is a southern Irish guy and he, for want of a better word, says "yous", because that's the plural in Ireland for "you lot". He said, "Yous sit down," "Yous get back in there," all that sort of thing. That was taken to be offensive. No, he did not use any overtly racist term.'

Dorling also maintains that it was not Gazi who took his team off the field but the referee who abandoned the match:

'They entered the field of play. They said the referee was cheating. This was the management team from the benches and the subs coming onto the pitch all the time, so the referee abandoned the game. And the police were called because of the threats to stab people and things like that on the pitch. What came out after was these allegations that the referee was racist and the team withdrew their players from the pitch because of the racist referee. This commentary has been going on for three years. The problem is I've read all the paperwork behind it and that isn't quite correct. It was abandoned. It was only later that the assistant referee was accused of racism because he said "yous". The FA charged the Irish assistant referee and found the charge proven. They took that view because in equality and diversity, if you feel it's racist, then it's deemed racist, even if it's not. Unfortunately, the club went to the press, social media, and it was very much portrayed as [the actions of] a racist referee. I don't necessarily think he was racist. I think he may have been inept or having a bad game. The young referee was probably too inexperienced to handle a game of that volatility. Whatever it was, he wasn't able to handle it. Sporting Bengal United took this as a racist incident.'

In Dorling's version of the story it is Eddie Andrews who is the wronged man:

'The assistant referee is actually married to a black woman, his daughter is of "mixed race" and married to an Asian man and they have mixed-race Asian, Muslim grandchildren. So, he's the least likely person to be racist. He hasn't any fight left in him now. He can't go anywhere after an FA appeal. So he's given up refereeing. He is really quite upset that he wasn't supported. He feels very aggrieved, and actually it's caused him some mental health issues for a number of years. He's the least likely person to be racist for his own personal circumstances, but unfortunately it was interpreted that he'd said something that was offensive, and it's caused a real problem between the club and the league.'

And far from Michelle, her husband and the league management taking the side of Andrews, they were, she insists, just doing their job:

'Obviously, we have to sit on the fence and, until the decision was made, we had to support both the club and the referees. And that was seen as taking sides. I tried to explain to the [Sporting Bengal] manager. We have to be neutral; it is not a personal thing. And we've worked hard since then. We've created a campaign called 'Equality, Solidarity, Liberty', which is our anti-discrimination policy. Irrespective of anybody's personal characteristics, everybody is entitled to come to football to enjoy it in whatever capacity as a spectator, player, referee, manager, whether they're black, white, gay or anything else. You are not a black player, you are not an Asian player, you are not a white player – you are a player. We are trying to get that message across.'

Dorling, who has been 34 years in football, has had to cope with a male-dominated football environment:

'I've had discrimination in football for a long time as a woman. They [the men] don't necessarily understand that, possibly, I am as knowledgeable as some of the men in football. And it's taken 20 years on the Essex Senior League for them to understand that they can come to me because I understand. Previously, they used to phone up and ask to speak to my husband, and when they couldn't, they would say, "Oh, sorry, love, it is about football," and hang up. Now they approach me and bypass him because they've built up an understanding that I'm knowledgeable about football. You have to get to that level of understanding now with racism and colour. I don't understand the colour prejudice side, I can't because I'm white, but I certainly have experienced discrimination in football. But I also think sometimes people automatically think you're racist because you're white. Honestly, I'm very much against racism, any form of discrimination.

'My best friend is of Pakistani descent. Her parents were Pakistani born and then came over for a better life, but still stick to the old ways, and her father's very close to the actual ethos of the Church, sorry religion. I don't know if he's actually an imam but he's almost an imam. He is into religious teachings and all sorts of things. He's always over at the mosque. But they are very welcoming, she's my

WAITING FOR THE ASIAN DAWN

best friend, and she is brought up in traditional ways. Her family are very much engaged in the community, but also not against working with and being friendly with white people. Not to be frightened of differences.'

It is then that Dorling tells me what her best friend, the Pakistani, has told her about Asians: 'My friend, she says, the Asian community is completely racist.' As she utters the word 'racist', she emphasises it in case I should miss the implication:

'They dislike the Bengalis and they dislike this group and they dislike that group. It's complicated. Her sister met somebody at university that she fell in love with and married him. He was a Sikh. And coming from a traditional Pakistani family, you can imagine how that caused ructions in the family. She was a second daughter, so it was allowed. Had she been the first daughter, she would not have been.'

Michelle, who is of Jewish descent – 'I am a quarter Jew' – suggests non-whites should learn from how British society's attitude to the Jews has changed:

'In the twelfth century, England persecuted Jews and threw [Jewish] people off a cathedral [a reference to the 1190 York massacre when Jews gathered inside the castle committed suicide rather than be butchered by the mob]. But in the twentieth century, they fought a world war because somebody else was doing some of the things that they did themselves hundreds of years ago. So, I think we need to change society. And if we can do that, we'll find we won't have these incidents, but unfortunately we're dealing with people and personalities.'

So how does the Essex Senior League propose to combat racism? Have a strong anti-racism message, says Dorling, but:

'On the flip side of that, what we're also trying to say is people's opinions of you only matters if you value their opinion. So, if they call you a black somebody or other or you know, anything offensive, don't react to it because if you react, you're giving them that edge that they wanted. They wanted to upset you, they wanted to impact on your life. Their opinion doesn't matter and we are trying to educate people to not let it affect them. Turn it on its head, so it doesn't affect people.'

By not reacting, believes Dorling, 'They won't do it, because they're the ones that are going to look stupid every time they say that or whatever they call you.' Listening to Dorling it is very clear that for some white people the response to racism hasn't changed in 50 years. Dorling in 2021 is suggesting the same response to racism that managers suggested to the likes of Chris Hughton and Brendon Batson in the seventies and eighties. And we all know what impact that had.

Imrul Gazi sounds weary when I mention Dorling's views about combating racism and her best friend being Pakistani:

'So what? It doesn't matter that you are Jewish, the fact is that your face is white. The reality is, unless you've actually experienced racism, unless you're a person of colour, you will never know what it feels like to go through what we go through on a weekly basis, on a monthly basis.'

And when I tell him about Dorling's defence of Eddie Andrews, he laughs sardonically: 'Regardless of what she thinks, we felt the way we felt on the day. Sometimes if something feels racist, it is usually racist.'

Nothing could better sum up the divide between a white woman and an Asian man on how they see race. For one, turn the other cheek when racially abused, for the other, words that feel racist are racist.

Imrul accepts that the overt racism of the seventies and eighties has disappeared 'It is not so bad now; it is a different type of racism we face. Now it's really under the radar. It is covert. It is little comments, little smirks, it's often the way they look at you. The comments they'll make on the side. The way they ignore you. I have had managers in this league not shake my hand. This happened a few seasons ago.' It is hardly a surprise that Imrul disagrees with Zulfi that things have changed for the better. 'Nothing has changed. I can't see any changes happening in the immediate future – in the next five years or so. In ten years we may start seeing a little bit of change. I'm hoping in another 15 to 20 years there will be a real change.'

Imrul Gazi's pessimism sadly appeared justified when it emerged that in 2020, Sathi Balaguru, a 12-year-old footballer of Asian origin, was racially abused when playing in a nine-a-side game for Pitshanger FC in west London. Having been tripped up, he was called an 'Indian boy' during a penalty incident. Also, another opposition player 'directed a racist Indian accent towards him'. According to Balaguru's family, the local FA provided little support and the opposition team did not apologise, although they have since claimed they did. Significantly, the story only emerged 16 months later when the *Guardian* reported that an 'upset' Balaguru had 'decided to speak out because he wants "everyone to have an equal chance" and that he was concerned that the handling of his case suggested his 'ethnicity may limit his progress in the game'.

FIFTEEN

HODDLE AND THE 'WHITE PAKI'

In 1998, soon after the World Cup in France had finished, a book on Asian football was published. It was called *Corner Flags and Corner Shops: The Asian Football Experience,* jointly authored by Jas Bains and Sanjiev Johal. The front cover had a picture of two Asian kids trying to head the ball against a background of a street called Gloucester Street which showed part of a shop. The back cover of the book had a joke about Asians playing football:

> Question: Why is it that India and Pakistan have never qualified for the World Cup finals?
>
> Answer: Because every time they get a corner they build a shop on it.

The book claimed to 'lay bare the cultural and institutional shackles that have historically denied Asians access to the last bastion of British football'. And it ended with two great English players confident the Asian football dawn was about to come.

In his foreword, Glenn Hoddle, then England manager, said:

> 'Whilst applauding the contribution of our black footballers, I must confess to being both surprised and intrigued at the lack of a break-through by Asian players into the professional game. Travelling extensively round the country, it is hard not to notice the skills and enthusiasm of Asian youngsters playing on car parks and waste ground round football stadia. Contrary to some popular opinion, these children are revelling in games of football, and not cricket or hockey . . . I firmly believe that we are now beginning to see a change in which the old stereotypes of Asian players are being broken down, and football

is realising the tremendous potential that exists in Asian communities. I look forward to seeing Asian players coming through at the highest levels of the game, with the ultimate aim of a place in the England team.'

Peter Reid, his England colleague, who endorsed the book, was definite there would be: 'Very soon you'll have the next generation of Asian lads coming through, I'm sure of it; just like once Laurie Cunningham and Viv Anderson started with black players.'

Twenty-three years have passed since the book was published and I am talking to Johal, now an established film-maker, and he tells me that the foreword came about because of David Davies, then head of communications at the FA. Davies told Bains and Johal, 'This is absolutely something that we at the FA want to promote and push Asians in football.' Johal recalls, 'They had begun to put a taskforce together as well. And they wanted to help, so they had Glenn write the foreword.'

The 1998 book had ended on an optimistic note with the authors talking about how Asian 'appreciation and aptitude for the sport were the equal or the better of their British counterparts'.

With no Asian Cunningham having emerged, it is hardly any surprise Johal's mood of optimism has long since vanished:

'I was stupid and naive. We are stuck in the same moment as in 1996. When we wrote the book, the [problems about] inclusion of South Asian footballers included such stereotypes as: They don't have the right diet. They eat food with too many calories. Their religion gets in the way. They pray too often and that prevents them finding time to practise and play. Their parents push them into business or education. They are more academic; they're better at maths and accounting and computers than they are at sport. When you read and listen to the kinds of reasons why South Asian footballers themselves are saying that they haven't been picked, and what's been quoted back, these are the same stereotypes that we were talking about 25 years ago. The racism experienced by black players is different to the racism experienced by South Asian players. The stereotypes applied to black people have all branded their physical propensity. That they have speed, they have strength, they have athleticism. And what do brown people get? Oh, they're wristy. They are good with numbers, they're good academically and there's also the kind of crafty brown man stereotype as well.

Johal, the son of immigrants who migrated to this country from Punjab in the sixties, was born in 1972 and grew up in the wake of Enoch Powell's speech, down the road from Smethwick, the seat Peter Griffiths won for the

Conservatives in 1964. One of the slogans [during that election] was, 'If you want a nigger as a neighbour vote Labour.' 'Going to school,' recalls Johal, 'we were getting shoved, spat at, called "Pakis", "wogs", "niggers". Sometimes my mum would have to come out and push them back, so that we could get through. As you parked your car, people would come and surround it. My dad had to come out and fight the skinheads.'

Johal, like many immigrants, has wrestled with his identity and because of his Western musical tastes was sneered at by other Asians as a 'white Paki':

> 'Until the age of nine or ten I had short hair. Then I had a topknot until the age of about 12 or 13. And since then, I have worn a turban. You go through the early teenage angst of wanting to be the same as everyone else; wanting to fit in. And bear in mind at my school, a mixed school, predominantly white, there were Sikhs, Hindus, Muslims but very, very few turban wearers, maybe two or three in the whole school. But because I had white mates, I didn't listen to bhangra music, I listened to U2, and I was called a "white Paki" by the Asians.'

But for all the problems he faced he was optimistic. 'As a kid walking down the street, I was thinking that we might have a post-racial society. I don't think we can for generations to come. I think we are yet to see the nadir, and then we've got to work our way through it. Hopefully, things will get better beyond that.'

By then, perhaps, a successor to Hoddle might find an Asian Anderson to pick for an England team.

SIXTEEN

ALWAYS LOOK ON THE BRIGHT SIDE

Riz Rehman, Player Inclusion Executive at the PFA, has any number of stories he could tell you about the racial problems he faced as an Asian growing up in this country.

His family moved from Birmingham to live in Sutton, Surrey, and he and his brother Zesh went to Cheam High, only for Riz, at the age of 13, to cope with the stark realisation that they did not belong to the mainstream white community:

> 'Zesh and I were the only Pakistanis in the whole school. There was only one other Asian, from Sri Lanka, and that was it. There were three blacks. That was out of 1,400 students. We had this thick Brummie accent. So, you can imagine, you're a 13-, 14-year-old with a Brummie accent and you got called "Paki" most of the day. There were times when we were chased home from school. That must have been around 1994, 1995.'

What makes this story particularly poignant is that his father, Khalid, had actually moved from Birmingham to London because he felt there would be more opportunities for football for his kids. In doing so, Khalid had defied his own father, leaving the family business, a superstore, to come to London:

> 'His father didn't really let him play any sport. The focus for my grandad was education, the business. My dad was different. Dad was a cricketer. He loved cricket. He tried to play for Warwickshire, and

said to himself, "When I have kids, I'm going to make sure that they do education and sport." '

Riz and his father knew that the world they were in did not believe Asians could play football. 'My dad actually did his coaching badges because he wanted to learn more about the game and coach us in football, which he did.' But at the final coaching session, when he asked the assessor why there were no Asian footballers, the assessor looked at Riz, ten, a midfielder and Zesh, nine, a central defender, and said that, good as they were, they would not make it. And then the white coach trotted out the usual stereotypes of Asian football failings:

No. 1: Asian players are scared of the weather. No. 2: You've the wrong diet. No. 3: The parents push them to education rather than sport.

But Khalid persevered and, as Riz found, even in Cheam and despite being called a Paki, 'Once the football trials started, and once they knew that we were good at football, we got accepted.'

Zesh became the first British Asian to appear in the Premier League. 'He played 500 career games and he's helping other kids. Zesh has been successful in terms of what he wanted. He was told he would never make it, but he made it.'

Riz was not that successful:

'I was playing Sunday league football when I got a trial at Fulham when I was 14. Then I got picked up by Brentford and I was there from 14 to 21. I broke my leg at 17, then my scholarship was deferred to my third year. I came back from that injury, I got a professional contract, but my leg didn't really feel the same. So, I started playing more the non-league route: Crawley Town, Hampton and Richmond.'

But during this football journey Riz did not encounter any racism. And this is why he wants people to look on the bright side on the question of Asians breaking into the top leagues of this country. However, both clubs and Asian parents have work to do:. 'It needs more clubs reaching out in the community and looking for talent. And the parents need to know – which they don't at the moment – where to take their kids. You can't only take your kid to the local golf centre and accuse scouts of not coming to watch. They need to know which teams have links with professional clubs. They have to do that work. It's too easy to point the fingers at everyone. My dad in the 1980s used to drive us four or five miles out of town so we would play in the white leagues, the tough leagues. We didn't just play in the Asian community with our friends or neighbours. You have to break out from your own little leagues. If you're serious about your son or daughter, you have to do this.'

So, would he agree with the Tony Sewell report on race that there is no institutional racism? His answer could have been scripted by Terry Westley:

'Listen, there are kids in the system now, who are 13, 14, Pakistani Muslims living in white areas, playing for Premier League clubs who have already got a scholarship. Clubs don't care whether you're Pakistani, Sri Lankan, Indian, Chinese, whatever you are. If you're good enough, you're going to come through. I'm sorry, I can't say it's racism.'

Riz accepts that parents of Asian kids do have a problem:

'When they take their son or daughter to the academy for a trial, they don't see other people that look like them, they don't know who to ask the questions to because there's not many Asians. That's changing because we're developing and creating a network that's never been there and no one's ever done it before.'

Riz Rehman, who has worked for the PFA for eight years, is talking about the peer-to-peer mentoring programme, launched by the PFA in February 2021. Work on it had been going on behind the scenes for about two or three years:

'You will have a 14-year-old connecting with a scholar, a 14-year-old connecting with a senior player and with their parents for that inspiration. A 14-year-old connecting with a 16-year-old who's sort of going through that same sort of journey. This will be with fellow Asian players and also non-Asian players as well. I select them. The clubs are very helpful. The clubs have basically invited me in.'

But with only 15 British Asian players across the four professional divisions when Asians make up 7 per cent of society, when can we expect the Asian 'Viv Anderson moment'? And that is when it turns out that Riz's estimation is not far away from that of Imrul Gazi: 'Being realistic we're probably about another ten, 15 years away. There are players in the system now that might come through before that. But there are not enough at the grassroots to really come through. When the black players came through, they came through in their droves at every level, and that's what it needs.'

Riz agrees that there are still unexplained problems with regard to Asian involvement in football, particularly getting Asians to watch the game. Riz's club is Aston Villa but Villa Park, despite being surrounded completely by Asian homes, does not see many Asians going to watch the matches:

'I don't know why that is. I think now you're seeing more fans. I used to go to Villa Park in the early nineties with my brother. My dad used to take us all the time. I never suffered racist abuse when I went as a spectator. Others have. Again, I'm not sure, maybe we just missed the racism. But I'm sure it happened. Me, my dad and Zesh, we didn't suffer any racial abuse when we sat in the Holte End watching Villa.'

However, Riz is all too aware that racist, stereotypical thinking can surface all too suddenly from the most unexpected quarters. This has had an effect on his mentoring programme and affected its launch date, which had to be postponed because of one such unexpected racial problem:

'We tried to get it out in November, December 2020. But that's when Greg Clarke came out with his comments, when he was talking about Asians working behind the scenes in the IT department and so on. I didn't want to come out and talk about it alongside something so negative, so we just waited.'

Riz accepts that Greg Clarke's comments showed that there was a generation which still thought in terms of the old stereotypes. 'The homework needs to be done.' One area where the homework has been done is, amazingly, in sporting boardrooms and executive offices. The result has been dramatic.

Changes I could not have anticipated back in 1996.

TURNING THE SPORTS WORLD UPSIDE DOWN

SEVENTEEN

A TALE OF TWO HALVES

ajid Ishaq, the managing director of Rothschild, looking very professorial with his luxuriant beard, is walking in a big, wooded area in North London with a very unspoilt hilly park on the other side. His house backs on to the park where the wooded area is. Had it not been for Covid we would probably have been lunching in an Indian restaurant or meeting, where we often have before, at Rothschild's offices in the City. But now he is taking time off from doing yet another deal to do a Zoom call with me. I am keen to talk to Majid because he represents a remarkable Asian involvement with sport, one that is rarely talked about yet shows how complex the relationship is between sport, race and society in modern Britain.

As Majid talks to me, I think back to the first time I met him at the Rothschild offices. Majid had been instrumental in helping the Glazers buy Manchester United, and the stories of what he and his colleagues, Robert Leitão and Richard Bailey, did convinced me that without Rothschild the Glazers would not have secured the club. Within this complex financial saga there were all sorts of wonderful vignettes, some of which read like a movie script. This was the first time I heard about Donald Trump's Mar-a-Lago club. It was by the pool of Mar-a-Lago, which Trump as US president would later make world-famous, that Majid and his colleagues met the Glazers for the first time.

I had met Majid in the middle of Ramadan, and, as a devout Muslim, he was fasting. So, while I had happily tucked into the coffee and biscuits that Rothschild served, Majid did not touch anything.

Majid, a season ticket holder at the Stretford End, has been a Manchester United fan since 1976, and is steeped in the history of the club and proud to call himself a red.

For Majid the pandemic may have meant not going to matches, but he says with pride, 'You know the last game I went to was when we beat City 2-0 at home, which was the last game before the lockdown more than a year ago.'

I had first met Majid when Rothschild advised the Glazers on their take-over of Manchester United. That has been followed by Majid doing several other deals. Now, as he walked round the park, he reminisced:

'We acted on the sale of Aston Villa, Blackburn, the acquisition of Liverpool, advised Arsenal on stadium financing and various Kroenke deals, Tottenham on their stadium, Wimbledon on their debenture issue and the FA when it was considering the offer from Shahid Khan, owner of Fulham, to buy Wembley.'

Yet in all this, his colour has not come into it:

'When I've walked into a boardroom I have never, ever, felt any form of prejudice towards me. Now, why is that? Is that because I'm walk-ing in, having got a level of credibility, and carrying the Rothschild card, the senior individual who knows more about all of this stuff than the people sitting across the desk from me? Now that might have a part to play. So, even if they did have a level of prejudice, or bias, they are listening to me because I'm speaking from a position of authority, of experience. They have got to because it's in their interest, and a lot of the time it's about their financial interest.'

Majid feels this has a long-term impact on other people of colour: 'The fact I'm doing that, and I'm in front of these people and they see me operate in that manner, is a massive positive. Because you hope you're educating them a little bit for the next person [of colour] that they come across, maybe in a very different situation.'

As I listen to him, it strikes me we have a great paradox. An Asian Raheem Sterling or Marcus Rashford is nowhere to be seen on the football fields of England, yet in the boardroom Majid is like one of those managers – Jose Mourinho in his pomp perhaps – whom football club chairmen turn to whenever they are in trouble. Majid may not have fulfilled his great ambition to become a footballer, but in the world of sports business, just as scouts track a player they covet, so Majid's prowess and achievements are passed round and sports organisations in need of financial advice come calling. Tottenham did and so did The All England Club:

'Wimbledon wanted to speak to us principally in terms of funding the roof for Court Number One and also setting the pricing for the Centre

Court debentures that were being sold. I met the whole Wimbledon team, and we made a pitch. One of the things we suggested was you need to go out and market yourselves a bit more. We told them you don't realise how valuable a product Wimbledon is. How valuable your debentures are. We said you need to advertise in the *Sunday Times*, because that is the best paper to advertise this kind of stuff. And we gave them comfort and confidence that they could increase the price of the debentures not by 5 per cent, not by 10 per cent, but nearly double it. We priced it at £50,000 and they had the highest renewal rate ever from existing debenture holders.'

The debenture issue raised around £100 million.

Tottenham had for various years struggled with plans to finance a new stadium which it considered essential if the club was to compete with its rivals like Arsenal, who had got a new stadium, and move forward. But none of these plans had worked:

'My understanding of Tottenham had been they've tended never to talk to advisers or take advice. Daniel [Levy, the Tottenham chairman] is a very capable individual. I knew an ex-banker who worked in his commercial department. He had said, one day, to Daniel, or to Matthew, his CFO, "Look, I know you don't like bankers, but you should meet Majid because he's not like most other bankers, and you will find it helpful just to chat through what you might want to do and over what time period. And there's no compulsion to do anything after that." So, I went to a game where I met Matthew and Daniel. We chatted about a few things, and I gave them some of my views and perspectives and we got on. And Daniel felt comfortable and took us on as advisers. Tottenham, probably, took us the longest because there were so many issues in terms of funding for the stadium.'

The result was spectacular, leading to Levy reincarnating White Hart Lane as one of the best football stadiums in the world. His only problem has been the football has not matched the stadium. The pandemic, a situation which no sport could have been prepared for, has led to many more sports organisations sending for Majid. But for all the news the sports business generates, it remains small, still only 10 per cent of what Rothschild do; much of Majid's time is spend on traditional City work like Initial Public Offerings, floating companies on the stock market. But it is the sports business that gives him particular pleasure.

So how is it that an Asian, a devout Muslim, is so highly prized in this country's sporting boardrooms whereas on the field of play in almost all sports there are hardly any Asians? Are those who say British sport is institutionally racist being too simplistic?

In all our conversations over many years, Majid and I had discussed many issues but the issue of race in sport had never come up. Now, as I raise the question of race, Majid broadens the subject:

> 'How diverse are we as a bank? We are very diverse in some respects and less so in others. When you talk to anybody about Rothschild they will immediately go, "Very traditional, very white, very male." But today there are three people who run the UK business: there's a Jewish guy called Alex Midgen, there's an Indian guy called Ravi Gupta, and there's me, a Muslim. And our managing partner globally is Robert Leitão, who is of Portuguese origin.'

During the Glazer takeover, Leitão would joke about his name, saying, 'I might have an unpronounceable name, but I have a big reputation.' In Manchester United circles it was common to refer to him as 'the foreigner'. But while Rothschild may be much more diverse than any football club, Majid points to a black hole in his organisation:

> 'As an organisation we have very few black people. And given that in London there is a large black population, that is striking. But if you had asked that same question of Rothschild 30 years ago, it wasn't Majid Ishaq running the place, and it wouldn't have been, and there would have been very few brown people. Maybe one or two. And today there are probably 150 bankers, and we have in the UK about 700 people, which [in percentage terms] is significantly greater than the Asian population in the UK. Why? Because most Asians are very education-focused and therefore there's a greater propensity for more of them to come through.'

However, he adds a rider, which emphasises the complexity of the Asian community in this country. 'When I think of Asians, you do have to differentiate them: it is most of the Indian and Sri Lankan communities who are very education-focused and come through.'

That, I tell Majid, is very like the medical field, which the pandemic has highlighted through the many TV interviews with so many Asian doctors in prominent positions. He says:

> 'You are absolutely right, Mihir. In those organisations things have moved on. Why am I where I am? Because I came through the education process and went through that system. Then you come to a

point, and you can have a debate that you need to be given a chance; somebody needs to take a chance. But if you're good enough, you will probably find your way through – providing there isn't deep rooted institutional racism. I don't think there is institutional racism in a banking context. In the commercial world if you are bloody good and you make money for people, people will pay you for that. So, what's gone wrong with sport? With sport if I look at participation and those playing professionally, you see two things: you see lots of black players excelling at sports, and they are clearly over-represented in terms of proportionality. That is no different from why there are many more Indian doctors. That is natural. You then say, "OK, that's got them through to the point of participation and players and being professionals. What about managers, what about administrators in the game etc?" '

Majid answers his own question by posing another question:

'If you turned to Stan Kroenke at Arsenal and said, "Who would you want to appoint as a manager?" he would have no issue with what colour that person was whatsoever, let me tell you. Or if you asked him, "Who would you want to appoint as a board director?" I genuinely, today, would not see an owner of the top teams having a prejudicial view on those questions. Owners want the best 11 players on the pitch. I would argue, certainly with the bigger clubs, the same goes for the manager, notwithstanding the statistics are not great about black managers managing the big clubs. As you go down into the lower leagues, lower divisions, owners of lower division clubs, what is the situation? Can you see the owner of Millwall appointing a black manager? Or a black director on to his board? Maybe less so.

'Where I think things are a little bit muddier, maybe even today, is where you don't have that same representation within the various FA councils, the county FAs, because you've got 60-year-old white blokes in those seats and they're not actually there making money and it's not about making money. And my only experience of that was when we sat there with the FA Council discussing the potential sale of Wembley to an American Pakistani Muslim called Mr Shahid Khan.'

Khan offered good money, well over £600 million, but the council decided it did not want to sell Wembley to the Fulham owner. Majid recalls how that day when the council met to consider the Khan proposal, as he walked into the council chamber, he noticed that, apart from Paul Elliott, there was hardly a black face and no Asian faces. An FA Council dominated by white men does mean, says Majid, 'It is easy for them to look for people in their own guise, and this is the unconscious bias, where you appoint somebody that looks somewhat similar to you. It is just natural to have some level of unconscious bias. But I don't think it is as widespread as people might think.'

Twenty-two years ago when Majid had first joined Rothschild he had wondered how far he would progress:

'Rothschild is a very Jewish organisation, and I was a Muslim, and I still am a Muslim, who on a Friday would want to go to Friday prayers at the local mosque, and in the middle of Ramadan will want to leave work early and come in a bit late. Rothschild has enabled me to do all of that without any problems. The fact that it is a Jewish bank means they understand some of those values. If I'd been at a non-Jewish place maybe that would be less so. Am I surprised? I probably am a little, Mihir, I probably am a little.'

His experience has made him conclude, 'If you're very capable, you're very, very good at what you do, you get opportunities, actually, in this country.'

Nothing in Majid's background suggested he would end up becoming a banker, let alone running Rothschild. His family, originally from India, migrated to Pakistan at the time of partition:

'My dad came over here from Pakistan. He was originally a science teacher in Pakistan but having failed to get a job as a science teacher, ended up working in a mill up north, which is why we ended up in Huddersfield.'

Was that prejudice?

'That probably was, because his qualifications and everything else were just not recognised, and that's why my dad's elder brother, who's a radiologist, left the UK and went to America. My dad never really talked about some of the prejudice and racism he faced. The one thing my dad instilled in all of us, me, my brother and my sister, was education. And that's probably why, ultimately, I didn't become a footballer.'

But while he knew he could never play football at the professional level, let alone put on the red jersey of Manchester United, he continued to play amateur football and faced a lot of prejudice:

'One of the teams I played in had a lot of black players and we played once on a Sunday in deepest Dagenham. And deepest Dagenham in the eighties, Mihir, was a hotbed of racism. Yes, there was the National Front. When you talk about underprivileged white people, there was a whole bunch of those people in Dagenham.'

In some ways, the most interesting aspect of Majid's success as a financial adviser to football clubs is the wonderful insight it provides into the contrast between the experience of a brown football fan and a brown banker at the very same football ground, Anfield, the home of Liverpool:

'When I was growing up in the seventies, if you looked at the crowds at football, there were very, very few black or brown fans at any Liverpool or Everton game. Manchester United had a few more. Liverpool had been phenomenally successful as a club, but forget about brown faces, you saw very few black faces. I had been to Liverpool as a youngster, I was probably 12 or 13 at the time, in the early eighties, and I was chased around the ground being called a Paki.'

Nearly 25 years later Majid is back at Anfield, but this time he is carrying a briefcase and has a Rothschild card: 'And I was walking into Liverpool with George Gillett, acting as his adviser as he bought the club. And by the way, as a Manchester United fan, that was hard enough, but obviously I'm going to be the consummate professional.'

Not only were they not now chasing Majid, 'the Paki', but:

'I go even further and say, today, Mihir, what the local fans think about Mo Salah and his faith, I find amazingly positive. All those years ago I was going to Anfield feeling very vulnerable. Today, Liverpool fans are singing songs about Salah as a Muslim in a mosque; that would have been unheard of then. Anfield from the late seventies, early eighties to now, has moved on so much. Now that doesn't mean, Mihir, that every single fan in that stadium is of the same opinion. The reason why I'm saying this is that as a fan I encountered racial prejudice, even at times from Manchester United fans. I came out of the United–Barcelona Champions League semi-final at Old Trafford, when Paul Scholes scored that goal that took us to the 1999 Champions League final, and on our way home we encountered racist abuse from fellow United fans. This, arguably, was one of their most positive days and that's 1999, the year of the treble. I have also experienced racist abuse at Chelsea and at West Ham when I've gone to these grounds to watch Manchester United. When I then turned up years later, sold West Ham to Sullivan and Gold, been to Chelsea for various meetings and discussions, I was received with all due courtesy. All that is reflective of the fact that within any walk of life there are going to be people who have not just unconscious bias, they have very conscious bias.'

So why this great contrast?

'I think most likely that is the case, Mihir, because I think they [the people in the boardroom] are more commercial and they have done well in their lives, and therefore they don't have that same level of prejudice. When I've walked into football clubs, or into football associations with a business hat on, it is to bring them something that they don't necessarily have. But why is it when I walked out of Old Trafford as a fan, or I've gone to Chelsea or to West Ham, I'm getting direct racist abuse? It's generally from somebody who is from a different stratum of life, who perhaps has not had a very successful life, who perhaps has struggled on many counts, and needs something to air his grievances at.'

Success in sport, says Majid, can often change racial attitudes.

I have just mentioned to Majid how amazing it is that football fans can be, and often are, racist but, at the same time, they accept foreign ownership from any background and any colour and love it if the owner is successful. Indeed, they can forgive a brown successful owner when they will not a white one. This was illustrated when news of the disastrous European Super League proposals emerged in April 2021. Manchester City, Manchester United and Liverpool were among the six English clubs (Tottenham, Arsenal and Chelsea being the others) that supported the idea. Fans rose up in revolt, and the fans of Manchester United were so vociferous in their opposition that they invaded Old Trafford, forcing the postponement of the match against Liverpool. Fans of Liverpool, while not going that far, were also very critical of their owners. In contrast, Manchester City fans, while opposed, did not vent their anger on their owner. What is interesting is that Manchester United and Liverpool are owned by white men, the Glazers and John Henry's Fenway Group, and Manchester City by Sheikh Mansour, a brown man. What is even more crucial is one of the points Manchester United fans made – and have always made – that the Glazers have never made any contact with the fans. Such was the vehemence of the protest that the Glazers were forced to come out of their shell. Yet Sheikh Mansour has never appeared in public. But for City fans what matters is that his money has brought the club success on a scale they have never experienced before. Majid's response was:

'I think that's fair to say that they accept foreign ownership if it brings their team success. It is guaranteed, because it's a reflection of society,

that within their fan base they will have a number of fans who probably have prejudicial or racist views. But by and large, if you have a
successful team people don't care who the owner is. When it was
mooted that the public investment fund of Saudi Arabia was going to
buy Newcastle, those fans were looking forward to ownership from
Saudi Arabia more than the ownership of Mike Ashley [a white Eng-
lishman]. Because they would view it as success for their team.'

The irony here is that at a club where, as we have seen, in the eighties black
players received horrendous racist abuse, which included being spat at, a
largely white fan base was hailing the arrival of a brown owner from the
Middle East – provided he brought money and success. As Majid had found,
money often mattered more than race.

In some ways, the most telling story of how, in sport, the search for money
can overturn conventional ideas of race and prejudice came when Majid
dealt with Doug Ellis. This was when 'deadly Doug', a nickname given to
him because of the ruthless way he sacked his managers, finally sold Aston
Villa:

'It was straight after the United deal with the Glazers that I did the
Aston Villa deal. I was advising, God rest his soul, Doug Ellis: 83 years
old, been in the war, done everything and here was I, a lot younger
than I am now, whippersnapper, talking to him about how to go about
selling his beloved club. And, Mihir, he listened to me every step of
the way. And he took the advice at some critical moments, including
whom he should sell it to, etc. And that's a really good example of the
behaviour of people who you may have thought might have some kind
of bias. Now the slight difference with him was that Doug had been a
businessman ever since he left the army. He had set up a travel business selling holidays to Spain. So, an interesting question is that if you
are in the business world, is there a natural tendency to ignore all of
those prejudices and so forth because you're just blind to it?'

One thing has intrigued me. Has Majid ever thought of changing his name?
'No, not at all, never ever.' He feels his name gives him a unique status.
First, he often has to correct people when they pronounce the name Majid:

'You only need to say it a couple of times and then people [get it] and,
you know what, Mihir, the other thing, and I'm going to say it in this
way, you become more memorable. Because there is only one Mihir
Bose. I kid you not, there is only one Majid Ishaq. But there are a
number of John Smiths in the City, and I've met a number of David

Jones, but I couldn't remember which one is which. But with a name like Majid Ishaq, you do become memorable.'

So, can we get to a non-racial world?

'Can you ever get to a world where there is no prejudice? No, because it's human nature. But can you get to a better place where sport can help to educate more people and bring people together? The answer has got to be yes. Sport can play a huge part in it.'

As Mahdi Choudhury can testify.

EIGHTEEN

LEGALLY SHATTERING SPORTING MYTHS

Mahdi Choudhury's career shows how you can fulfil the Asian parents' classic dream of my son the lawyer, yet have a career in sport which can be both unusual and striking.

In May 2021 the 41-year-old was appointed Assistant Secretary (Membership) of the MCC. It meant a rare brown face in an organisation that has always been proud of being the home of cricket but has always presented a very white face. Mahdi's journey had started in the classic Asian tradition of 'different career interests', as Greg Clarke, then chairman of the FA, told MPs.

> 'I started as a private practice solicitor. I got into sports through the legal route, sports law. [Mahdi, having read French and Russian at Birmingham University, went to law school in Nottingham and then did a sports law postgrad at King's College London.] I got a job in sport with the British Olympic Association just after London had successfully bid for the Olympic Games, in early 2006. They required a second, junior lawyer for sport regulatory and intellectual property work. I worked very closely with LOCOG [London Organising Committee for Olympics and Paralympic Games]. At that time the organisation was not that diverse.'

Choudhury being the odd non-white at LOCOG was significant, for it showed that when it came to race there was an enormous gap between the face London presented to the world and the real face back in London. It had won the bid to stage the 2012 Olympics claiming to be the most diverse of all the great cities bidding for the Games: Paris, New York, Madrid and Moscow were the other cities. Ken Livingstone, the then London Mayor, had told members of the International Olympic Committee meeting in Singapore, where the decision was taken, that London was more multicultural than New York. More languages were spoken in London than in New York, and during the Olympics no national team would be friendless in London, as people of every nation lived in London. Seb Coe, the bid leader, had made much of the fact that his mother was of Indian origin. But apart from Coe's Indian connections, the face of the bid was uniformly white, and Choudhury was the rare non-white to be found in the bid's team headquarters in Canary Wharf.

Choudhury, whose Bangladeshi Muslim parents migrated to this country from Sylhet, describes himself as an 'in-between generation':

'My grandfather managed a tea plantation in the hills in Sylhet, Bangladesh. My dad came over to the UK in the early sixties. My parents went back and forth. My sisters were born in Bangladesh. They grew up there. Then my dad decided to bring the whole family over, and I was born in Stockport in the seventies, in an area that had a very strong Asian community. Then we moved to a different part of Manchester which was predominantly white. Our neighbours when I was growing up were white professionals. I had a very mixed upbringing.'

However, he remained closely connected to his roots. 'My parents both maintained strong connections with the Bangladeshi community in Greater Manchester. My dad was chairman of our local mosque in Manchester and part of the Greater Manchester Bangladeshi Association.'

It may come as a surprise that Choudhury took to sport. 'My father, like people from our culture, had a massively hard work ethic. He would be in the restaurant he owned, the Passage to India, working during the day and evenings or doing the accounts in the morning. I also used to help in the restaurant from a young age.' Mahdi's father's career was one of social mobility in this country. For almost 15 years, after arriving in the UK, he had worked as a waiter in an Indian restaurant, but always had ambitions to own it – and eventually did. But he also loved sport, which meant Choudhury was brought up to think sport was very much part of life:

'My dad enjoyed sport. He loved his cricket. He liked watching football. He was a Manchester City fan. He used to serve all the City players when he was a waiter in the Grand Hotel in Manchester in the sixties. Our mosque was next to Maine Road, and I went to Manchester

Grammar School, which is literally next to Platt Lane [the old City training ground complex], so we used to watch City.'

Choudhury himself resisted the lure of City and became a United fan.

As Choudhury tells me his story, it becomes clear that there are many things that set him apart from many of his contemporaries. There was his skin colour His fair skin may be due to his ancestors having some Arabic roots. But his fair skin did not mean whites did not think of him as a brown man. 'No, they definitely did.' His exceptionalism was also emphasised by his size. At six feet one inch he is unusually tall for a Bangladeshi. On the football field he was the tall, strapping Asian lad, playing centre forward. 'I was the odd man out. I was the only person of any South Asian origin playing in the league that I played in.' And his mates were white:

'All my friends in primary school were white as it was a predominantly white area. I was very lucky to have very close primary school friends. They took me to the football club and the cricket club. We ended up playing sport from the age of five, all the way through to me leaving for university. We played in the same cricket and football teams all the way through my childhood. I had a whole set of friends who formed the first XI of the football team and the third XI of the cricket team. We were just mates, and I never really got any grief. My white friends used to come to our house for Eid. Generally, they respected my race and the culture I grew up in.'

The only time Mahdi met people of colour on the sports field was when his cricket team played Bolton Indians or Deane and Derby. 'These clubs were Asian and West Indian clubs. That's when I played against teams where the majority were people of colour. The Bolton Indians provided fantastic tea, samosas, bhajis and things like that. We always enjoyed that.'

Mahdi did encounter racism as a kid, but more on the football rather than the cricket field. This highlighted the class divide in Britain, which in his case proved more pervasive and powerful than race:

'The players who I played football against when I was a kid were from inner city Salford, Moss Side, etc. and from deprived backgrounds. I think they were probably brought up in a different way to the kids I used to play cricket against. On occasions, I was verbally assaulted, racist remarks were made. Roughly up to the age of 16 it would happen two or three times a season.'

Growing up in Mrs Thatcher's Britain in the early and mid eighties, with the National Front prominent, it was inevitable he faced overt racism.

'Racial slurs against Asians were still quite prevalent when I was young in the eighties and early nineties.'

The really surprising thing is how Mahdi got into rugby league. For Mahdi it was 'not exceptional', just part of childhood. 'When I was at primary school, I played for a rugby league club for a while. I used to go with my mates. They used to drag me along. I would have played any sport. I am a sports nut.'

Mahdi is on the board of the European Rugby League, a position he felt was important for his career but which was a very unusual appointment for a person of Asian background: 'Rugby league is probably not the most diverse sport from an administration perspective. There are, of course, black players alongside those of mixed ethnicity and those from the Pacific Islands, but I am probably quite an anomaly as an administrator in the sport.'

Mahdi is aware that lack of diversity is a problem in British sport:

'In Olympics and Paralympics sport, it is definitely the case that national governing bodies' staff composition is not reflective of the diversity in the UK population, and that those who do work within NGBs [national governing bodies] do tend to work in the support departments (e.g. finance, legal, IT) as opposed to the performance teams.'

Does this not suggest institutional racism?

'I personally don't believe there is institutional racism, but in some areas I would say there is unconscious bias. There is often a tendency in sport to employ people you know. And a lot of it is people you are connected with. There is unfortunately not a huge amount of diversity within the organisations that I interacted with. When I was a CEO, I was regularly the only non-white person sitting around the board table or in a meeting. On occasions, I have received comments that were not politically correct. To be honest, a lot of the time I have been desensitised to that.'

Mahdi, who admits he did not find it 'difficult to break down doors and get through to the next level', knows much more needs to be done to make sport more diverse:

'If you look at the demographics of Team GB and Paralympics GB, you have certain sports where there is greater diversity because of the nature of the sport, because of the participation levels from grassroots upwards. Athletics is like that. Combat sports is probably one as well, where you do get people of South Asian, black or mixed ethnicity backgrounds. But if you look at your traditional sports like hockey, fencing, sailing, equestrian and rowing, the composition of the elite squads is not reflective, in terms of diversity, of our population. And that's because of tradition and lack of opportunity for people. That's changing and there is work going on. The wider sports system does appreciate that work needs to be done, and some of the sports that I have mentioned have worked hard to improve in this area. But it is a very stiff challenge to make progress.'

The way to do that, argues Mahdi, is diversity at the top of sports:

'From an administration point of view, there needs to be greater diversity in the boardroom. That is more important than diversity at the middle management level, because it will create diversity in terms of recruiting people from different backgrounds. You will get much more ethnically diverse organisations if those at senior executive levels, the ones responsible for recruitment, have a lens on the importance of having a diverse workforce. From a playing perspective, the focus on diversity needs to be at grassroots participation level – you will then see athletes, coaches and performance staff at the elite level . . . It will take a long time. How long? I don't know.'

Mahdi has never wanted to be appointed to a sports organisation so that as a person of colour he can be paraded as evidence of the organisation fulfilling their requirement to be diverse.

'I have been approached for certain non-executive roles and I have challenged people as to why they have approached me as I believe I have not had the relevant experience or expertise for a particular role. In some situations, I feel there is pressure to get the diversity numbers up.'

But does he feel that, being the only non-white in a boardroom of whites, he is assumed to be the spokesman for people of colour?

'I look at it both ways. I want to be judged for my own abilities. I don't want to be given any sort of preferential treatment because of the colour of my skin. At the same time, I feel a great responsibility as someone in the sports world to mentor people. If I've got a young person with an Asian or black background who wants to get into the sports world, I want to help them and give advice and see where I can help fit them into this high-performance system. So, in some respects I don't mind being asked to do stuff because of the colour of my skin because it might help someone else.'

Mahdi accepts that a person of his skin colour without that legal expertise that he had might even now find it more difficult to become a sports administrator.

'I think we have made some progress because of the measures that have been taking place at an administrative level by the governing bodies. Can we get diversity across the sports we talked about? I don't know. Traditional boundaries need to be broken down in terms of mentality.'

The reaction to George Floyd's death may help break that down and Mahdi admits:

'I am surprised it has had a major impact which, again, I think is positive because it's opened up a stream of conscious people. It has filtered down to my peer group. I have got a lot of white friends and they have talked to me about it, about how I feel about it. I am Asian, not black. I guess they are talking to me because it is an issue of institutional racism. How genuine it is for some people, I don't know, but in some other people it's just opening their eyes a little bit to my experience, your experience.'

Mahdi can see much merit in the Rooney Rule:

'The Rooney Rule where it is appropriately applied, not just making the numbers up, can only be a good thing. For me it's something that will give people the opportunity to present themselves and alter opinions. It gets round that unconscious bias point. If I'm interviewing candidates for a job and I see a name that doesn't look right, I might just chuck that to one side because that person doesn't fit a stereotype. In that respect Rooney Rule is good.'

What the Rooney Rule cannot change is the name of the person applying for a job, and in recent years there has been much research into what happens when largely white-run organisations get applications from people whose names are not the traditional white-sounding ones. There is evidence to show that an applicant who has a name that is not the familiar English ones of Smith and Jones, and is Patel or Mohammed, or some other ethnic one, may find their application tossed into the bin. This has led to organisations like the English Cricket Board (ECB) having blank applications where, to prevent any unconscious bias, the person in the organisation assessing the application does not know the name. Mahdi, who is in a civil partnership with an Englishwoman, has given his children double-barrelled surnames to reflect both his culture and his wife's culture and to have flexibility in their lives. This means that if they wanted to drop one of the names, they could, possibly the Choudhury part of their name, and sound more English.

Such measures may make sure unconscious racism when it comes to job applications are dealt with. But, the other glaring contrast in our sport is more difficult to deal with; that while our football fields may tell a wonderful story of diversity, teams with a majority of black players are playing to crowds that are almost uniformly white. Mahdi says:

> 'Has there been the integration between cultures and between nation-alities and assimilating into British society? That has been a bit slower than some of us thought it would be, to be honest. I've got lots of family and friends who live in Rusholme. You will know well from your days of covering football that around Maine Road there is a huge Bangladeshi community. They don't go to the football. Cricket is slightly different. You do get a lot of people from the Indian sub-continent, South Asians, watching the cricket.'

Mahdi admits, 'I go and see United and you can sometimes hear racist chanting.' He would not want his children to be subjected to that sort of abuse. He is also well aware that football is segregated: rival fans are not allowed to sit together because the authorities fear this would provoke violence. Yet one of his most memorable sporting moments was at The Oval, when Bangladesh beat South Africa in cricket and he sat amidst South African fans; there was no question of any violence between Bangladeshi and South African fans.

As our conversation is ending, I mention to Mahdi that because of my views on race, refusing to see it in simple black and white terms, I had been called a 'coconut', a derogatory term meaning brown outside, white inside. Mahdi's response is that he had also been called a 'coconut'. With a laugh, we joke that 'We should open a Coconut Club and offer membership to those who qualify. Once the pandemic age goes, we should have regular meetings of the Coconut Club. Well, maybe we should be a Coconut Cricket Club.'

With Mahdi now ensconced at Lord's, perhaps we could even have a 'Coconut Club' match at the hallowed Nursery End of the ground. And one 'coconut', who would walk into the team, is one of the most prominent Asians in British sport and quite likes being called a 'coconut'.

NINETEEN

COCONUTS AND THE R WORD

I t is almost towards the end of our hour-and-a-half-long conversation that I find Sanjay Bhandari, chair of Kick It Out, and I have suffered the same abuse. Not racial abuse from whites, such as being called 'Paki', as Bhandari was by social media trolls within minutes of the announcement of his new job, but abuse from fellow Asians.

I had told him I had been called a 'coconut' by the younger generation of Asians. Bhandari immediately says, 'I have been called that many times,' and with that he laughs.

It is the laugh of a calm, measured man. This should come as no surprise for Bhandari knows all about how the world of the second-generation immigrant can be far more complex than that of the first generation and is always a question of balancing many things.

Bhandari learned this lesson of balancing early from his father, Om Datt, who on the day he got married did something unheard of. The year is 1948, and India has been free for a year. Om Datt is having an arranged marriage which means he only meets his bride on the day of the marriage. Datt's family expects the family of his wife to pay a dowry. But Om Datt does not believe in dowry. However, he does not reject it, but asks for only one rupee. For Bhandari this was his father laying down a principle and from which Bhandari says he has learned a lot:

'The dowry system did have a sound legal basis. You weren't allowed to give any part of your estate to your daughter. So, once they married, this was their share of the estate. It was meant for the daughter, not for the in-laws. It has now become a demand by the in-laws. I still have that rupee. It is worth about £9 now.'

This was not the only way his father broke the mould. His decision to leave India for Britain was also not the classic immigrant story of seeking economic prosperity in a foreign land. His father came from a good family business background. But he did not want to be involved in the family business and emigrated to Britain in 1949. 'He wanted', says Bhandari, 'to make his own way.' Bhandari's father settled in the Black Country and established a business selling clothes, curtains and drapery 'on tick' as it was called:

> 'You would go round selling clothes and curtains. And the people who bought would pay off a pound a week. And then the person running the credit round would come around with their tick book. They would tick it off in the book.'

Bhandari's uncle, his mother's brother whom he calls Mama, acted as the tick man going round houses collecting money. Everything worked fine until 1964 when tragedy struck. 'He was collecting money on the tick and he got strangled by two black guys trying to steal his money. They were convicted in Stafford Assizes. Between conviction and sentence the death penalty was abolished. They got life imprisonment.'

His uncle's murder had two dramatic consequences:

> 'That is the reason I was born. My brothers are six and eight years older than me. My parents were not going to have any more children. But when my uncle died my parents decided to have another go for a girl. It was a girl they wanted. I was the boy they didn't want. My uncle's death resonated through the family. My Mama was married. He had kids. They blamed my father because my uncle got killed working for my dad. They cut themselves off from my mother. I've never met them. My dad did not want to do credit on tick any more. He had never drunk but he took to drink and died an alcoholic. My father was on holiday in India in 1984 with my mother, the first time they had gone to the country together, when he had a heart attack and died.'

Bhandari heard of his father's death through a bad telephone call from India. As he tells me the story I think that I heard of my father's death also via a telephone call from India and the very same year, but he was old and had been ill for a long time. His father having died a bankrupt put his mother on widow's benefit. With Bhandari only 15 his life growing up was now a huge struggle. But nevertheless, he ended up at Peterhouse, the oldest of the Cambridge colleges, studying law. And three people, two white men and one white woman, played a crucial role in this:

'I passed my 11 plus in 1978–79 to go to grammar school but I couldn't go because it had just become fee paying. But when I was 13 or 14, two of the teachers in my comprehensive school intervened. My deputy headmaster, Mr Palmer, who had been at a grammar school, and my English teacher Mr Clark, said, 'You have got potential. We don't have a sixth form here. We don't have people who do A levels here. When they do they go to the local college. You're better than that. We'll give you some extra support.' Actually, one of them even said, 'You should think of Oxbridge. We should try to help you to get into the grammar school in the sixth form.'

Both Palmer and Clark were white. But even with their encouragement Bhandari would not have made it to Cambridge but for the white woman. She was Margaret Thatcher, who came to power in 1979, when Bhandari was still at the comprehensive, and introduced the Assisted Places Scheme. This enabled Bhandari to go to Wolverhampton Grammar School between 1984 and 1986 with the grant paying for the school fees, travel, uniform and meals.

He soon fulfilled his teacher's prophecy of going to Oxbridge and at Peterhouse he met another white man but he could not have been more different from his comprehensive teachers. Maurice Cowling, a historian, was a Fellow of Peterhouse and says Bhandari, 'He was a prominent eugenicist. He was one of the influential historians of that time who provided academic cover for more extreme eugenics theories.' Bhandari was to take his revenge on him. 'In my third year my room was next door to him. Sometimes I would deliberately leave my music on loud and leave my room just to annoy him.'

Growing up in Wolverhampton in the 1980s he was very aware of the skinhead menace, which was very strong, and often crossed the road to avoid them. So, was he never assaulted? 'Couple of times but I always kept it quiet. The worst one was when I was about 12 when a white kid at my comprehensive during a break pinned me against the wall. It was frightening. I was determined not to let these fascists get to me.'

Bhandari paints a vivid picture of how his world changed as he moved from comprehensive through grammar to Cambridge and then the City, reflecting the class structure of British society:

'If I took a Sergeant Pepper-style snapshot, like the album cover, then for every year of my life from the age of six or seven years old the background will get whiter and whiter and whiter. As I got older I started to see fewer and fewer black faces because I was climbing up the social strata. I go to my comprehensive, it has loads of black and Asian kids. Go to grammar school, quite a few Asian faces, not a lot of black faces. I go to Cambridge and there are a few Asian faces, in my year at my college probably one or two of them among 150 students. No blacks in my year at Cambridge. We had only just gone co-ed – Peterhouse was one of the last male colleges. The year before I went there they started taking women in, who were predominantly white. Then you come into the City and it gets even worse.'

Bhandari, who came to the City after the Big Bang, in 1990, trained as a lawyer at Herbert Smith, 'known as the Manchester United of litigation', and then worked for a number of firms ranging from law to accountancy including Baker McKenzie, KPMG and Ernst & Young from 2007 to 2019.

Bhandari's experience in the City has convinced him that:

'Discrimination in the City and other walks of life is more subtle. People never say anything to your face. It goes on behind closed doors. There were certainly some glass ceilings but also it's just the unconscious biases that you see in the City. You have these models of what makes a leader where people describe the leadership traits. They very often describe the traits of white men.'

Interestingly, in order to bridge cultures and help white people understand Asians, Bhandari has never felt he needs to change his name Sanjay:

'My dad did. When he did the market stall, everyone called him Pete. For a short time a friend of mine called me Jay using not the first half of my name but the second half. Nobody else. And I have never given any thought of changing my name.'

What makes Bhandari's story exceptional is that while working in the City in his 'spare time I became a stand-up comic. It started when I was at Baker McKenzie and carried on at KPMG.'

The catalyst was a speech he gave at the National Convention for Alcoholics:

'I was an alcoholic. I started drinking when I was 15. About three weeks after my dad died I had my first drink. You name it, I drank it. Started off with beer, then moved on to white wine and then whisky. Black Country beer was very good. It became part of my everyday life. Initially it was difficult to give up. Now it is just something I don't do. I have been in recovery for nearly 19 years. I don't touch a drink at all.'

Soon after he gave up drink he spoke at the National Convention for Alcoholics. On stage in front of 1,000 people he wore a thin, hands-free microphone that stretched down his cheek. Bhandari decided to start his talk by making a joke about it, 'It's funny having one of these mics because 'Oops! . . . I Did It Again' was my catchphrase drinking.' The audience laughed and afterwards someone suggested he should think of becoming a stand-up comic.

Bhandari did his stand-up comic routines in the evenings or at the weekends, 'My firm knew. Some of the people would come along to watch me perform. I was only doing the beginners' comedy circuit. Never went beyond that. I did it upstairs in pubs, back rooms. I would do a gig and earn 10 or 20 quid at the door.'

Being an Asian, 'did not even register':

'It is almost like a concentrated form of football, because football is a narrative. In football it is about getting the ball and putting it in the opposition net and stopping it going in your own net. Comedy is equally a narrative. In comedy, the only thing that matters are the laughs. It is a very egalitarian environment. If you have a good gig that is great. If you have a bad one it is okay as well because you are learn-ing. It taught me a lot about life. If you've got something, you share it. People will like it or not like it, but it's not fatal. It made me more relaxed, more resilient.'

He also joked at his dad's expense:

'My father deliberately did not teach us any Hindi, Punjabi or other Indian languages, because he didn't want us to grow up speaking English with an Indian accent as he thought that might hold us back. The joke I always tell is he did not want us to speak in an Indian accent, but we grew up in Wolverhampton so I speak with a Black Country accent that makes us sound more stupid than in any other accent. So, he didn't hold me back with an Indian accent, he just held me back with a Black Country accent.'

However, despite being born in the Black Country, he did not support Wolverhampton Wanderers. The reason is simple: 'Our local MP was Enoch Powell.' Bhandari was born the year of Powell's infamous 'Rivers of Blood' speech. Instead, he supports Manchester United, influenced by his uncle Prem and his favourite cousin Mukesh.

Bhandari's journey to become the chair of Kick It Out was also very distinctive. Having been part of the government review on ethnicity for property companies he was invited by the Premier League in 2015 to become a panellist for the equality standard they had created. In 2019 with Herman Ouseley, who had set up Kick It Out, deciding to leave and Bhandari looking for a change, this seemed the very natural next step.

Bhandari is well aware that the football world now is very different from when Kick It Out was set up in 1993. But for all the changes that have come, Bhandari identifies three major issues of 'systemic biases' that have existed 'for 30, 40 years and which pretty much haven't changed':

'The first one is leadership. Leadership teams in football are broadly white and male and a little bit older generally. The second one is coaching, which traditionally, not exclusively, comes from the playing side. So, you'd expect with somewhere between 25 and 30 per cent of players being black, that would be reflected in coaching, but it isn't. It is somewhere between 4 per cent and 6 per cent and the excuse that they are unqualified is not really good enough. Probably about 8 per cent to 10 per cent of them have UEFA B licences but they still can't get a job. So that is a statistical anomaly. And then the last one is Asians on the pitch. It is a myth that the pitch is meritocratic because loads of black people have been successful. Asian people have not been successful and are not on the page and the statistical anomaly is very clear. The way I explain it is that in this country, there are three times as many people of Asian or mixed-race heritage than there are black people in this country.'

Then raising his voice Bhandari says:

'There are 100 times more black professional footballers than there are Asians. Well, the numbers being quoted are 25 to 30 per cent black professionals and 0.2 to 0.3 per cent Asians. If that's right, that's 100 times. So, if you express it in that way, that means there are three times more Asians in this country, 100 times more black people on the pitch. I am not saying this to denigrate black players. I am saying there is something happening there. In many of the areas in football, I see lots and lots of reasons to be optimistic but to be candid, I have not seen the desire or the acknowledgement that [the lack of Asian players] is a problem, or the solution to it. So, I'm not optimistic about seeing more Asians in football in the professional game, because I don't see the action that's being done to understand where the problems are, of where the barriers are. I am not seeing in a systemic way any plan dealing with areas of diversity and inclusion of that specific problem. The FA has got some initiatives, but I'm not convinced that there's anything that is connected. More importantly, ultimately they have to be driven by clubs and I am not seeing concerted efforts.'

His pessimism has been increased because he is convinced, 'Asian people are suffering unconscious bias at the academy level.' And what is more, journalists are not interested in covering the story:

'I have heard at least half a dozen parents telling me, "Yeah I have got kids in the academy and they [the coaches at the academy] are saying, 'Why should I spend time with your kids when you're going to want to be a lawyer, or accountant.'" They [the academy coaches] will never ever say anything equivalent to a black parent. They will never say to a white parent, "Why should I waste time with your kid when you will want them to be a feckless, alcoholic benefit cheat?" They would never do that because that would be a lazy stereotype of working-class people. But they are very comfortable with that lazy stereotype of middle-class Asian people.'

Bhandari has heard this story from 'at least six parents' and one of the clubs involved was 'a top six club. I've told that story to probably half a dozen journalists in the last year and no one has ever written it. Nobody ever talks about it. It tells me people don't think it's an important issue.'

Bhandari talking in this vein reminds me what Herman Ouseley told me some years ago when he said he thought there was institutional racism. I expected him to agree with Ouseley but he does not:

'I am really careful when I use the R word. I want to drive change and in order to drive change, you have to be in the room with people and you have to not label people. Racism is the worst of all words. People don't mind being called a sexist, or they might mind it less being called sexist than racist. So, I tend to refer to structural bias, systemic biases. Language like systemic and structural bias actually goes across all strands. So, systemic biases covers racism, sexism, homophobia, discrimination towards disabled people – it actually covers the whole gamut for anyone in a minority or in a protected characteristic. Anyone who's underrepresented, or in a minority community, tends to suffer from structural biases. It isn't actually just about racism. It also tends to be an easier conversation to have because I'm not labelling someone and I'm not stigmatising someone. So, I deliberately do not use phrases like institutional racism or structural racism, because I actually do not think they help us with what I want to do, which is to create change.

'I use the R word very carefully, because it has become weaponised. And I don't think that's the way in which you get change. You get change by engaging people in a dialogue, and suggesting solutions; I think that's the way to drive change. I would rather be in a room talking to someone than outside the building shouting at them.'

It is towards the end of our conversation that when I say I had been called a coconut, Bhandari reveals that he had been called that many times. It does not faze him. If being called a coconut leads to changes in attitudes to racism, then Bhandari is happy to be called a coconut.

TWENTY

THE TURBAN, OSAMA AND THE HIJAB

Turban

In 1996 when I published *The Sporting Alien*, I had a chapter called 'Jack and his Turban'. It had the story of Jack who was invited by Terry Westley to Luton's school of excellence. Jack, born in Hitchin, living in Baldock, sounded like any of the hundreds of other boys who aspired to the school of excellence. But Jack was very different. He wore a turban and Jack was not his real name. His name was Jagjeevan Dosanjh who had become Jack because his teachers could not pronounce his real name.

Jack was almost the classic second-generation child. Bedfordshire was home. Jullundur in India, from where his father migrated to this country in 1975 – he worked in a factory in East Ham – was just a place to visit. His father's sport, hockey, had never appealed to Jack. His friend, Gurjeet, a fellow Sikh, had introduced him to football when he was about nine. Later, prompted by Gurjeet, Jack played for an Indian side, Letchworth Khalsa, a Sikh team. 'Soccer is my first love.'

Jack quite enjoyed six weeks of training at Luton's school of excellence, although most of the people he played with were older and the sessions every Thursday night emphasised that the English game sought boys of strength. 'We played in the gym, not a full-size pitch, which meant tight space and you needed strength. If you had strength you did all right.' Not easy for Jack who was five feet ten inches and confessed, 'I don't have much strength. My upper body is not that strong. I like running at players and I have got a lot of pace.'

Even before I had spoken to Jack, Terry had told me that Jack was 'a pleasant enough lad but not up to the standard'. And then there was Jack's need to pursue his nine GCSEs. But while his parents did not mind his playing, they were not, he said, like 'black parents who encourage their children in sport. My parents say concentrate on work. Given the choice I would rather be a professional footballer than have a degree.' Yet he was not driven by a burning ambition, saying, in a matter-of-fact, almost resigned, tone, 'If I don't make it, it is no loss. I shall do my studies.'

At Luton where most of the other players where white, and one or two black, he had faced no prejudice. 'There were no jokes about my turban.' Terry had said, 'He has a turban but that is neither here nor there.' Indeed, for Jack the worst moment of racism came on the streets of London. 'Six months ago we were going to London looking at shops. We went on the subway in London, to go to King's Cross and St Pancras. Some people came by in a car, opened the window and shouted racist remarks.'

His loyalty to the England football team was not in doubt. 'I support England, I was born here,' he said in a tone which implied I had asked him a stupid question. But, 'If India play England I want India to win.' However, this does not matter much. 'I don't really know much about cricket.'

If that is how a Sikh saw it in 1996, how do Muslims see things in the twenty-first century?

Osama

When I ghosted Moeen Ali's book, there was one story he was very reluctant to talk about. It concerned what had happened to him during the first Ashes Test of 2015 at Cardiff's SWALEC ground. Moeen's manager Kamran Khan had repeatedly told me it was an explosive story and finally I got the chance to sit down with him and get him to tell me.

England were fielding and with Moeen leaking runs, the England captain Alastair Cook had just taken him off. An Australian player gleefully said to him, 'Take that, Osama.' Moeen on hearing those words had gone very red and had never been so angry on a cricket field. The player concerned who had denied saying it, claimed Moeen had misheard and he had actually said, 'Take that, you part-timer,' as a way of mocking Moeen's pretensions to be a spinner. Moeen was much amused to hear that, for as he told me, 'there is a world of difference between the words "Osama" and "part-timer" and I could not have mistaken the two.'

Moeen did regain his composure, came back to bowl well and took a crucial wicket. England went on to win the Test which was a launch pad for winning the series and regaining the Ashes. However, when I wrote it up for the book, while the incident was mentioned, Moeen would not let me name the Australian player. What consoled Moeen was his teammates were appalled he had been called Osama and that the English fans would not dream of calling him that.

Moeen's rise as England's most prominent Muslim cricketer since the Nawab of Pataudi senior played for Douglas Jardine's team in Australia during the 1932–33 Ashes series casts a very interesting light on both English society and cricket.

He has emerged when the country, as was tortuously illustrated during the Brexit debate, is seeking to define its role in the world, and where sections of white society are still adjusting to the presence of large numbers of non-whites amidst them with, as we have seen, a young footballer having a beard like Moeen likely to have it pulled by a white opponent and told he is Osama. It is against this background, very different from the world of the Nawab of Pataudi senior, that Moeen has become in the eyes of the English cricket supporters one of their own and whose beard is the subject of celebration not of fear he is an alien. What makes his story even more interesting is that during this, Moeen himself has been on a remarkable journey discovering what he considers his true Islamic faith and in the process casting a light rarely shone on little known aspects of British society.

I was eager to follow his journey and this meant talking at length to Wally Mohammad. Moeen had met him on a very cold, rainy day in Birmingham on 2 August 2006 when he was playing for Warwickshire against the West Indies A team touring England. Moeen sitting by the window saw a man, with a beard, make salaams to him. Moeen was intrigued that he looked West Indian. Was he, probably, a convert to Islam, Moeen wondered? Moeen put some apples and oranges in a tissue and took them to him. The man was indeed a convert, a West Indian whose parents were Pentecostal Christians. Talking to Wally I began to understand how this Muslim convert had made Moeen, born a Muslim, find what Moeen now calls his true Islamic faith. Moeen's family are Sufis, a branch of Islam I have great admiration for. Wally told him that Sufism was not part of the original teachings of the prophet Mohammed, it was something which was introduced later on.

Like all his family members, Moeen wore a chain round his neck called the taweez, said to contain verses of the Koran and worn to protect the person as a lucky charm. Moeen had already had doubts about it when an Arab he had met in a mosque had asked him how he could take the taweez to the toilet if it contained verses from the Koran. He had opened his taweez, found it was empty and stopped wearing it. Wally did not wear a taweez and reinforced Moeen's view that it was not Islamic.

Moeen's own heritage gave me insights into immigrant societies in this country which is not much talked about. Moeen can claim to be at least a quarter per cent white. His grandfather had migrated to this country from Kashmir and in 1949 married an English girl Betty Cox, whom he had met at the Lucas factory in Birmingham. Betty had been married before, her husband, a pilot, having been killed in the Second World War, and this romance between a widowed Englishwoman, who knew nothing about the subcontinent, and a Pakistani immigrant was a touching story. Moeen was close to Betty's children from her English husband and spoke lovingly of an aunt called Anne, his dad's half-sister, and an uncle called Brett, his dad's half-brother.

That Moeen had an English grandmother would completely fox his teammates who could not believe that was possible. In 2015 Moeen went to the Desert Springs in Andalusia in Spain, where England had their training camp to prepare for the Ashes series. One evening, in the great British tradition, a quiz was organised and each member of the team gave the quizmaster a question which the rest of the team was asked to answer. Moeen's question was, 'My grandmother's name is Betty Cox. Who am I?' Nobody knew the answer and Moeen told me how when he stood up and answered the question, Andrew Strauss could not believe that a person of Pakistani heritage could have a grandmother called Betty Cox.

That a publisher wanted a book about Moeen also showed how far Moeen himself had come. In 2014, at nearly 27 years old, an age when many cricketers would have given up hope, he had made his Test debut, scoring a century in his second Test, albeit in a losing cause. Then, with his off-spin, he had turned the series against India, paving the way for a crushing 3-1 win after India had taken a 1-0 lead in the series with a win at Lord's. But despite this, in 2014 he was still an Asian cricketer. I had first met him at a function to honour Asian celebrities and arranged to interview him. I then did the weekly 'Big Interview' for the *London Evening Standard*. But it required a lot of persuasion to convince my sports editor that Moeen would be a good Big Interview subject. All this changed on 31 July 2017.

That afternoon on the fifth day of the Test, Moeen became the first English spinner to take a hat-trick in a Test for 79 years. What was even more remarkable was that he did it at The Oval where no bowler had ever before taken a hat-trick and timed it so well that the ground was staging its 100th Test.

Suddenly, from being an Asian cricketer with a beard he was dramatically transformed into a national treasure. Less than a week after the hat-trick, the *Guardian* devoted nearly two pages to an interview with him. Within two months he made the cover of the weekend *Times* magazine with a picture of him looking resplendent in his beard alongside the headline 'England's Best-Loved'. I did not need to lobby editors to write about Moeen. It was one of my publishers, who had many decades ago published my first book, who approached me with the idea that I contact Moeen and get him to agree to write his autobiography. Moeen was keen I write the biography but the publisher felt it would be better as an autobiography with me ghosting it.

I was fascinated to learn how Moeen's faith dovetailed in with his cricket and the effect it had on his fellow, white, English players. After he had taken a hat-trick he had driven home to Birmingham. Hoping to get some colour I asked him what he had listened to as he drove home. I expected him to say he had listened to the radio which was full of Moeen's achievements. But to my surprise he told me that he never listened to cricket on the radio. Not even a single ball. Instead, he listened to lectures or talks on Islam. He listened to the Koran a lot in his car. He tried to memorise it as much as he could. That made him feel wonderful and meant a lot more than the hat-trick.

And his white English teammates had adapted wonderfully to accommodate such a devout Muslim in their midst. The routine after a victory such as the one at The Oval is well set. The victorious England team assemble for a group photograph, a bottle of champagne is uncorked and sprayed all over the players. But Moeen not only does not drink, he does not even touch alcohol and would not want to be near alcohol. So, as the England players celebrated, Alastair Cook shouted out, 'You know, make sure Moeen gets in the picture first and then we can spray.' It was only after Moeen had walked away from the group photograph that the champagne bottle was opened and the players sprayed with it. For Moeen it meant a lot and was a touching show of respect for him and his religion. What happened when the players returned to the dressing room provided further evidence of how a largely white team with its own hallowed customs adjusts to its devout Muslim teammate. The tradition was the players would sing a song which went:

Oh Sally, Sally come home tonight
You've been looking round, but you never found
The love you needed for so long
Oh Sally, Sally come home tonight

For Moeen, having had his celebratory Coke, the start of the singing was the time to go home and leave his teammates to their singing. And this meant leaving his best friend in the team, Ben Stokes [Stokesy as he is known], belting out this call for Sally.

In some ways the relationship between Ben Stokes and Moeen tells us a lot about how British society is becoming multicultural. Contrary to Stokes's public persona, Moeen finds him gentle and kind. The two rib each other and Moeen can anger Stokes so much that Stokes can even shout at him, but this does not affect their friendship. The bond between the two was illustrated when Stokes made sure Moeen got his hat-trick that day at The Oval. Moeen had taken two wickets with two balls. The problem was he had taken the second wicket with the last ball of the over. Stokes was due to bowl the next over and South Africa were nine down so Stokes would be expected to try and take the wicket to give England victory. Instead, Stokes did not try and take a wicket in that over. However, the problem was that Stokes was bowling to Maharaj who can bat and it was very likely he could get a single. This would mean Moeen would bowl his hat-trick ball to Maharaj and not Morne Morkel, the number 11, whose batting skills are very limited and was less likely to prevent Moeen from taking his hat-trick. But Stokes reassured Moeen. After Stokes had bowled his third ball to Maharaj he told Moeen, who was fielding at point, 'I will make sure you bowl at Morne Morkel.' This is just what Stokes did. Moeen bowled to Morkel, got his wicket and made history. Stokes was also the one most outraged by Moeen being called Osama.

Moeen's acceptance by cricket watchers would reach out beyond England and connect England and South Africa in a remarkable way as was demonstrated in 2015 in the Cape Town Test. Ben Stokes scored a magnificent double hundred and so did Hashim Amla, the South African captain. The Test saw a singing duet between the South African and the English supporters. The South African crowd, who were in one part of the ground, sang what they call the Kolo Touré song. They would rise and sing, 'Hashim, Hashim, Hashim, Hashim, Hashim, Hashim, Hashim Amla,' and then sit down. In response, the Barmy Army, who were in another part, would get up and sing, 'Moeen, Moeen, Moeen . . . Ali,' and sit down. Moeen thinks this went on for hours and both Hashim and Moeen smiled and waved to the crowd. Here were two Muslim cricketers, both with beards, one of whom [Amla] had been called a terrorist by Dean Jones, the former Australian cricketer during a commentary, albeit in a whisper which unfortunately was caught on the microphone. But now they were being hailed by a largely white crowd. And this in Cape Town off whose shores is Robben Island where Nelson Mandela had been jailed for years. Moeen capped this by telling me the story of what A.B. de Villiers had said to him after the series. 'I'm going to tell you something. I sing the song to my son and it's the only thing my son goes quiet about. That's the song my son sings most of the time. So, when my son is playing cricket, he says, "I'll be Hashim

Amla, you be Moeen Ali," or he'll be Moeen Ali, I'll be Hashim Amla. And we both sing.'

For A.B. de Villiers' son it would make no sense that Moeen had once been called Osama in a Test match. And by this time his beard, which had once caused disquiet, was no longer a matter of debate or raising the question of what constitutes being English.

The debate about the beard had started when, going into his Test debut at Lord's, Moeen was asked about his beard. He replied that it had to do with representing the people of his faith. This had prompted Michael Henderson to write that 'a man who belongs to a team and draws attention to his beard as a symbol of his faith is opting to stand out'. Yet when cricketers had worn the crucifix no such question had been raised about their identity; if anything it was seen as a man of faith turning to his God as he had every right to.

The best example of this comes from Jack Fingleton's *The Greatest Test of All*, describing the first-ever tied Test, between Australia and the West Indies in Brisbane in December 1960. In this cricket classic Fingleton described Hall bowling, arguably, the most dramatic last over of any Test. It was four minutes to six, and Australia needed six to win and had three wickets in hand:

> 'I will never forget the sight of Hall, a magnificent specimen of a man, as he came back slowly to his mark to begin this last death-or-glory over. He wears a cross on a chain around his neck and I could see him fingering the cross as he walked. I could imagine him saying a prayer; "Please, Lord, I'll do my best – you know I always do – but what I want is a miracle. And yet not one miracle but two or three, please Lord!"'

Hall got his three miracles as three Australian wickets fell, the last a run-out by Solomon of Kline off the fifth ball, tying the Test, something that had never happened before in Test history.

Nobody made anything of Hall making a religious gesture. Fingleton certainly did not, and if anything emphasised it. But Hall was a Christian, and after retirement he was ordained a minister in the Pentecostal Church, the one Wally Mohammad's mother had belonged to. This 1960 Brisbane Test was in religious terms between two Christian nations. In such a contest a player wearing a cross would not be seen as exceptional and no journalist would have asked Hall why he was wearing a cross. But in 2014 Britain, Moeen's comment about his beard raised the question of whether he was an alien. The fact that it did raised questions about how the British see religion rather than Moeen using cricket to advertise his religion. Britain rightly advertises its secularism allowing different religions to practise and preach. However, it is a Christian country where the monarch is both the head of the state and the Church. In fact it is a Protestant country in that no British monarch can marry a Catholic, let alone a non-Christian. All ceremonial state functions are held in an Anglican church. It would be unthinkable to have state functions in a church of any other Christian denomination. British politicians talk of this being a Christian country and the need to preserve its Christian status. In such a country a Muslim displaying what he sees as a symbol of his faith, a symbol most people are not familiar with and about whose religion most people know little, raises the question as to whether he is one of us, or can be one of us. And given the Islamic terrorist threat, it ignites fear that such a person may be an alien, a threat to the British way of life. It is this unfamiliarity, stoked by intellectuals and writers raising questions, that prompted the journalist to ask Moeen the question. He would not have dreamt of asking Hall, or any other Christian cricketer, why he was wearing a crucifix. In fact a Christian not being allowed to wear a crucifix on a cricket field would be seen as a threat to society.

However, by the time I came to write Moeen's book, it was clear that English fans did not find the beard a threat. They had accepted it to such an extent that they began to sing 'The Beard that is Feared', celebrating the diversity of the nation. Moeen could feel he was part of England and his beard did not set him apart.

Hijab

Rimla Akhtar could not be more different from Moeen Ali, except for their common passion for Liverpool, Rimla having modelled herself on Jamie Carragher, the great Liverpool player. However, she admitted to me that, following 9/11, she faced problems, even from her own Liverpool supporters. 'It was at the Carling Cup final at the Millennium Stadium against Chelsea [in 2005]. We lost. I was wearing my hijab and I had comments by my own fans, about being a terrorist.'

I met Rimla Akhtar five months after she became the first Muslim woman on the FA Council in June 2014. In a body which FA chairman, Greg Dyke, had famously said is 'overwhelmingly male and white', Akhtar was seen as the ideal role model for the Asian community. The child of Pakistani immigrants, who has been wearing a hijab since she was 11, nobody had to tell Akhtar about discrimination:

'I'm born and bred British, a Londoner through and through. I grew up in the eighties when there was a lot of racism in the community. I experienced it at first hand. We were the first family to move into a particular area that was white, so with that came a lot of verbal and physical abuse. My two older brothers were beaten up on the streets. Sport was the one area where I felt nobody cared about the colour of my skin or the fact that I wore a piece of cloth around my head, or my gender even. It's where I was accepted. Everywhere else I wasn't.'

We had met at the Pret A Manger near St Paul's. On the table in front of us was a column by Rod Liddle in that day's *Sun* suggesting that the recent rise of anti-Semitic attacks might be the work of Muslims. 'Oh gosh,' said Akhtar in horror as she read the paper. 'It's unfortunate that such comments are made. I don't like to be apologetic about being Muslim. Unfortunately, there are always people out there who will stir up hatred.'

Then Akhtar added sadly, 'I spent the first half of my life fighting some of the issues that came with being Asian. Now the second half of my life has been spent dealing with Islamophobia.'

But this fight had not dented Akhtar's conviction that sport can provide an answer to society's problems. This belief lay behind her successful campaign to get FIFA to accept that women should be allowed to play football wearing hijabs. 'My work', she said, 'is not finished. Men who wear turbans or Jewish men who wear the yarmulke still have the same problems. This is about allowing everyone to be included in sport. This is a problem across all areas of sport. There's no hiding that there is sexism in sport. We have a lack of women right across all levels of management, playing and coaching. It shows the closed nature of sport in general and this includes the media. It's an indictment of sport as a whole.'

Our talk invariably referred to the lack of Asians in football and it was interesting that Moeen's name came up:

'We have a real problem. There is a lack of role models. Moeen Ali is now in the cricket team. For years, we've had Monty [Panesar]. We've not seen it in football and that's one of the challenges.'

What was interesting was that, unlike many other Asian leaders I had met, she accepted that Asian parents also had to do more. 'In Asian communities, education is put first. My brothers went through that as well. We are the children of immigrants to this country and sport was treated as a hobby.'

But, while Akhtar drew encouragement from the fact that these issues are at last being discussed seriously, she confessed that, 'There is a long way to go to get to a place of parity. There is a lot of work to be done. The structures of football need to change a lot. It will take a few years before we get there. Possibly ten years.'

Laurie Cunningham, Brendon Batson and Cyrille Regis, dubbed the Three Degrees by their manager Ron Atkinson, posing with the real Three Degrees American pop group at the Hawthorns in 1979 in a photo shoot organised by Atkinson. *Mirrorpix/Alamy*

Gareth Southgate, the England manager who played his football when black players were told to suffer racism, has shown remarkable awareness of racial issues. Here with Raheem Sterling, the new generation of black players who refuse to turn the other cheek to racism. *Charlie Forgham-Bailey/Alamy*

Adam Lallana of Brighton taking the knee, an important gesture against racism which started in 2020 after the death of George Floyd and the rise of the Black Lives Matter movement. *Paul Hazelwood/Brighton and Hove FC*

Brighton using the Premier League match against Wolves in December 2019 to show solidarity with the LGBT+ community in conjunction with Stonewall's Rainbow Laces campaign. *Paul Hazelwood and Brighton and Hove FC*

Imrul Gazi, the manager of Sporting Bengals who has confronted racism in grassroots football in London, feels it could take another fifteen to twenty years before we get a non-racial sports world. *AZ Images*

Tom Loizou, a Greek Cypriot who because of his looks has been called a 'Paki', took his Haringey Borough players off the field in a FA Cup qualifying competition match in 2019 against Yeovil following racist abuse of his players. *Nigel French/Alamy*

Samei, a young Asian boy with his mother, celebrating success at grassroots football in London in March 2020, holding out hope of ushering in a non-racial sports world. *Zulfi Ali*

Isa Guha, the first women of Asian heritage to play for England, now a highly respected commentator on *Test Match Special*, is proud of her cultural duality of being both Bengali and British. *Tony Marshall/Alamy*

Michael Holding, one of cricket's greatest fast bowlers, has persuasively argued that racism can only be eradicated if the untold story of black achievements is finally made known. *Richard Splash/Alamy*

Ebony Rainford-Brent, the first black woman to play for England, broke down at a Sky meeting when discussing race which led to her and Holding making a seminal film on race. *Ashley Western/Alamy*

Azeem Rafiq, whose cricket held such promise, but whose revelations about racism in Yorkshire cricket unleashed an earthquake from which English cricket is still reeling. *TGSPhoto/Alamy*

Majid Ishaq, managing director of Rothschild, at the age of twelve was chased round Anfield being called a 'Paki' but is now welcomed into the Anfield boardroom and is the most sought after financial adviser in the sports world. *Majid Ishaq*

Mahdi Chowdhury, a lawyer of Bangladeshi origin who is Assistant Secretary (Membership) of the MCC, believes there is unconscious bias and that sports organisations are not very diverse. *MCC*

Lewis Hamilton, whose response to racism for many years was to do his talking on the track, following the death of George Floyd decided that he wouldn't 'keep quiet about unspoken racism in this country.' *James Moy/Alamy*

Graffiti mocking Raheem Sterling's wealth prompted by media stories of black players showing off their wealth, reporting which Sterling has criticised and contrasted with how wealthy white players are treated. *James Malone/Alamy*

Alex Williams, the former Manchester City goalkeeper who suffered horrendous abuse in the 1970s and 1980s, now lectures school kids on tackling racism. *Manchester City FC*

Donna Fraser, four-time Olympian and now the UK Athletics' equality, diversity and engagement lead feels that 'some white people don't quite understand' the experiences of people of colour. *Allstar Picture Library/Alamy*

Scott Lloyd, chief executive of Lawn Tennis Association, with Andy Murray, agrees with Pat Cash that tennis is a white middle-class sport and that for a white person it is difficult to understand what it is to experience discrimination on a daily basis.
James Jordan Photography

Young kids taking to tennis as part of the LTA's Inclusion Strategy launched by Lloyd in May 2021 to help tennis reach out beyond its traditional white Middle England heartland.
James Jordan Photography

Emma Raducanu, whose victory in the US Open in 2021 made her the first qualifier to win a Grand Slam singles title in the open era, is proud of her Chinese heritage. *James Jordan Photography*

Chris Hughton, unique among black ex-players, has an array of impressive managerial portfolios including three Premiership clubs. He feels racism will always be there but is encouraged that more black coaches are coming through. *Graham Jepson Photography*

Chris Powell, who played with Southgate at Crystal Palace when black players were just breaking into the team, was racially abused by fellow white players but is now part of Southgate's coaching team. *Graham Jepson Photography*

It was revealing when I asked her if quotas would get more ethnic minorities involved in football coaching and administration:

'For me, quotas are a short-term strategy. I wouldn't want to be selected because I'm a woman, because I'm Asian or because I'm Muslim. I would like to be selected on merit. I've had people really close to me, relatives even, who have said, "You do realise that you're being included just because you wear the scarf." In the long term, it's about making the sports environment more inclusive. That's what's lacking right now. We need to get an inclusive mindset as well as action on the ground. This is not about placing people from the black, Asian or the LGBT community into particular positions. It's about saying, "We want to make sport more representative of the community, more diverse and therefore more successful." '

The success of Moeen Ali and Rimla Akhtar shows we have moved a long way since 1996 and Jack and his turban. However, while they may not represent a fundamental shift in society it does demonstrate that British society is more nuanced than a simple binary discussion about race and religion might suggest. The barriers that divide communities remain, but these barriers are not iron walls and it would be a mistake to dismiss the breaches that have been made as of no significance.

TWENTY-ONE

PRESERVING BENGAL IN HERTFORDSHIRE

I t is towards the end of our conversation that Isa Guha says, 'I know Bengali history is a rich history with some of the most incredible thinkers – something that I am incredibly proud of. I am desperate to immerse myself in it. There is so much to know that I need to take it in stages but I would like to read a bit more about Bengali culture, so, if there is anything you can send me that would be very nice.' I promise to do so and send her a couple of books and cannot resist including one of my own books. Guha's desire to learn more about her Bengali roots has been the result of what she calls 'a lot of personal introspection' as a result of the Black Lives Matter movement. Not that she has not been aware of her Bengali heritage or proud of it. Indeed, Guha's is a story of the first woman of Asian heritage to play for England – and now a commentator on the programme that defines an English summer for every cricket lover, *Test Match Special*, as well as presenter on BBC's Test and ODI cricket – being proud of her Bengali heritage while feeling firmly rooted in today's Britain.

Our conversation had started with another duality, the one imposed by the pandemic. We cannot meet and I am speaking to her on the phone on a winter's morning in London where, to add to the cold, there is concern that Boris Johnson's much talked about road to freedom may end with another lockdown, as it soon did. I am very envious of Guha as she is in Australia getting ready to commentate on the 2020–21 Australia–India series which is about to start. I would love to be there, more so as my Indian publishers have just signed a contract with a British publisher for a revised British edition of my book on the history of Indian cricket. But when I ring Guha it turns out that the pandemic has converted her Australian summer into a scene from a disaster movie. Guha and her husband, Richard, are in their sixth day of quarantine in a Perth hotel. 'I can't open my windows. Can't leave the room.'

But she only has to start speaking of her Bengali roots for me to feel that we have much in common. Her dad comes from Kolkata, the city I was born in, her mum from Comilla, in what is now Bangladesh and in the days of the British Raj used to be East Bengal, where my parents came from. When I ask her if she can speak Bengali she answers in Bengali *'Aami ektu ektu bolta pari'*, 'I can speak a little.' She calls her mother, Ma, the sweet Bengali word for mother, she calls her grandmother, Thakurma, which means mother's mother; the Bengalis have different terms for grandparents from their maternal and paternal side. And when she speaks of her upbringing in High Wycombe it is obvious that she has tried to perform the very delicate balancing act that so many children of immigrants find almost impossible: retaining links with their ancestral culture but still feeling firmly grounded in the new world their parents have brought them to.

In a Britain where so much is often made of Muslim girls wearing hijabs, which instantly mark them as outsiders, her mother's dress sense balanced cultural traditions:

> 'Ma wore a sari at times. But she also wore Western clothing and was happy to do both. Ma would wear a sari for Bengali occasions and attending typical Bengali events or Bengali friends' houses. Mum and Dad came from Kolkata in the 1970s. There was a group of friends who migrated with them to High Wycombe and the only extended family lived in Greenford, but they all became our link to Bengali heritage; as well as trips back to Kolkata, and visits from family around the world.'

As she talks of her mum wearing her sari, I think back to the time I first saw Guha outside of a cricket field. She had established herself as a vital member of the England women's team and had been nominated for the Sony Asian Sports Personality of the Year Award. Guha recalls:

> 'I remember I was on an England training camp and I had to go to Birmingham to receive my award. All of my teammates came with me and supported me at the awards event. I dressed up in a sari to receive my award from Akshay Kumar. I remember all of my teammates were in the audience, cheering me on. I really appreciated that at that time. I didn't see it as a big deal but it was.'

I was one of the judges for the award that year and was struck by the looks on the faces of her white female teammates dressed in elegant frocks as they saw this Asian woman in a sari walk up to receive her award. The hall was packed with people of Asian origin who did not need to be told what Guha had achieved or that Akshay Kumar was a huge Bollywood star. It was the white England players who looked like strangers watching with wonder at a scene they had never seen before. In that instant, Guha was educating her teammates about a culture they did not know existed.

For a Bengali, no meal is complete without rice and fish and the great Bengali dish is rice and hilsa fish, which they consider the most delectable fish in the world. So, did Isa grow up with this Bengali delicacy as I did?

'Ma cooked every single day. She moved to Kolkata at a young age after partition. My thakurma [grandma] was a singer. She started singing in her mid twenties. As she got older, her and Dadu [mother's father] would invite people round to the house and entertain guests with music sessions. Ma was quite young at the time and was asked to provide the teas and make the food. She cooked every day from the age of seven or eight so I was accustomed to fresh Bengali food from a really early age, like Ilish mach and mangsho bhat [hilsa fish and rice with meat], which I absolutely loved. She would intersperse that with making lasagne, fish and chips or a roast!'

Her name she admits:

'Still causes problems. It is difficult. Even Indians will actually say Eesa. Pretty much everyone I speak to I have to say to them, it is actually Isa (Eesha). That was a bit of frustration when I was younger. But did I ever think of changing it? I think when I was a teenager. Eventually I learned to be proud of it. Mum always used to say that when I was born, a nurse revealed the meaning of Isa to be "the determined lady" in German. Bengalis traditionally use 'sh' in a lot of their language so it got converted to "Isha" but it was down as Isa on my birth certificate so my parents never changed it. I grew up in a white British community and to be honest I enjoyed it because my parents made it feel very normal – their work colleagues and our neighbours were predominantly white and we had a good relationship with them. However, as a child I guess you want to fit in, don't you? Obviously I looked different from everyone else and I definitely felt at times that I should leave my roots at the door and prove that I belonged. My background and my roots weren't necessarily something that I talked about too much, potentially for fear of being judged or made to feel different. But I was also proud of my Bengali roots. I am very proud of both parts of my background. And so, growing up I became a sort of chameleon. When I was in a white environment I behaved as if I was British. But when I was in the Bengali environment, for example going to the Durga Puja, the great Bengali religious festival, in west London, I would act respectfully to fit into that environment. Did I ever experience racism? I definitely felt at times that I was stereotyped and anytime that happened I would try my hardest to prove I wasn't that way. Overtly racist comments you become conditioned to ignore, but I was fortunate that I didn't have to experience that often.

'There is definitely a phase I went through as a teenager whereby you are not sure where you belong. I guess that is true of a lot of teenagers but there seemed to exist a battle sometimes where I was trying to be accepted by white people but then vilified for doing that by some of the Indian diaspora. Bengali culture is generally quite supportive of mixing cultures so less so from Bengalis, but sometimes from closed communities.

'I feel I am constantly finding out things about my roots and culture. And it is really important not to shy away from that either. I think we are in a better position now to be able to celebrate what makes us who we are. Perhaps when our parents or families came over in the sixties or seventies, they felt a need to suppress that. Maybe they felt they were treading on eggshells and having to conform as a sign of respect. But now I think the world is creating a culture, certainly in the Western world, whereby differences are celebrated. Cricket did allow me to do that. When I was part of the England team I would talk about my Indian roots. When we would go on tours to India I would chat to the girls about the different things that they might experience when they go there.'

Guha's cultural duality was matched by her cricketing duality:

'It helped that when I was eight I joined the local boys' team. I was the only girl in a team full of boys. But also the only British-Indian in a team full of white British and British-Pakistanis. It was great to have so many different, diverse people within that team. And for me the thing that stood out more was the fact that I was a girl. I did not realise till I was ten that England had a women's team, and that is something a lot of other professional women of my generation would say. Mum and Dad never had any issue with me playing with boys or people from a different background and it was never really questioned.

So growing up I learned how to fit into that environment, and being a girl in a boys' team simply wasn't an issue for me like it was for some relatives. Mum and Dad very much protected me from that.

'Mum was very supportive of everything I did. I enjoyed chasing after the ball when my brother, who is seven years older than me, was practising in the back garden. My mum thought, "Why doesn't she go to the local club as well?" Mum reassured Dad that it was okay for me to play with boys. Dad eventually got involved as well and set up a women's cricket team, alongside a man called Bob Lester, because there weren't any girl teams around at the time. He saw my abilities and thought, "I want to push her forward," so he looked out for club teams for me to play in. I was lucky to be introduced to some very early on and I was eventually picked up for the Under-21 Thames Valley team when I was 11 years old.'

What helped Guha bridge the age gap on the field of play was that socially she was mixing with the older generation from a young age:

'Dad is a businessman, an MD of a commercial company, and from the age of 12 he was inviting me to dinners with some of his clients. Having to hold a conversation with adults as a youngster gave me the confidence to hold my own in that environment. Playing in a boys' team also gave me a lot of confidence. If you do anything out of your comfort zone it can give you self-belief. I got to play for England at a very young age too but that was an intimidating experience because I was the youngest in the team at the time and I didn't know a lot of the players.'

But the summer of 2020, following the death of George Floyd and the Black Lives Matter movement, made Guha rethink the question of fitting in. So what has changed?

'I think a combination of factors. Coronavirus has allowed a spotlight to be shone on these issues. It has been festering away for hundreds of years and the majority had not wanted to tackle the problem or palmed it off as not their problem. Suddenly everyone was at home and witnessed first hand the injustice in America. It galvanised people to stand up, take notice and try and create change. I think people have been empowered by what they have seen. They are now able to speak up about their own issues. The advent of social media has meant that people can say what they want to say without necessarily being silenced. It has encouraged people to feel less afraid of speaking out. There are many situations where you had to keep things to yourself or not bring it out for fear of being difficult in a particular environment. And this year and this summer [of 2020] has allowed everyone is to be a bit more passionate, to be a force for good. And they have recognised their ability to help.

'While my lived experience is different from what George Floyd and many others have faced, I definitely see it as a responsibility now to help create an environment that is inclusive of everyone. I have been very fortunate with cricket setting my path and I have always wanted to give something back. I definitely see an opportunity now to really create meaningful change with everyone working together. You can't create change until you have that. There will be people who are afraid of getting involved because it feels too much or they think, "It's not my responsibility." To flip it around, if every single person said to them-selves, "How can I make a difference?" or "Do I want to live in a world that harbours racism?" then change is never too far away. I am now in a position where I can talk about racism, which wouldn't have been the case five years ago and I feel very fortunate to be able to use my voice.'

This has made Guha look at how we can change things:

'I think there are many different levels to how we create change. Firstly, there is education. I have been made aware of a charity called Facing History. They actually set up a module to work with secondary schools, being able to talk head-on about racism but also educating students on the history of different communities and why people might feel the way they do. For years I played for England and I was really proud of being British singing the national anthem. Winston Churchill to me was a hero who led Britain to freedom and without that I would not have had the opportunities I do today.

'His legacy was created on the back of the Second World War. But only in the last five years have I been made more aware of his impact on the Bengal famine. That is something which is a real conflict in my head.'

The 1943 Bengal famine is one of the great untold stories of British colonial history, which even British historians find difficult to come to terms with. It killed 3.5 million Bengalis. This was the worst in twentieth-century South Asia, caused by dreadful incompetence on the part of British Raj officials, the local Bengal government and a reluctance by the British War Cabinet to divert shipping to take food to India. The Greek famine caused by the Nazi occupation killed an estimated 300,000. While Churchill resisted diverting shipping to feed Bengal, he was keen to get food to Greece and, at the

Cabinet meeting of 24 September 1943, Churchill made it clear that, 'the starvation of the anyhow underfed Bengalis is less serious than sturdy Greeks'. Churchill told his secretary that Hindus were a foul race.

Guha says:

'It is not to say I admonish Churchill. I think it is important to understand history, to be able to move forward and help people understand the repercussions of people's actions. And the education system, the way everything is put together, is designed to serve those in positions of power and privilege. This is what it is has been built on. And this is what we are trying to, I guess, change. Kids need to have that understanding or have the education of what has happened in the past so they might look at things in a different way and be able to change the future. It is about getting them to ask questions themselves about how they feel about a certain subject.

'I have been learning a lot about the Aboriginal culture, the oldest living civilisation, and one of their mantras was to pass on their learnings but also to look after the land for future generations. It's a culture we could learn a huge amount from. I like to see the positive side of things always because that is how Mum brought me up and that is how she was. With regards to British rule in India, understandably there are a lot of people in India who are still angry about it and rightfully so. While it brought about a lot of turmoil, she would always explain the positive things the British did too, so I had both sides of the story. Overall though I do think how history is taught is very important and unfortunately not the whole story is told in schools about the impact of British rule.'

Guha is aware that as a person of colour, a rejection can make you think race is involved:

'I remember when I got into the England team it was quite a big deal, and people made a lot of me being the first Asian woman to be involved. At the time, I was almost embarrassed to get that attention. For me I just wanted to play for my country and it's only in recent times that I have embraced the significance of it. When I was part of the England team I did not experience any overt racism directed at me. But there may have been times when I was conscious of being stereotyped. When I was playing cricket I didn't want to think I wasn't being left out because of my colour – I never let that thought enter my mind, although it may have entered the minds of some members of my family at times and it was something I had to manage. I think that is a constant battle for young British Asians or British kids who have a diverse background, that you always worry about the reasons why you are not picked or why you are dropped. And it becomes a complex. That is something that these young kids have to manage.'

Many people of colour often feel they have to be 50 per cent better than their white counterparts. But, says Guha, 'I never felt that. I just wanted to be the best at what I was doing.'

For Guha, being the only female in a male group or the only Asian in a white group has never been a problem:

'I feel comfortable with both as I was brought up that way. That has come from having been in those environments all through my life. I guess through having that mindset of wanting to be challenged, I am attracted to opportunities that make me a better version of myself through being in a different environment. However, I don't really think about being the first to do something; it just happens that way. Being the only girl in a boys' team definitely prepared me. Being part of a competitive environment educates you as well on how to try and be better too. It makes you realise that if you are not the best you can be, and if you are not pulling your weight in a team, then you will fall behind and let the team down essentially. A team environment is something I have always really enjoyed – seeing how I can get the best out of everyone together and celebrating each other's successes because of that. Being the only female in a male broadcast team you do want to prove yourself. But it is like any new environment you are part of. I didn't think it was any different in that respect. If I had gone to play for Bankstown in the Sydney Grade League, which was a women's team, I still felt the need to prove myself and wanted my teammates to accept me. I have always felt that way in any environment that I go into. To show that I am more than capable of doing the job.'

The result is that she now feels, 'It has got to the point where I am really content with what I am doing at the moment. Really pleased with how things have moved on.'

When I complement her on her voice, which she had told me that she did not like, she laughs and says:

'Interestingly I actually think my voice has changed significantly over time. You find a range. You understand how high you can go. How loud you can go. Understanding the different audiences helps. And working with my male counterparts has given me confidence. Going to Australia and working for the radio broadcaster Triple M was a pretty significant moment in my commentary career. In Australia for some reason I really enjoyed what I was doing rather than feeling intimidated sitting alongside some greats of the game in the UK and India. Then I got the opportunity with Fox Cricket. That was a pretty big step for me, being lead presenter with Adam Gilchrist and working alongside the likes of Shane Warne, whom I'd had the pleasure of working with a couple of times before. To be in that environment and the guys asking me what I thought of the game was really encouraging and made me feel that I had arrived. Male cricketers are vital to progress. They are the ones with the power to make you feel at home and I definitely had that on my journey. But I really started to back myself as a commentator when I realised I had Shane Warne's respect. He has got one of the best minds in cricket. For him to give me the time of day and respect my opinion was a huge confidence booster and I owe him a lot for that.'

Then with a laugh she adds:

'To be able to work with those guys and feel at ease in that environment definitely helped to change the perception of female commentators because they were encouraging me to give my opinions as well as have a laugh with me. I think that became a model which other broadcasters have taken on board. It has taken a while to get to that point where females are expected to be part of a broadcast now. Nobody ever thought that there would be two female commentators on major Test matches in the UK and now we have that – all we've ever wanted is for it to become normalised and kids growing up are now questioning why there isn't a female on the broadcast rather than why there is one – which is probably what their parents have drummed into them.

'In my opinion, not only is it good to have a representation of gender and cultural backgrounds, but to have a successful broadcast you need a diversity of personalities and I'm fortunate to be part of those environments in the role I have now which is incredible.'

Given how confident she feels, it is no surprise when I ask whether we will achieve a non-racial sports world that she says, 'I have seen enough to be positive about the future. So, I shall say yes.'

OUR RULERS' STRUGGLES

TWENTY-TWO

WHITE PRIVILEGE
AND THE BIG TANKER

I have just asked Mark Bullingham, chief executive of the FA, whether he feels the FA is institutionally racist. In the era before the pandemic age, this would have been an interview in his offices at Wembley, with a member of his press team present. Now we are on Zoom, Bullingham is at home, looking very relaxed in a shirt, and while a member of his press team is present taking notes, he is also at home. Bullingham's initial response to my question is what I would have expected: 'I don't believe the FA is institutionally racist.' This has been the traditional FA view with Greg Clarke, former FA chairman and Bullingham's boss, telling a Commons Select Committee that institutional racism was 'fluff'. But then Bullingham goes on to express opinions that I had not expected from the man running our national sport:

'But I don't believe that every area of our organisation is fully representative either. I would say that there is unconscious bias throughout the country. I think there is white privilege throughout the country and there are absolutely deep societal challenges that we have to get over.'

'Have you benefited from white privilege?'

'I think', replies Bullingham, 'every white person has benefited from white privilege.'

I cannot imagine any predecessor of Bullingham, and they have all been white, ever saying this. Admitting white privilege is one thing, doing something about it is another and here Bullingham is keen to point to what he has done. 'I do believe, equally, that we're making progress as a society against those [societal challenges].' He then spells out with some pride how quickly the FA had moved to launch its Football Leadership Diversity Code which like so much that has happened in sport in the last year was triggered by the killing of George Floyd.

Bullingham had seen the video of George Floyd's death, thought it was 'absolutely horrendous' and 'from our point of view, it put things on the agenda and allowed a momentum for change that we see something positive coming out of.'

The weekend after Floyd's murder in Minneapolis on 25 May he had a conversation with Paul Elliott, Chelsea's first black captain and FA Council member:

'We had a sense of frustration that things weren't moving more quickly in the game generally and decided that that was the opportunity to really seize on the momentum from that tragic event. We pulled together a letter quite quickly and sent it out to the whole football community, saying we were going to bring through a Football Leadership Diversity Code. That was actually not the traditional way of doing things in football. Normally you spend a few weeks putting together the terms of reference and getting everyone to agree. We managed to pull together a lot of key stakeholders within football, and within a matter of months, we had a leadership diversity code.'

The code lays down specific numbers of people from black, Asian, mixed heritage and females who have to be appointed to senior leadership and team operations, coaching staff for men's and women's professional clubs. And that the 'shortlists for interview will have at least one male and one female black, Asian or of mixed heritage candidate, if applicants meet the job specifications that apply.' Bullingham has no doubt, 'The Football Leadership Diversity Code will change the face of football and the conversation of leadership throughout the country. I think that will bring in genuine and long-lasting change.'

Bullingham feels we need to understand how football goes about recruiting people:

'The problem in football is that people have recruited in their own image. And, probably more so than most areas. Football is a very immature industry and the recruitment practices have not developed. It tended to be for senior positions, particularly, that people would be recruiting from their own network or, potentially, a slightly extended network. There is a merry-go-round of managers and staff being permanently recruited and re-recruited. Not that long ago managers were recruited, almost, over a cup of coffee or it might be that there wasn't even really a proper shortlist. Owners would just WhatsApp their ten best friends in football who would recommend someone they knew. I am oversimplifying it to make a point but I wouldn't say that for many senior positions, you get what you would refer to as the normal HR process. The talent is there in all areas of society but you have to encourage people to look for diverse pipelines of talent and then appoint the best candidate. We have seen a number of players from ethnically diverse backgrounds actually refuse to go on the senior coaching courses because they don't believe they'll ever get the opportunity due to these closed networks that have existed. Part of the Leadership Diversity code, almost one of the most important things for me, was to disrupt that established network.'

Bullingham's confidence that the Leadership Diversity Code can be a game-changer is based on the fact that when launching it, the FA had its own version of focus groups:

'The biggest thing for me, since George Floyd, was actually more listening. So, we pulled together a lot of different listening groups, from both within the FA and around. We had internal black listening groups, from our black employees, and then as part of the Football Leadership Diversity code, we had groups of players, groups of young coaches, we had a media group as well which obviously was a lot less diverse than some of the other groups. But then we also pulled together a lot of different representatives from clubs. We have found the best way of getting as many people as possible to take on the journey.'

Time will tell how far the clubs will travel on this journey, but the fact that it was launched as a result of George Floyd's death shows how dramatically things have changed for Bullingham since he took over the running of this huge tanker, as Brendon Batson calls the FA.

In March 2019, when his appointment was announced, while saying his 'to-do-list is long', Bullingham did not say anything about race. He was seen as the commercial man, who had got to the FA having been CEO of a sports and entertainment marketing agency, and in his three years at the FA had done such a successful job as commercial director that it had seen a 25 per cent rise in annual revenue. He talked about 'transforming the quality of amateur pitches, to doubling the women's and girls' game across the country, to hosting major international tournaments, to building digital tools to help volunteers across all areas of the grassroots game'.

The only reference to 'inclusion' was in the obligatory praise of his predecessor Martin Glenn for making the FA, 'a more modern, innovative and inclusive organisation'.

Yet a month after the Football Leadership Diversity Code was launched in October 2020, Bullingham was being forced to accept that on diversity there were several things wrong, and when it came to race, the views of the man at the very top of the organisation did not represent the organisation. On 10 November 2020, Greg Clarke, who back in March 2019 had so effusively welcomed Bullingham and also supported his Football Leadership Diversity Code, appeared before the Digital, Culture, Media and Sport Select Committee. Asked about the absence of prominent gay footballers within the game, Clarke said, 'If I look at what happens to high-profile female footballers, high-profile coloured footballers and the abuse they take on social media . . . they take absolutely terrible abuse.' In answer to a question by another MP he said, 'BAME communities are not an amorphous mass. If you look at top-level football, the Afro-Caribbean community is overrepresented compared to the South Asian community. If you go to the IT department of the FA, there's a lot more South Asians than there are Afro-Caribbeans. They have different career interests.'

By that evening, following an emergency board meeting, Clarke had resigned. Bullingham made all the right statements about how Clarke's words 'simply do not reflect the view of the FA, our people and the organisation we are today'. But Bullingham had worked with Clarke for over four years. Surely, I asked him, Clarke's views must reflect some people in the organisation:

'I don't accept that the views represented our organisation at all. We've got a far more diverse organisation than people give us credit for, certainly at an executive level. Our leadership is 55 per cent female and we've made great strides on the ethnic diversity of our make-up at all levels. To be fair to Greg, I would say that anything we've done to push the diversity debate in the last few years, he had supported. So, the comments were surprising to me. I genuinely can't tell you why he said what he did. They weren't things I'd ever heard him say before. I don't know where they came from.'

I can sympathise with Bullingham. Back in 2011 when Clarke was chairman of the Football League, I had interviewed him and with real passion in his voice he had said:

'In the entire league we have only one black manager, Chris Powell at Charlton. That is appalling. We need more black managers, more ethnic minorities, more women. About 60 to 70 per cent of our population is either female or of an ethnic minority, so we're talking about the majority of the UK population being disenfranchised.'

But if Clarke does not represent the true view of the FA, the fact remains, as Bullingham accepts, that the FA Council does not represent the diversity of our nation:

'It's obvious that the council and various committees that we have throughout the game don't represent society. There's no avoiding that fact. I'm not pretending it's diverse or representative of society. It is not. But we are making changes and we have put in place initiatives to change that, but it'll take time to come through.'

Bullingham may have been inspired to initiate the diversity code after George Floyd's death, but it was Tyrone Mings of Aston Villa and Wes Morgan of Leicester who initiated the taking of the knee before the start of all Premier League and English Football League matches. This despite the fear that the players could have technically been booked for taking the knee as it would have been seen as a political gesture. But just as the previous generation of players would not have contemplated making such a gesture, the response of the FA showed how much it has had to take the knee to player power:

'We had to make a decision when the players first started talking about it whether it was something that we would allow. We were very clear that we would allow it and we felt that players should be allowed that individual right to make that demonstration.'

So how did Bullingham feel about the FA being left behind by the players?

'I'm incredibly proud of the players and what they've done. Raheem Sterling's interventions were a long time before George Floyd and particularly in calling out the media, I thought that was so powerful. And the fact that Marcus Rashford has changed government policy twice is something we should all be proud of. He's a fantastic ambassador for the game really. So, I don't view it as a negative. But that's not to say that we don't think we should do anything ourselves – we should and we do.'

But while the FA may have had to follow the players in certain situations, Bullingham confidently asserts:

'If you're talking about tackling discrimination in football, we've taken leadership in many areas. If you look at grassroots in football, the problem was a lack of understanding of how to deal with racist incidents and we've brought in specialists throughout the county network to be able to do that. What we will see as a result of that, actually, is a higher level of reporting of racist incidents because we don't believe that many communities in the country have full confidence in the reporting methods. So, by bringing in these senior reporting officers, we will actually see a higher level of reporting. Then we've also increased dramatically the sanctions for players who make racist comments with a 12-match minimum mandatory sanction there. If you go through what we're trying to do on the terraces, we've done a huge amount of work in trying to increase communication, education programmes to be clear what's not right, to make punishments, to go to clubs when there are offences. We have no authority over fans but we do over clubs. We are taking leadership, and we are trying to do everything we can within our power to wipe racism out of football.'

Where Bullingham pleads helplessness is over social media. 'Probably the biggest problem we face and we have least control of would be social media. If you look at the volume of abuse, it's shocking and I'd say that that's been an ongoing issue for us for the last few years. And we spent two years speaking with the social media companies and all we've had back has been warm words and no action.' Bullingham is convinced what is needed is legislation.

So, can all the initiatives mean racism in football will finally be dealt with?

'I think they can absolutely make a positive impact. I do accept that some elements of it are generational. Clearly it's not gone away and it's a societal issue that we'll help to fight. I would love to believe that we could extinguish it completely, although I'm not sure that's realistic, but we'll definitely do what we can. We are fortunate within football that we have, aside from the lack of professional British Asian players, a diverse playing base and some brilliant role models who can help drive that agenda forwards. So I would say that in the past, sport has shown it can change and absolutely will continue to do so and we should embrace that.'

Surely race will always be a part of life?

'Will race always be a part of life or is it something that just gets increasingly accepted further down the generations? I mean, my kids are mixed race, and I don't see anyone's ever challenged or questioned them on anything at all. I'm not saying that from a naïve point of view, they're still quite young. And I'm not saying that race has completely diminished in society. But I do see it as something that was worse in older generations and I don't think we should accept the point of view that it'll always be that. I'm optimistic but not complacent. It still is an issue, both in this country and in many other areas, and we still have to do a lot to eradicate it.'

However, for all the optimism he exudes there is one area Bullingham will not venture into. I had told him that one feature of English football that has always disturbed me was legacy left behind by the racism and violence that marred the game in the seventies and eighties. This is crowd segregation with fans from different clubs not sitting together as they historically had, but in separate enclosures. I did not have do it when I went to football as a student in the seventies. It was not necessary in rugby, cricket and in all other team sports. It was introduced by the football authorities at a time when they were in denial about racism and fan violence. So, would Bullingham not like this anomaly to end?

'Well, we don't have it in women's football and actually the atmosphere there is generally great. A women's Super League match is brilliant. It's quite a different feeling actually as it's far more of a familiar, family atmosphere. Do I see a day when it could end [in the men's game]? It isn't something I've thought about other than in the context of women's football and being pleased that it's not there.'

Bullingham's answer was revealing. It seemed to recognise that there are limits to what he can do. The big tanker may be turning, albeit very slowly on race and inclusion, but on this issue it cannot change direction.

TWENTY-THREE

THE UNEXPECTED
REVOLUTIONARY

W hen the RFU offered me Sue Day as the ideal person to talk to about race and inclusion, I must confess I felt I was being fobbed off. Although she had 59 caps for England, she is now the chief financial officer and I was not investigating the RFU's finances. Moreover, her additional title, the RFU's executive team lead for diversity and inclusion, has a touch of being the person who ticks the right boxes. I was hoping to speak to Bill Sweeney, the chief executive, but with England having had a dreadful Six Nations in 2021, interview dates with Sweeney were always being overtaken by unfolding events, and I had to be content with Sue Day.

This being the third lockdown of the pandemic, it was another remote conversation. Day had begun by flattering me, saying she had asked for a long conversation with me because she wanted to pick my brains. Yet the first ten minutes suggested this would be another talk with a chartered accountant, a profession I know well having qualified as one. I would learn little that was dramatically new. Like so many rugby players I have interviewed, Day made the required obeisance to the game. 'Rugby has given me so much. It has taught me all of the simple life lessons about leadership. You name it.' That she was 'incredibly passionate about diversity and inclusion'; 'getting kids from disadvantaged backgrounds and all different cultures and geographical areas playing rugby'; 'when I got the chance to join the RFU it was a brilliant opportunity'; and that the RFU had had 'a diversity inclusion strategy slash plan' even before she arrived at Twickenham three years ago. She compared the RFU favourably with

KPMG, the accountancy firm she had left to come to Twickenham, which when she left had 'one black partner out of 600. The more senior you get in the corporate world, the less diversity there is.'

The first hint that Day was prepared to look out of the box was when she admitted that 'being totally frank with you, we have a long, long way to go in rugby. I hesitate to shout about greatest achievements, because honestly, I don't think we've got enough to shout about yet. On diversity and inclusion I'll give myself a five, because it was a very slow start. It definitely wasn't good enough to start with. There are so many other things going on, but it is far too easy to let ourselves get distracted. There's loads of work to do.'

A couple of weeks earlier I had spoken to Stuart Barnes, who had lived up to the description of a Corbynite given by Stephen Jones – an old friend and the *Sunday Times* rugby correspondent. Barnes, the former England international, had made himself 'unavailable' to go on the 1974 British Lions tour to apartheid South Africa and, unlike many rugby players of that generation, has never hidden his views about rugby's shameful racist past:

> 'You have to look at the roots of rugby. It does emerge from the public schools and from the empire, from a system where racism was used a lot to increase the wealth of this country. Effectively the empire exploited race and rugby union was very much an empire sport. If you look at the countries who play it and take France, Argentina and Italy out of the equation, it's the white Commonwealth. It is the Commonwealth where Australia have had their race issues with their indigenous people, as have New Zealand, obviously South Africa, and that has been the roots of the game. We used to say wouldn't it be great when South Africa are back, isn't it terrible that they aren't. The great Lions team of '74 shouldn't have been there but they went there.'

When Mandela died, many people in rugby who were on the 1974 tour wrote glowing tributes to Mandela without mentioning their own part in supporting apartheid by touring there. Barnes was one of the few to highlight such hypocrisy. And a long-time resident of Bristol, he supported the pulling down of the Edward Colston statue. 'I am delighted that there were white people heavily involved in pulling it down. In this instance the actions were absolutely right. It was time.' When I mentioned to Day that Barnes felt rugby had not changed and was not likely to, her first response was nervous laughter. But then she answered in a way Barnes could have scripted:

> 'Rugby is a microcosm of society it is built on. It is built on systems that are still unequal, colonial, patriarchal systems, just like politics

is, just like the corporate world is. And it is incredibly slow to change, or indeed there is very little emphasis to change. The only way that it will change is if a load of us in it really push for change. I'm here to be part of the change.'

This process of change would mean that when a kid from a school in a deprived area who had not played rugby turned up at a rugby club they would:

'Find leaders in those clubs who look like those kids and so when they look around, they feel part of something. If an Asian kid turns up and he sees every coach is white, and every person on the committee's white, and when a girl turns up and she sees all the coaches are men and all the committee members are men, it is much harder to feel like you belong there.'

But the revolutionary thoughts harboured by this chartered accountant only emerged when I asked, 'Is this country institutionally racist? Is rugby institutionally racist?'

'Every institution that we are part of in this country has been built on racist structures. [In] all of the structures in our society, or the institutions within it, and that must include us, there is institutional racism and if we try to shy away from that, then we will never change it. That doesn't mean that the individuals within the organisation are racist but it does mean that outcomes have happened which are unfair, which are racist. We end up with far fewer people from ethnic and diverse communities in positions of power and so on and so on.'

So, you would say, there is some institutional racism in the RFU?
Day laughed nervously and said:

'I'm really scared of saying that, because I'm not sure what you're going to do with the words and I'm trying to do the right thing. There's a context. My personal belief [is] that there's racism built into all of our institutions in this country, including the RFU.'

Day had been president of Wasps, had captained England, so how many members of her English team would echo her views?

'I'm worried now that you think I have some extreme views.'
To reassure her I said, 'No, not extreme views. You've got different views.'
'What do you think is different about them? Do you not think that most people think that there is some racism?'

'No, they don't,' I said. 'I think you'll find a lot of people feel all this stuff about inclusion is nonsense.'

'Most of the women', responded Day, 'that I played international rugby with by the very fact of being international rugby players in the late nineties can very clearly see some of the systemic inequalities that exist within sport, so I imagine they would support my view that systemic inequality existed and still exists. Whilst things are getting better, there's still a lot to do.'

'But isn't there white fatigue?' I asked. 'Some white people feel we had slavery, we had empires. All that is over. Why are they still banging on about it?'

'I don't. I am sure there must be people who feel that. What should we do about that?'

'The only long-term answer is to look at history and explain it.'

'Well the conquerors write the history, don't they?'

They do indeed and I narrated a bit of rugby history:

'The problem is that the wider historical knowledge is not known. So, English rugby fans know the Calcutta Cup came about because the two Calcutta clubs, unable to find players to play rugby, melted their silver to make the Cup. But the reason they could not find players was they did not want to play with Indians. That is the reason rugby was the one British sport that never took off in India. That history needs to be told.'

Day murmured, 'That's interesting.'

What, I wondered, was the reason why Day, a white rugby player, had developed such views on race?

Day replied that it was because she had experienced the wrong side of privilege.

Wrong side of privilege? But Day had gone to St John's, Oxford.

'Oh yeah, I'm not saying I'm underprivileged. I'm saying privilege in its broadest sense. There are structural inequalities in our society that are driven by race, that are driven by gender. So, I've ticked those boxes, have been on the other end of that and have probably seen a little bit more of it. Everywhere you look there are very clear illustrations of the fact that things haven't been fair. You look at senior positions at every organisation across the land and they're really white. I'm not a white supremacist and therefore the only reasonable explanation to me is that something systemically doesn't work. That means I guess you've got to try to make a difference in all those different places; not everybody has a fair chance to progress. Then you start to think about what it is that caused that. So then you talk to people about it and read about it and so on.'

So, would Day accept that there is white privilege?

'Absolutely, yes.'

When Day says she knows about ticking boxes of being underprivileged she is not wrong. For hers is the classic story of overcoming obstacles of class and gender to go on to play rugby for England. Day, who grew up in the West Midlands, just outside Dudley, went to a state primary and a state comprehensive and says:

'It was hard to become a player in the first place because, as a woman, sport was hard to be part of. I played football at primary school and I wasn't allowed to play on the school team. I just remember this intense feeling of unfairness. I was a supporter of Wolverhampton Wanderers and grew up with Steve Bull and Andy Mutch. I think probably the fire in my belly was lit when I was about ten and couldn't get into the school football team. The reason I was given was just that I was a girl. There wasn't a girls' team and girls couldn't play in the boys' team. This wasn't an area where the boys played rugby let alone the girls. I didn't even see a rugby ball until I went to university. The biggest struggle for me was just doing it, knowing it existed in the first place. When I picked up a rugby ball I was 20. I saw a match on the telly, and then I saw it again at university.'

I cannot believe that an England international first played the game at the age of 20:

'I was probably one of the last of the generation where you could pick up the ball at 20 and still be an international, probably because so few girls were able to play because it simply wasn't in the schools. My generation tended to be a lot of crossover athletes. People who had been good at another sport and then found rugby, often at university. That's different now. The generation of women internationals playing now usually have played for much, much longer.'

Day became a rugby player when, while studying at St John's, Oxford, where she did French and Spanish, she went to Barcelona for her year abroad:

'I got dragged along to the rugby club when I lived in Barcelona, because I couldn't find a hockey club. It was just sort of love at first play. When I came back to university there was a team and then I moved to London and there were plenty of teams. It turned out to be my game and I was quite good at it. The struggle for me was trying to balance being an international player and the career.'

George Floyd's death filled her with:

'A sense of exhaustion. I don't have the words for it, it just gives you a sinking feeling in your stomach, doesn't it? The unfairness, the outrage. I know that's something that happened to somebody in a different country but there are inequalities, structural inequalities that exist, where we are and where we live and that we can all do something about, and it's incumbent on all of us, in those little spheres of influence, that we each try to make a difference.'

Day had surprised me that rather than being a desiccated calculating machine, as I had feared she might be, she was prepared to think outside the box, showing how certain mindsets in rugby were changing. I would not have anticipated that 25 years ago. And certainly not in rugby which, as Barnes says, is yet to come to terms with its past as in its fervent support for apartheid South Africa.

The question is: are Day's views a minority in the RFU?

'I genuinely don't think so. I appreciate the perceptions of what rugby is. I have found the RFU itself to be really open-minded and to be welcoming, and when I bang on about diversity, inclusion, to be there with me; when I raise it, and I'm not the only one raising it, I find people asking me questions, not telling me to be quiet.'

But to change, the RFU would have to begin with its own organisation where, as Day says, of the over 400 people employed by the RFU, '95 per cent are white'.

There is a lot of work ahead.

TWENTY-FOUR

MIDDLE ENGLAND'S
ULTIMATE WHITE GAME

'**Y**ou have to be Middle England, middle-class to play tennis in this country. It is absolutely a white middle-class sport.'

The man telling me that is Pat Cash, the Australian who won Wimbledon in 1987. It is November 2009, and we are sitting at Queen's Club in London's Barons Court, watching a real tennis match, a qualifier for the British Open. I am interviewing Cash for my 'Big Interview' column in the *London Evening Standard*. This remark by Cash provoked a strong response from the Lawn Tennis Association (LTA). Soon after the interview appeared in the *Evening Standard*, the LTA got in touch with the then *Evening Standard* sports editor, Steve Cording, and outlined all that they were doing to make tennis an inclusive sport open to all races.

Here we are 12 years later, and I am talking to Scott Lloyd, the LTA chief executive, on Zoom. Lloyd is at the LTA headquarters in Roehampton wearing a blue T-shirt and looking very relaxed. On another screen is his head of communications, Ben Wiseman, with whom I crossed paths when we were both at the BBC. I have just told Lloyd what Cash told me about tennis being 'a white sport'.

I expected Scott Lloyd to dismiss Cash. But instead he says, 'I would agree with Pat Cash.'

Perhaps I should not have been surprised by what Lloyd said.

On 12 June 2020, in an open letter following the Black Lives Matter movement, Lloyd had made dramatic admissions about the lack of inclusion and diversity in British tennis. In the letter, if not exactly in those words, he endorsed what Cash had told me in 2009: 'There persists a perception in this country that tennis is a sport for the middle classes or the elite – that is not the case in other places around the world, and it doesn't need to be the case here.' The letter had begun with a mea culpa: 'We haven't done enough.' Lloyd had gone on to say:

> 'Actions are needed – not just words . . . We can't just simply say that tennis is a sport that is open to anyone and expect things to change . . . On behalf of our sport, I apologise to anyone who may have been a victim of abuse . . . What we also have to realise, however, and that has been at the heart of the agenda in recent weeks, is that as much as we can ensure overt instances of racism and other forms of discrimination are not tolerated, we are part of a society where things are not equal. Racism, and wider discrimination, is structurally ingrained in our society, and so the effect of racism is still very much evident and pervasive within our sport . . . The death of George Floyd and the global movement it has mobilised needs to be a turning point for us all . . . Many of us cannot pretend to understand what it is to experience discrimination in a way that many others do on a daily basis and have to spend their lives fighting against it. What we can do is to listen. We all need to challenge ourselves, whatever our role in tennis, to listen to truths which may be hard to hear, and to ask ourselves how we can be an ally to those whose experience is more negative than our own.'

What made Lloyd's confessional letter so interesting was that it came after years of any number of LTA initiatives to reach out beyond its white Middle England heartland. Lloyd's open letters were an admission these initiatives had clearly not worked, but it also showed that with Black Lives Matter producing such a massive moment in British sport, the LTA was smart enough to see that the wave was coming and was trying to get ahead of it.

By the time I spoke to Lloyd he could claim he and the LTA had come a long way since his open letter. Two non-whites had been appointed to the board. In May 2021 it issued the 2021–23 Inclusion Strategy. It had chapters headlined, 'Inclusive Leadership and Governance', 'People Empowered to be Inclusive', 'Tennis Looking and Feeling Opened Up', 'Targeted Interventions for Greater Diversity' and 'Holding Ourselves to Account'. The picture selection was the PR department at its best. The opening page had a picture of a boy with Down's syndrome kneeling down, one hand holding a tennis racket, the other fist clenched celebrating a victory. The foreword by Rachel Baillache, the LTA Board Inclusion and Diversity

Champion, spoke of the LTA's desire to 'truly reflect the diversity of the communities around us'. The first page of the two-page foreword was of a blonde, smiling Baillache, and the second page ended with a picture of two young women in hijabs holding tennis rackets. The various chapters had other pictures including a young black girl in a hijab and other happy young black girls and young black men playing tennis which were meant to show how the LTA was reaching out to a country very far from a white one.

In his foreword to the Inclusion Strategy, Lloyd had admitted 'that people's experience and perceptions of our sport at a day-to-day level can too often make them feel like tennis is not for "people like me".' But while he agreed with Cash, Lloyd would not accept that tennis was institutionally racist or that there was white privilege in tennis.

Is this denial? Or is there some merit in what Lloyd claims?

As Simon Briggs, tennis correspondent of the *Daily Telegraph*, has pointed out, race in tennis is complicated:

'If the people administering the game in Britain are largely mono-chrome, the same cannot be said of the players. In last year's [2019] Fed Cup tie between Great Britain and Kazakhstan, only two of the six women on the home team were white. On the men's side, Paul Jubb and Jay Clarke – who are both black – figure among the five players who are receiving Pro Scholarship Programme funding. As for the best juniors, the two National Academies – based in Loughborough and Stirling – will have five students from minority backgrounds out of 20 when the new school year begins in September [2020].'

And the reality of life as a black or brown tennis player in Britain was:

'Not a story of outright marginalisation. Numerous BAME players – from Heather Watson to Arvind Parmar – have built lengthy professional careers . . . The issue is more one of belonging – or a lack of it. A high proportion of elite tennis players tend to be outsiders, often the offspring of first- or second-generation immigrant families. Yet the people who run the game are drawn from a narrow demographic: white, middle-aged and middle-class. Eight or nine years ago, a couple of coaches went to Yorkshire's county Lawn Tennis Association with a plan to set up a regular clinic in a predominantly BAME area of Leeds. "The response was positive," said one of those coaches, but then one of the councillors said, "What are we looking at here? What's the selling point? Hip-hop tennis?" And you realise how much further there is to go.'

Briggs described what had happened to Josh Ward-Hibbert, once ranked among Britain's ten best juniors, achieving a record service speed of 133 mph during the Wimbledon boys' event but now a professional shooting guard with the Leicester Riders basketball team. He told Briggs how 'tennis was the Caucasian sport and basketball had a lot more black kids playing' and that race and prejudice was 'a subject that I have dealt with for the majority of my life. I never had racist comments shouted at me on the tennis court, not in this country, but it was difficult at times because you found yourself being stereotyped. Certain things were said – that I looked like a rapper. Not anything malicious, but that kind of thing was quite common. Sometimes I felt like I had to bite my tongue.'

Serena Nash, who was Britain's number one junior at 16, but had given up 'her dream of a career in professional tennis', told Briggs that, 'As a teenager, I was the only black girl from Yorkshire who was playing at a national standard. It puts a different kind of pressure on you, to represent your community and do well, to hold yourself to a certain level of standard.'

Lloyd admits that the tennis coaching workforce is male-dominated, 'with those from an ethnically diverse background or with a disability also under-represented.' So how does a black coach feel about the state of British tennis and the fact that it is white?

Justin Layne's story has the feel of Andrea Levy's classic novel *Small Island*. His father's arrival in the UK, probably, predated the arrival of the *Empire Windrush*, the historic ship which brought the first significant number of Caribbean migrants to this country. His father arrived from Trinidad and in this country met Layne's mother, a white British woman. They could not have been more different but, in the classic story of opposites attracting, fell in love:

'My parents married in the sixties. It [an interracial marriage] was incredibly rare. There was tension. My grandparents never ever accepted him. In my grandparents' place he was allowed but far from welcome. They never really understood [the marriage]. My father had to put up with the fact that his in-laws didn't accept him. My uncles and aunts who are still around were all accepting of my dad, it was only my grandparents. He talked to me openly about the discrimination he faced from my grandparents and every now and again he would speak of the discrimination he faced when he first came in. My parents definitely did have bad experiences. My dad is not alive but my mom's [dad] is still alive. The marriage worked very, very well. I think sometimes something like that [different background] makes it.'

But while his grandparents did not accept his father, 'They accepted me 100 per cent. It was really interesting.' What makes Layne's story all the more interesting is that his own mother used the term 'half-caste'. 'My mum', says Layne, with surprise in his voice, 'until recently used to say "half-caste". For her it wasn't a derogatory term, it was just what she had grown up with, historically.' So, did she call Layne 'half-caste'? He says, again sounding surprised, 'Yeah. We're talking only three years ago, both me and my sister saying, "Mum, you can't say that," and this is my mum, who is the least racist person, obviously, in the world. She would say it just because she didn't realise [what it meant].'

Layne, whose own colour is what 'they call it in the Caribbean mix-up, or mashup', had an upbringing which was very different from much of the Windrush generation:

'My parents came from a middle-class background. Even within the class society of Trinidad, my dad was relatively upper-class and his family was pretty well off. I got into tennis because I was really fortunate that my parents had good jobs, and we had a big garden. I saw tennis on TV, my mum used to play tennis and I said to my dad, "I want to play tennis." Where we grew up there were chalky grounds, the stone chalk. So, my dad went to the gardens, dug up some chalk, crushed it in a bowl, made a paste and painted white lines on the grass and made a court in the garden.'

This difference to the Windrush generation was emphasised by the fact that they lived in Cambridge, which was then uniformly white, and yet Layne didn't encounter racism. His one bad experience due to race in his whole life came when he went to the United States:

'We were in Tennessee playing a tournament. It was an LTA-funded trip in 2000ish and I walked into a bar with the British team. I was the only black person. I had just got through the door and everybody looked at me. The guy who had walked in front of me said, "We'd better go, pretty quickly." It was clear that I shouldn't have been in that bar. I have never experienced any racism in tennis.'

It is how Layne distinguishes racism and stereotypical thinking that is fascinating:

'In some ways, it can be an advantage to be black. People think black men are faster, rightly or wrongly. Was I put into a category because of how I looked? Not just my colour, but my physicality, then yes. You can't see someone that's six foot one, obviously athletic and not think rightly or wrongly, they are going to be a good athlete. It's very, very hard not to do that. And governing bodies are always looking for good athletes. So, if you are clearly a good athlete, or look like one, you will get preferential treatment to somebody that doesn't look like a good athlete. And this is a form of racism but it's very positive. If you are a race that people think is going to be athletic, then that's a huge advantage when you're getting any kind of selection.'

But does that not discriminate against, say, an Asian?

'Yes, it does.'

So how has Emma Raducanu, born to a Romanian father and a Chinese mother, emerged and made such a startling impact?

Layne brushes this aside saying, 'There are always ways around that. She is of mixed race but I really don't think there's anything stopping any race doing well.'

Yet, he agrees with Cash about tennis being a white, middle-class sport:

'I do agree with what Pat said. I'm going to separate participation and performance. So, participation is just playing for fun without the aim to maximise potential and playing level. On participation I don't think it has really changed. Tennis is a middle-class sport, and predominantly white in participation. [As regards] performance, trying to be the best we can possibly be, I'm not too sure that was ever the case. In performance level, the number of black or mixed-race players is higher than in the general population, and it certainly wasn't a barrier for anybody I knew.'

But this difference between participation and performance, admits Layne, does cause a problem: 'I might coach a youngster but when he wants to go to a club he finds he's the only non-white person there.'

Layne speaks from experience, having worked on programmes such as 'Tennis for Free':

'This was an inner-city tennis initiative about 2000. It was with the view to widening the net and, perhaps, producing great players. Basically, we went into inner cities and got kids playing. We did tennis in a park where it was very rare to find somebody white in a lot of those sessions. Loads of interest. It didn't work because once the things finish, there isn't a place for people to go which is a reflection of themselves, a reflection of their culture that they have outside of tennis.'

Scott Lloyd has made much of LTA initiatives like 'SERVES' and 'Open Court'. Layne says:

'To make this [the initiatives] really work, what you need to do is to make sure that when the people who have been to these initiatives go to a club, there are loads of other people who look whatever race they are.'

Interestingly Layne himself has never found this a problem. I read out to him what Rodney Rapson, a mixed Asian former coach, had said: 'Nobody from a BAME background is going to be comfortable walking into Queen's Club and feel accepted in the next few years.'
Layne says, sounding startled:

'Oh, I know what he means. If you were to walk in and you're the only black, Asian, Japanese player there, now I can see that is going to be a harder bridge to overcome than if you go somewhere and it's more mixed. This is a societal change which is beyond the LTA.'

But Layne himself has 'walked into Queen's Club, walked into the All England Club and I felt accepted, but I realised that I might be the exception.' And if his experience at his club in Cambridge is any guide, then the problems of race and inclusion in tennis are both more complicated and provide hope of tennis changing from an all-white world.

After 20 years as coach and also doing fitness training, the 42-year-old is now head coach at Cocks and Hens:

'I think it's either the oldest club in the country, or one of them. You couldn't get a more archetypal club. It's all white people. We've got two black members, maybe five or six Chinese members, six of Indian or Bangladeshi descent. But if you took the population, Cocks and Hens probably has the membership that reflects the population for each of those races. So how do you go beyond that?'

Yet, when Layne first went there he was welcomed:

'I walked in there to have a meeting with the chairman and while I was waiting for him I had two different groups say, "Do you want to come and join us for a game?" They had no idea who I was. They had no idea if I was even a member, and they'd never seen me before because I've never been there. But they saw somebody in tennis cloth-ing and thought let's get him involved. And these were white people. And then I thought I really liked this club. That was 2018.'

After this it comes as little surprise to hear what Layne thinks when I ask him if the LTA is institutionally racist or there is white privilege:

'No. It is not the LTA's fault and it's not inherent in what they're doing. It's just inherent in society. There's no more inherent racism within the LTA than there is in the country at large. Almost everybody has racist beliefs. That is what we are fighting against. That is the real barrier at play, not tennis.'

However, he does not hold out much hope for LTA's Inclusion Strategy as, he says, society will have to change for tennis to become really inclusive.

In this view, while a Raducanu can emerge, she will be an exception and tennis will still remain, as Cash put it, middle-class and white.

TWENTY-FIVE

ATHLETICS'
LIGHT-BULB MOMENT

Donna Fraser, the four-time Olympian and UK Athletics' equality, diversity and engagement lead, has started our conversation by saying she is glad it is a Friday. She, like many, has been working from home and says,' It is getting rather tedious. But hey-ho, at least I am safe and well, so I should be thankful.'

Fraser's reference to the light-bulb moment comes when I ask her, 'In your organisation, if a white person was told they had white privilege, how would they react?'

'We've had that conversation within the race programme. It was in July 2020 after George Floyd. When white privilege was discussed, some people got it and others didn't. For some it was a light-bulb moment thinking, "Oh, I understand it now; I never saw it that way."'

'Is it difficult for a white people to understand what being a person of colour is?'

'Yeah. It is a different experience. They don't have that experience. They don't have the emotion that someone of colour would have gone through on a day-to-day basis. One off you can pass that off. If an individual of colour has experienced that kind of racism or microaggression on a day-to-day basis, it does become tiring and wearing. I do think some white people don't quite understand that because they don't have that lived experience.'

What makes my conversation with Fraser interesting is that her own experience of race is in stark contrast to many other sportsmen and women of colour I have interviewed over the years. Born in Britain to parents who migrated to this country from the Grenadines in the sixties, she heard her parents tell her what life was like for black people when they first arrived here:

> 'Seeing signs saying, "No, blacks, Irish or dogs" definitely was the norm for them. Not being able to get skilled jobs, despite having the skills to do them. My dad was a carpenter and did masonry. My mom was a nurse.'

Yet, growing up in the seventies in Thornton Heath in Croydon when the National Front was strong in that area, Fraser says, 'I never experienced racism in this country.' As an athlete, specialising in the 200 and 400 metres, she was never called names and did not have to put up with bananas being thrown at her as black footballers did. 'Definitely not within my sport. Some of the older athletes may have but I definitely did not.'

There were two occasions she suffered racism but both of them were abroad. The first was in 2008:

> 'I was running the 200 [metres]. And when we stepped out on the track, bottles and so forth were thrown on the track, whether that was because of my colour, because I was female, I do not know, but that was the only time.'

Fraser will not name the country. 'It's not fair to do.' She will only say it 'was a Muslim country in the Middle East'.

There were also problems in Potchefstroom, the stronghold of the Afrikaners in South Africa. 'There were stares and I heard snidey comments. Not just me. Other athletes may have experienced a lot worse than me, but I just had an uncomfortable feeling.'

In Britain, in stark contrast, the picture might have been scripted by the British Council to advertise a warm, cuddly Britain, where kind-hearted white women help young black girls fulfil their dreams:

> 'I became a runner because of my primary school teachers who were white women. They were Miss Hughes and Miss Hindshaw. I actually wanted to be a doctor, and my parents were really support-ive of that. But I loved running and they [my teachers] immediately spotted my talent. They were hugely encouraging. Miss Hughes had always told me to be determined in everything that you do. That stuck with me.'

So dramatically different was her upbringing that she avoided being stereotyped because of her colour. As we speak, in front of me is a book written by Jon Entine, an American Emmy-winning producer, entitled

Taboo: Why Black Athletes Dominate Sports and Why We're Afraid to Talk About It. In the last chapter entitled 'A Genteel Way to Say "Nigger"?', Entine says, 'Black domination of sports is so pronounced that a kind of reverse racism has set in' and gives an example of how white guys find it difficult to become cornerbacks for NFL teams. Entine concludes his book saying:

> 'The scientific evidence for black athletic superiority is overwhelming and in accord with what we see on the playing field. By and large, athletes who rely on the ability to sprint and jump at endurance sports trace their ancestry to West Africa; East and North Africans are best at endurance sports, particularly distance running . . . It's time to acknowledge and even celebrate the obvious: It's neither racist nor a myth to say that "white men can't jump".'

When I mention the book, Fraser says:

> 'I would have heard stories when I was growing up in the sport that black athletes are the sprinters and white athletes are the long-distance runners. That's simply not the case. Now you're seeing the difference. Now you're seeing black athletes in field events, shot-put, javelin and you're seeing white athletes be really good at sprinting. For me personally, the only thing I would have heard was, "Golly, you've got an advantage because you've got long legs. It's not fair." But not because I'm black. I was never told my race gave me an advantage in running. Absolutely not.'

However, even as Fraser makes this confident declaration, there were many other athletes of colour, much younger than her, telling a very different story. This was highlighted in a March 2021 BBC Sport video entitled: *Let's talk about race: Black athletes on their experiences*. Miriam Walker-Khan interviewed Fraser, double Paralympic champion Kadeena Cox, and world 4 x 100 m silver medallist Imani-Lara Lansiquot.

Lansiquot, who was born 25 years after Fraser in Peckham, had suffered horrific racial abuse. 'Racism isn't something that just existed in 2020. It's always been there. And I've definitely gone through situations in and out of GB kit where I felt less than comfortable because of the colour of my skin.' She confessed how before the killing of George Floyd, she had 'personally felt quite scared' to talk about the racism she had suffered. 'Because you don't want to be put into a box or you don't want people to lash out at you for speaking out.'

Lansiquot had already gone on record with Sky News about the racism she had suffered: 'I was representing my federation, I was dressed up in my kit, I was doing an event for a sponsor of the federation, and a member of staff actually referenced me as a "monkey". That was my first real experience of overt racism.'

Cox said:

'One of the things that really does annoy me is just comments on my hair. Like "Your hair's not tidy," or "Ooh, what's this?" . . . But you know, as a black female, you do learn to just brush these things off, which isn't the way it should be.'

But in Fraser's reply we heard the voice of the woman who in the 2021 New Year Honours List received an OBE for services to equality, inclusion and diversity in the workplace. Miss Hughes would have been proud:

'It's for us to take responsibility ourselves and step up and say, "Actually, no, that's not right, what you just said. Are you aware that you offended me?" and so forth. And giving the confidence and creating that environment [where] people feel comfortable challenging back.'

When I spoke to her, Fraser reinforced the need for dealing with white people having problems with racism, with patience and understanding. 'When you are talking about things where people feel uncomfortable either taking on board, or they don't, you have got to understand. You won't always convert people to your way of thinking.'

The problem for Fraser is that she has quite a job converting her own organisation, the governing body for athletics in this country, to become a more diverse body. Fraser accepts that for all the diversity of track and field athletics, 'within the organisation we don't quite replicate that.' She emphasises steps are being taken to change but admits, 'We [have] still got a long way to go. And it's not just ethnicity we need to look at; we've also got a disability arm of the sport, the power athletes as well.'

A big problem is at the grassroots:

'At the grassroots and the clubs there are definitely some issues that have been identified. There are practices which we need to work with the clubs in terms of unconscious bias and engaging with the community that they serve. An example may be the committees. We are a very old sport. We have a very traditional way of running the sport going on for many years. It will have to change. Because society has changed. That is definitely being looked at at the moment.'

The problem Fraser is talking about is that at the local clubs a lot of the leadership is white male.

'The ones that I have worked with and met that has been the case. However, there are some great clubs like the Harriers who are doing a huge amount around the whole conversation regarding ethnicity.'

What really pleases Fraser is that in race:

'Athletics haven't got as many issues as football has. Our athletes do not get verbally abused when they step out onto the track. That is not something that we have to focus on. We were hugely supportive of our athletes when the Black Lives Matter [movement] kicked off last year. If they wanted to take the knee, or make any other gesture at the British championships, we were supportive of them. We definitely are in a different space compared to football without a doubt. Now, if we were in that same space as football, we wouldn't stand for it. And the reason why I say that is that we, for example, launched our LGBT+ network, a year or so ago, and we were the first to do that. We're now the first to set up a race equality network within athletics.'

But for all its dominance over football on race and inclusion, Fraser is well aware that even on the sporting field there is one area it is failing. Athletics hardly has any Asians:

'That is an area that I'm passionate about making a difference. There are a number of factors there. Cultural barriers. And of course, there aren't any, or not many, Asian athletes out there. There are no role models potential athletes can look up to. We have one Asian coach in in the NGB [National Governing Body]. Actually, one of our osteopaths is Asian, and as part of this race equality network, that will be the area that we will be heavily focusing on.'

I would have expected Fraser, who worked at EDF Energy for 19 years and chaired the black Asian minority ethnic network, to leap in and try and set this right. But it soon becomes clear that here her own colour holds her back. It also immediately highlights the problems of lumping all those who are non-white as BAME: black, Asian and minority ethnic. For Fraser there is a huge divide in this supposedly unified world of colour that she dare not cross:

'I couldn't go into the [Asian]communities and talk about this, so we will need someone who already has those links to have the conversation. I don't know enough about the culture to be talking about [it]. I am not fearful of being treated badly, but I suspect the barriers would go up. [They would say] What do you know about our culture? I don't, and I wouldn't want to disrespect anyone in any way whatsoever. So, I need to have someone who is from that community and has connections to start those conversations and help me understand what we need to do better as a national governing body so that the doors are open. We need to do some work in that space. Definitely.'

I add that, 'And, of course, within the Asian community, there are differences. A Muslim woman, who might want to perform in the hijab, might face certain problems.'

'Absolutely. All the sporting manufacturers are starting to realise that for them to catch such communities, they have to change the ways they manufacture their sports kit.'

While Fraser is optimistic about the future, she recognises that because of the drugs problem in athletics, the race issue has often been ignored by the game's governing bodies. 'It is not apparent that the whole racial bad behaviour is as high on the agenda as the drug issue and the gender issue.'

But one thing that makes athletics a more welcoming place for her is that she does not carry the burden of representing her community. Her every action is not judged by the colour of her skin but how she performs, and she draws a revealing distinction with business:

'The team atmosphere within athletics always worked for me. That was my second family, but within my business career I was, probably, being judged more on the colour of my skin rather than for the skills that I bring to the table. It was the incident of the George Floyd murder that definitely catapulted a lot of conversations, both in my organisation and people that I know of. It is sad that it took that for this to happen, but in a positive light it is happening, and people have been more open about having a conversation around race where that wasn't the case two years ago.'

That even in athletics, that has always presented itself as the most multicultural, multiracial sport, the light-bulb moment should have come as a result of the killing of a black man by a white policeman in America, something hardly uncommon, shows how much race had been swept under the carpet over the last few decades.

But, perhaps, that should not come as a surprise as Mo Farah's views on race illustrate.

In March 2011, I had interviewed Mo Farah, who the previous July had become Britain's first European 10,000 m champion. The story he told me was how Britain had helped a little African boy from a war-ravaged continent find the fulfilment on the track he could not have found in his native land.

His English at first was limited to a couple of expressions – 'Excuse me', 'Where's the toilet?' – and he spoke Somalian, which he still speaks. But 'The kids did not give me a hard time.' And living in London he, the black boy, was no different to anyone else. 'I did the normal things you do, going out with your friends, going to the cinema'

It was a kindly, white man, his school coach, Mr Watkinson, who was the decisive influence in making him realise his future lay on the track:

> 'If it wasn't for my school coach, I don't think I'd be running at all. I would still be trying to play football and would have gone nowhere. He said I was good at running and he was going to pick me for the running team if I came to the trials. I came to the trials, and I won it, and then he put me in the cross-country team against other schools.'

His running did mean this child of Africa made the journey back to Africa – albeit only as far as Richmond Park. 'I did my hill sessions on Saturday at Richmond Park, and I used to see these Kenyan athletes running around Richmond Park. I knew the Kenyans were the best. I was kind of running all right, but I wasn't anywhere near the Kenyans. My agent, Rick Simms, said to me, "'On your days off, live with the Kenyans."'

But while Farah shared their African origins, he could see his Western upbringing had made him different. 'These guys have had it so tough. I was born in Africa and left at eight, but I didn't get any running there. We lived a normal life in London. For these guys, life is so hard. If they don't make it, they don't make enough to feed their family. That's what motivates them.'

Farah's decision to emulate the Kenyans would bring him success, culminating in London 2012 with his becoming an Olympic legend. He would add to his gold in London with more golds in the Rio Olympics, become a four-time Olympic gold medallist and be knighted. Race was never mentioned in our conversation.

However, a decade later, in July 2021, Farah told the BBC that he had suffered some dreadful racist abuse on social media. 'I've had some shocking [messages]. I've had "You don't belong." It seems like it's getting worse.'

And such is the malign influence of social media that many of those who administer our sports, particularly our national game, football, are beginning to despair about how to cope with it.

TWENTY-SIX

ARE WE LOSING THE ANTI-RACIST FIGHT?

'I've always been slightly uncomfortable as a 50-something white male talking on matters of discrimination because I have not suffered it. It is an issue that has never directly affected me. It is hard to experience or understand fully what it is like to suffer racism if you haven't suffered it. I can empathise and I can sympathise. I can play my part in helping to eradicate it, but until you have actually suffered it I don't think you can really feel it. That's why I think it's really important that the players like Marcus [Rashford] and Raheem [Sterling] speak out. But I think it is equally important players like Jordan Henderson, or our captain Lewis Dunk, are side by side standing in support of them because that is absolutely critical to get the message across that it [racism] is unacceptable to everybody, not just the black people. It is really important that the white players and black players are side by side on this issue alongside white administrators and black administrators and Asian administrators. It is important that the message comes from everybody, not just one section of our community.'

The man saying these words to me, Paul Barber, a football administrator, has in the last 25 years worked at various levels of the game at different organisations – the FA, Tottenham Hotspur, Vancouver Whitecaps FC – and is now chief executive of Brighton. But while he may not be a one-club administrator, he is a one-club fan and shares a common love with me for Tottenham Hotspur, where for a time he was chief executive:

'I still love the club. We have beaten them twice now in the last two seasons. After our victories, Daniel [Levy, the Spurs chairman] will look to me as if to say, "Well, you know you are a lifelong Spurs fan. How do you feel about that?" I always say to Daniel, "I don't know whether to laugh or cry." I am delighted for Brighton, I always am, because they pay my wages, but I'm also sad as they [Tottenham] are not at the level that I think they should be.'

Barber's words recall a time when English football had not become poisonously tribal. Barber has vivid memories of growing up in the seventies, having Sunday lunchtime conversations about football where his family members had very conflicting loyalties across the North London divide:

'My maternal grandfather, who was an Arsenal fan, would talk to me about going to Arsenal one week and Tottenham the next in the forties and fifties. There was hardly any away travel and also not a lot else to do at weekends. Most of the banter over our Sunday lunch table was about football. While my grandfather was an Arsenal fan, my daddy was a Spurs fan, I was a Spurs fan. And then my uncle, my mum's brother, floated between Spurs and West Ham. Although he was much more of a sixties child, whereas I was a seventies child, he was a little bit torn between them. Tottenham because it was the closest team to where we grew up and West Ham because it wound up my grandad. I grew up in Edmonton. Middlesex Hospital to White Hart Lane is half a mile and the maternity ward in which I was born, you can actually see from the Tottenham Hotspur boardroom in the new stadium. Can you believe that?'

Barber regrets the passing of this world but what depresses him is that football is still having to deal with racism:

'The first thing I'd say is we are in 2021 and it saddens and frustrates me that we're still talking about these issues. In fact it feels worse than ever actually, particularly the use of social media to abuse players. Unfortunately, abuse comes through also straight into email channels to clubs on a regular basis. It is not just racist, it's discriminatory language across the board – it's sexist, it's abusive. The language used by people can at times be downright nasty.'

What makes it worse is that these abusive emails coming to the clubs, unlike those on social media, are from people signing their names:

'This is what bothers me. Some people, and again this might surprise you, write from their work email addresses which I find more than astonishing. Because it makes them very easy to trace and potentially threatens their careers as well. We seem to be going backwards not forwards at a time when we genuinely thought we were beginning to move in the right direction. Sadly, we have still got a mountain to climb.'

For Barber the solution is:

'A combination of carrot and stick, of continued education and sanctions. There has to be education because there are some people who need that education and will need it at quite an extensive level. But education is not enough on its own. There are people who have been educated and, for whatever reason, decide that it's appropriate and acceptable to do it. We have got to start making these people realise that there is a punishment for behaving like this. Those sanctions should be serious.'

And that means treating social media platforms as 'publishers. Where they are libellous, where they are defamatory, there needs to be some accountability and where they are discriminatory and where they are racist there needs to be potentially criminal accountability.'

Since the pandemic, the football authorities have been pressing the government to introduce legislation and while the Queen's Speech in May 2021 promised such legislation as this was being written, it was not certain that there would be anything on the statute books.

It is when Barber contrasts his own upbringing to what is happening now that makes him think that in tackling racism we have not gone forwards but backwards. He grew up on a council estate in North London. 'I wasn't fortunate enough to grow up in an environment or an education system where I went to the best university or anything like that, so my education has come from self-learning to some extent, but also because of the way my parents brought me up, just to be decent.' He had West Indian and Asian neighbours:

'We didn't actually think too much about the colour of each other's skin. We were all just friends. One of my best friends at school was a young West Indian kid who happened to live in the same road. We played football in the street. We enjoyed each other's company. Ironically, having grown up in a working-class area of North London where there was quite a big racial mix, it wasn't in those days anything like as toxic as it feels in some places now. That really worries me. Something's happened along the way to sort of almost disharmonise certain communities and it saddens me.'

While Barber says 'all administrators currently in football' share his outlook that colour, religion and sexuality do not matter he admits as far as people sitting around the boardroom table are concerned, 'predominantly it is still white males".

For Barber, players taking the knee before a match marks a seismic shift in attitude on how to combat racism compared to the seventies and eighties:

> 'Then it seemed from the outside looking in, not being a player or an administrator at that time, that this was very much a problem for ethnic minorities. Garth Crooks, Chris Hughton, Cyrille Regis and those guys were almost shouldering the burden of what was going on and [the racism] directed at them. Now white players are saying no. "These guys are our friends, our colleagues, our teammates. They are human beings and we stand alongside them." That's very powerful. During my time in football, players have become far more active in saying no. And I think we've got to this point now where the most recent generation – which is the Raheem Sterlings and the Marcus Rashfords and players of that standing, backed thankfully by white players of equal standing – have said no.'

But there are some players who do not take the knee and not all fans accept taking the knee as appropriate. While the Millwall fans booing of taking the knee made the headlines, there were a few Brighton fans who also objected:

> 'It shocked me to hear that when we first started taking the knee and Black Lives Matter was on the shirts, we got emails of protests from some – a very, very tiny minority of people – who said it was inappropriate that our players should be doing that. It's almost like a parallel universe that they live in. "This is not a big deal, is it?" That is their typical refrain. Come on. Actually, the fact that you don't think it is a big deal is racist in itself. [They say] "Well no, I'm not racist. I am not saying that I would do it but I don't see there's any real harm, what some people are doing." It's quite incredible how this sort of rhetoric still exists and I've had some email exchanges on this.'

Barber then narrates an incident at the Amex Stadium which shook him:

> 'Two years ago, in an Under-23 game against Tottenham at the Amex, two people in the crowd, Brighton supporters, abused Tottenham's black players, even though we had black players of our own in the side that night. There were probably fewer than 1,500 present at the Amex. These people were prepared to do so in such a small crowd in a

stadium where we've got some of the best technology in the country, knowing that we can easily identify them, we can easily arrest them, as we did. And then subsequently sanction them. If they're prepared to be that brazen in that environment, they would be prepared to do far worse in a crowd of 30,000, where they will feel that they've got almost the cover of everyone else around them. And that shocked me to my core: (1) because it was us; (2) because it was an Under-23 game; and (3) because it was directed at Tottenham players when we had black players of our own in the side that night. It is an example of that parallel universe I'm talking about. Okay to be racist towards players of another team. You tell them the black players of our teams also see that. And their response is, "They won't be affected by that. I wasn't having a go at them. I would not have a go at those players in our team." This, almost bizarre way to rationalise this kind of behaviour, is quite scary. But sadly, this isn't just a football problem, this is a society problem. Football is a subset, and unfortunately it's an opportunity for some of these people to vent their feelings. That's sad and frustrating but it means we have a responsibility of our own to try and play our part in dealing with it.

Not just racism

Paul Camillin has much to be happy about. He has grown up in Brighton all his life, loves living in that seaside town, supports Brighton and Hove Albion and since 1998 has been head of media at the club. He also is a firm believer that 'sport is a vehicle to try and educate people'. But he confesses that, the 'one thing that really scares me is the racist person who sits there and he is clever enough not to blurt it out, because he knows he would be removed from the ground, but he still goes home believing it. We get into strange territory here, but do you challenge that?'

Camillin's memories of racism in football go back to the eighties. It is a memory of a match Brighton played at home against Liverpool:

'I remember my dad attending a game at the Goldstone Ground and coming out of the east terrace which was right next to where the away fans were. He told me of a black fan in the away end which was quite rare. Back then you didn't see a lot of black people in a crowd at football. There were two Brighton fans racially abusing him as they were both walking up either side of the fence segregating the fans. At the top there was a policeman, a senior officer, who said nothing. But there was a police line between the home and away fans. And just as the two Brighton fans and the black visiting Liverpool fan got to that point, he pulled the line out. He watched as the black away fan, who my father said had the physique of a heavyweight boxer, dished out some retribution. I am not condoning violence but the policeman turned his back to it and the racists got what they deserved. But that just shows you the mentality of the police and the mentality of those fans back then in the mid eighties. Under the very noses of a senior police officer, two so-called fans felt it was okay to abuse a rival fan based on the colour of his skin.'

His own memories of racism are from the end of the twentieth century:

'When people would throw bananas on the pitch, it happened at the last-ever game at the Goldstone. I heard fans make monkey noises. And people would just pretend it wasn't happening, as did the commentators. I was at Southend in 1998 and I had just started working at Brighton. I was at the away end with some friends, and there was a group, who I suspect were National Front supporters, or some incarnation of it. Self-styled "lads" and quite intimidating. They were constantly abusing the Southend black players. And I remember turning to this group and saying, "Guys, look, please stop this, it's not right. We've got black players playing out there for Brighton and you are here to support Brighton. How do you think they feel?" The response was, "Yeah, but they are playing for us, aren't they? They're okay." This was the sort of mentality you were up against. We had to move to another area of the ground because we feared that we might be attacked by this group of thugs. And that's what football was like in 1998.'

What depresses Camillin is how, when fans come to football, they think they can behave in a way they would not elsewhere:

'If you come into a football stadium, there should be a minimum level of behaviour that is the same that would be expected of you in the street, in a nightclub, if you are at work or in the supermarket. People should be able to go to a football match, without the fear of being abused. I remember listening to a black lady speak at a Kick It Out event, and she recounted that she could not walk to work for fear of abuse. Why should she have to think about what route to take to work because "that's where I'll get the least amount of abuse, or I won't get spat at." Why should she have to walk an extra half a mile to work to avoid such hatred and abuse? It's shameful when you sit down and think that a person is saying: "When I was growing up I had to judge my route whenever I walked somewhere to avoid being spat at." It makes me sad. It makes me upset. I have never had to do that and I do find it so hard to comprehend. Sadly, the reality is that this is still the way of the world.'

As a white person he may not have suffered from the racism directed at black fans, but he has agonised how it has affected people who are not white:

'I wonder how many people like yourself who wanted to go and be a sports journalist, or like our former manager Chris Hughton, who wanted to be a professional footballer, actually said, "Forget it, I'm not going to do that because I don't want take all that abuse." Chris told me many times that he was brought up to turn the other cheek by both his parents. I have huge admiration for him for that, but it is not right. He shouldn't have had to have done that. It was his way of coping, his mechanism. But at the same time, that was the time of his life that was almost robbed from him by a racist undercurrent that existed throughout society.'

While he is convinced, 'The coverage of Black Lives Matter was correct and right,' he regrets that:

'We went from years of not covering the abuse minorities suffered, to suddenly highlighting everything. It was not so long ago that people went to football or watched football on TV and heard the crowd making abusive noises or racist chants and TV commentators did not even mention it. I wonder how black people felt watching that on TV. If you are a father, and you have a young black family who love football, surely you wouldn't want them to be exposed to that. For years people did nothing. And then all of a sudden now it is being taken more seriously. But we have all been guilty of not doing enough. It's brilliant what's happening now because it's educating people and educating young people. So, until racism goes away, keep taking the knee, wear the T-shirts, wear the pin badges. But back it up with action. If you see someone misbehaving it is not good enough for the rest of the world to sit by and let it happen; we must take affirmative, lawful action.'

The added complication is social media as was illustrated when during the 2020–21 season Brighton lost at home to West Bromwich Albion:

'I spent several hours on Saturday and Sunday dealing with abuse that our players received on Saturday because we lost the match, a football match. Because a player, who happens to be black, missed from the penalty spot. A frustrated football fan calls him a useless N-word and puts a monkey symbol on an Instagram post for having the audacity to hit the post from the penalty spot. Three separate posts, two were from the same person. One was from a second person. That was not the only abuse he got. That was just three bits of racist abuse, but there was a lot more general abuse. What people are saying in football grounds and on social media, they wouldn't get away with in a workplace, they wouldn't get away with in a restaurant or other walks of life.'

Camillin is convinced that social behaviour has taken a turn for the worse as a result of the political battles we have had in the last decade:

'Chris Hughton used to say, you will never eradicate it completely. I felt we had made terrific progress and then Brexit happened, and all of a sudden you feel a little bit like you're back to square one. I think we saw an uptick of racism in the stadium on the back of Brexit. It almost gave people the freedom, the confidence – I hate using that word, but that is the right word – to be racist to people in the stadium. And then we saw Trump in America, Boris Johnson and other politicians here. And this horrible, divisive politics. I'm not a fully fledged socialist, because I believe that people have to have ambition and goals in life – but I genuinely believe there's a standard of living that everybody should have. And with that goes a standard of behaviour and a level of respect we are all entitled to.

'It makes me cross, because you see people go on right-wing protests, and clearly their views are racist, yet they'll tell you they're not. But they are. And I bet you they use the underground to get there. If they feel sick or say they get punched in the face in one of the marches, they'll be at a local A & E. They probably go to have a curry of a Saturday night with their pals, after football or one of these marches. All those industries across the UK that I've just mentioned would not be where they are without the immigrants in this country. The public transport networks across the country, the NHS, the local Indian restaurant in the High Street – all part of what is brilliant about a multicultural British society. So many brilliant things in this country have been built on immigration, going back to the end of the Second World War and the Windrush generation. Our Premier League is the best league in the world. Why is it the best league in the world? It is the best league in the world because all the players from around the world want to come and play here. And as for the England team, it's never been as multicultural as it is now. I have more pride in what our players have done off the pitch than anything they can ever achieve on it.'

This makes him doubt whether racism can be completely eradicated:

'Sadly, I think there are people who are beyond educating. You won't change their mind. I think racism is always going to be there – I hope I am wrong, but it's always going to be in a dark corner. Hopefully, it can be pushed into that dark corner and stay in that dark corner and not rear its ugly head. Racism will remain because sadly I think there is that element within human nature. And it is bred on fear and small-mindedness. I am optimistic about tackling racism, but not eradicating it. I hope I am wrong, and one thing that gives me hope is that history usually shows that eventually good tends to overcome evil.'

While many football clubs are surrounded by houses where minority communities live, Brighton, says Camillin, 'in terms of ethnicity is 88 per cent white British'. But 'we have a large LGBT population in Brighton and Hove.' Camillin is very proud that: 'We celebrate it every year at Gay Pride.' However, this does mean that Brighton has problems with homophobia:

'A few clubs have had this problem of homophobia. Most notably ourselves, Watford, because Elton John was chairman, Manchester City, bizarrely, I think because of the gay scene in Manchester, Birmingham as well for similar reasons. These clubs were targeted by rival fans. It's pathetic. Homophobia went unchecked for a number of years. This would have been happening even in this century. The sort of comments that would in the past have been termed as banter not so long ago. The gay community was being forced to come to the grounds incognito. It was only really in the mid noughties when it came to a head and people started to take it seriously. We started to address this problem at Brighton and our supporters club did a huge amount of work in this area. At the beginning of the century we started to tackle it amongst supporters, and pushed for criminal prosecution.

'At Brighton, we encouraged members of the LGBT population locally and made them feel that they can come to enjoy watching football. We asked members of the LGBT community to come and experience the game and provide us with feedback. It was a Monday night against Stoke City. And most of the stuff they moaned about was stuff that all football fans moan about, like queuing for a burger or getting out of the stadium to the train. It was fantastic to read that the whole experience was much better than they thought it might be based on their perceptions. As a football club our aim is, at the very least, to represent the community we have in terms of ethnicity, gender, sexuality and other characteristics.

'The challenge for us is to encourage a diverse group of fans to follow clubs. We need more women to not only come to the games, but to feel comfortable coming to games. We know traditionally and culturally football is a male-dominated sport, but times change and you have to evolve. There's work to be done there. Society is no longer about 2.4 children and the 1970s time-warp mentality that the husband goes out to work and the wife is cooking the dinner.'

But if that is yesterday's world, there is one aspect of that world Camillin would like to recall, a world when football was not tribal and fans could applaud the wonderful play of opposing teams and even their goals. The days Barber's grandparents enjoyed. But Camillin and Barber know those days will not come back, not helped by the way football is now projected in the media with its celebration of tribal loyalties.

TWENTY-SEVEN

CRICKET'S UNBRIDGEABLE RACIAL DIVIDE

The first time Azeem Rafiq, the former Yorkshire cricketer, was called 'Rafa the Kaffir' by Matthew Hoggard, his Yorkshire teammate, he could not understand that. 'For two years of my career my nickname was Rafa the Kaffir. I actually did not even know the meaning of the word "Kaffir" [in the sense they were using it]. In our religion it is a non-believer. I actually thought they were saying that.'

In Islam, to call someone a Kaffir is very serious and can have dangerous consequences. But Rafiq came from a religious family and had been to Mecca for his haj, the pilgrimage all Muslims are meant to do at least once in their lifetime.

So how could he be an unbeliever? It was some years later, when Yorkshire were investigating Rafiq's allegation of racism, that he realised that Hoggard was not using the word 'Kaffir' in the Islamic sense but in the way apartheid white South Africans had traditionally used it to denote non-white people and justify the racist superstructure of the white nation:

'When I found out what it meant from the investigation panel I was like, "Wow. How was that allowed to be my nickname?" These are not guys who have come from small towns. These are guys who played international cricket. Travelling the world. They knew exactly what they were saying.'

Racist remarks directed at him and others ranged from 'smelly Paki', to 'nigger' and 'elephant washer', although he clarifies that he himself was never called 'elephant washer'.

What caused Rafiq the greatest pain was that he was made to feel like an outsider:

'There would be little things, so-called banter. [This included being called a "Paki".] As we went through the years the incidents started getting more frequent. It was the culture. That feeling of not belonging. You started going out. Drinking. I remember in 2012 I made a conscious effort to start doing that. But even when I did I felt my presence was still something that could be used as a joke. I was left countless times outside a bar in Leeds crying on the nights out in 2012–13. Nothing was done. People were aware of the terms that I am talking about. There is no getting away from that fact. I wish I had stopped it myself.'

I am speaking to Rafiq on Microsoft Teams in August 2021. The Yorkshire report into his allegations of the racism and bullying he suffered in Yorkshire cricket, which took nearly a year to come to a conclusion, has yet to be made public. Yorkshire have admitted Rafiq was 'the victim of inappropriate behaviour' and offered him their 'profound apologies'. He is speaking to me from Karachi, the city of his birth, and he tells me of the pain he has been through:

'Before speaking out I have been in pretty dark places. The last 12 months have been very difficult. I wish I had come out earlier. But if I had spoken earlier, say I had spoken as a 19-year-old, would anyone have listened to me? Probably not.'

In the weeks and months that followed, Yorkshire played a curious cat-and-mouse game. They claimed they could not release the report for legal reasons but published a summary. This admitted Rafiq was the 'victim of racial harassment and bullying', but only seven of the 47 allegations were accepted. However, there had been insufficient evidence to conclude the club was institutionally racist. Then a story leaked out that Rafiq had been called a 'Paki', which the investigation had concluded was 'friendly and good-natured banter'. This lit the fuse. Sponsors walked away, the ECB took away Yorkshire's right to stage international events and the Health Secretary, Sajid Javid, called for 'heads to roll'.

Yorkshire heads did not roll for some time, but within days, heads of many in the land, some with no interest in cricket, hung in shame when, at 9.30 on Tuesday morning, 16 November 2021, in the committee room of Portcullis House in Parliament, the Digital, Culture, Media and Sport Select Committee held a hearing on the racism in Yorkshire cricket. This had all the hallmarks of a parliamentary inquiry into a major political cover-up.

When I was speaking to Rafiq in Karachi he was in a kurta of the type Imran Khan wears. Now dressed in a suit, he was shown walking towards Portcullis House, before sitting down in front of the MPs to give evidence. His evidence was detailed and devastating during which he cried.

Rafiq alleged some of the best-known figures in Yorkshire cricket – players, coaches and administrators – had used racist language or bullied him. Others, said Rafiq, while themselves not racist, heard what was being said and did nothing. In this category was one of the greatest names in contemporary Yorkshire and English cricket, Joe Root, the England captain. Rafiq had told me, 'I played with Rooty in under-age sides. We go back a long way.' Rafiq had captained Root both at Yorkshire level and when he led the Under-19 World Cup squad.

Rafiq had made it clear that while Root never used racist language, he was present on nights when Gary Ballance, a Yorkshire teammate, who went on to lead the side and become an England batsman, would call him 'Paki'. Root did nothing. Root had denied that he saw any racism. Rafiq told MPs:

> 'He might not remember it, but it shows how normal it was in that environment, in that institution, that even a good man like him doesn't see it for what it is. It's not going to affect Joe but it's something I remember every day.'

It illustrated a profound truth, the huge divide between how a white man, however good and well intentioned, might not see racism when a brown man, who suffers from it, remembers it vividly. Yorkshire, Rafiq said, had thought, 'Little old Azeem Rafiq, nobody will believe him.' It was clear, even as he was giving testimony, that now there was no question of the world not believing. The next day's *Daily Telegraph* had over its masthead, 'Cricket's Day of Shame. England stand accused on day of bombshell racism revelations'. Rafiq's story had made such an impact that this prime spot, which is meant to draw in readers, was considered more important than the story about how the Church had helped a Liverpool suicide bomber, who was seeking asylum, to convert to Christianity to avoid being kicked out of the country. That story had a picture showing a very concerned Archbishop of Canterbury, Justin Welby, but this was overshadowed with a picture above the masthead of Rafiq wiping his tears as he spoke to the committee.

The scene in the committee room had its curiosities. In modern, diverse Britain, these explosive details of racism and bullying by whites of a brown man were heard by an all-white committee of MPs who looked bewildered and at times did not know how to react. Only one other brown man spoke during the three-hour hearing, Lord Kamlesh Patel, who had just taken over as head of Yorkshire cricket.

In January 2022 the Culture Committee released its report and, after praising Rafiq for his testimony and criticising those who had tried to distract attention by focusing on his anti-Semitic comments, Julian Knight, the chairman, set out clearly what not only Yorkshire but English cricket needed to do:

> 'We are watching closely and fully intend to ensure that cricket cleans up its act. We recommend that the Government ensures that any future public funds for cricket are dependent on continuous, demonstrable progress in getting rid of racism in both the dressing rooms and the stands'.

Three months after Rafiq's testimony the Culture Committee was told by Anuj Dal, the Derbyshire cricketer, that the racial slur 'Kevin' was used, 'outside of Yorkshire . . . Asian players were stereotyped as being lazy. I remember specific hand gestures that were made for players of colour and comments made while senior members of staff laughed along.'

Never before had cricket, or for that matter any sport, been so heavily taken to task on racism by those elected to govern us. But that this should have been necessary in 2022 showed how far cricket had always shielded the problems of racism endemic in the game.

Enemies of Promise

It should all have been so different for Rafiq. He had been brought here as a child of ten, by parents who were passing through to settle in Canada, before changing their minds and deciding to settle in the UK, as Rafiq's uncle, his father's brother, lived in London. Giving evidence to the committee, Rafiq could not have sounded more like a native-born Yorkshireman. And such was his early promise that instead of his words producing cricket's day of shame, it looked as if on the cricket field he would produce glory that Yorkshire and England would be proud of. Nine years ago, then 21, it seemed he would be the first Asian Yorkshireman who would make his mark on English cricket. He captained the Yorkshire Twenty20 side, which contained Root and Ballance, winning all the five completed matches he captained, and that year Yorkshire, who reached the final, recorded their best year in that competition. *Wisden* had a picture of Rafiq celebrating in triumph. He even supplanted Adil Rashid as Yorkshire's first-choice spinner in all formats. Rafiq told the committee he did not want his son to play cricket and Roger Hutton, the departing chairman, admitted that Yorkshire cricket was 'institutionally racist'. Within days, Tom Harrison, chief executive of the ECB, described Rafiq's testimony as an earthquake.

This was to prove an apt description although, as can happen with earthquakes, Rafiq himself was the first one to be caught up in the aftershocks. Two days after his testimony it emerged that when he was 19, in an exchange of messages with another Asian cricketer, he had made anti-Semitic remarks. He apologised immediately and, while some felt this cancelled his racism testimony, most recognised that even a man who had sinned was entitled to demand that the harm he had suffered should not be disregarded. The earthquake aftershocks were to prove more devastating for the ECB and Yorkshire.

Realising it had to act and with the situation worsened by the miserable performance by Harrison in front of the committee, a week later the ECB announced a 12-point plan of action to tackle racism, backed by a £25 million fund, which would include reviewing dressing-room culture. This was a culture which Rafiq said had seen Asian cricketers told to sit near the toilets. Two weeks later Yorkshire sacked 16 members of its coaching staff, and then a few days afterwards, lured Darren Gough, their former international cricketer turned successful media pundit, to become acting managing director of cricket. Patel promised to rediscover the real values of the White Rose County. But had these real values not led to this scenario? The great irony is that Yorkshire, which prides itself on being 'God's own country', could have set the standards of inclusivity and diversity in English cricket but instead had encouraged a system that brought back to cricket the racial prejudice of the Raj.

Racially segregated Yorkshire cricket

For almost half a century since the 1950s, immigrants from India, Pakistan and Bangladesh had been making Yorkshire their home. They played cricket but none of them made the Yorkshire team. Through the 1970s and 1980s on my visits to Yorkshire, I heard two contradictory stories. The white cricketers denied there was any racism and insisted the reason there were no non-whites in the Yorkshire team was because they did not play for the right clubs, the clubs that had traditionally formed the cricket pipeline for the county.

The Asians told a story of denial and how to play the game they loved they had had to set up their own clubs. Eventually in the 1980s they set up in Bradford their own tournament called the Quaid-e-Azam Sunday League, named after the founder of Pakistan, Muhammad Ali Jinnah, 'to combat', as the League's website puts it, 'what was felt to be limited opportunities for Asian cricketers in league cricket'. For all the talk of hallowed White Rose values, Yorkshire, far from combating such a racial development, allowed it to flourish. So much so that now there is a second Quaid-e-Azam League in Bradford with a similar one named after the poet Muhammad Iqbal, who coined the name Pakistan, in Sheffield. In effect, more than 75 years after the British Raj ended, in Yorkshire racially segregated cricket has been allowed to flourish, in some ways even more racially segregated than it was in the Raj. It is as if Yorkshire wanted South Asians to feel that the Raj, at least on the cricket field, still existed. To complement this racism at grass-roots level, at a first-class level Yorkshire for decades took pride in refusing to open up its game to all races and nationalities as the rest of English cricket had done.

Since the 1960s, the start of summer would see black and brown overseas cricketers from the West Indies, Pakistan, Sri Lanka and India arrive in droves to play county cricket. But the doors of Yorkshire cricket were closed to them and Yorkshire prided itself on the fact that it was still the only pure English county. It was only in 1992 that Yorkshire allowed a non-white player to enter the Yorkshire dressing room. Even then it required special pleading by Solly Adam, an Indian-born businessman who lives in Dewsbury. He had long dreamt of the day when the Yorkshire dressing room would finally have a non-white player. He got his opportunity when the white player Yorkshire had selected, Craig McDermott, the Australian fast bowler, got injured. Adam urged the Yorkshire committee to sign Sachin Tendulkar, India's star batsman. Adam found that only one or two on the Yorkshire committee were in favour of breaching this last colour bar in English cricket, with Fred Trueman making no secret of his racism and calling it 'stupid'. But eventually Adam's plea that Yorkshire players who had not shared a dressing room with 'a coloured bloke for 128 years' should finally do so was heard.

Then Yorkshire seemed to be putting its past behind it. I was part of the media group that accompanied Tendulkar as he was welcomed by Geoffrey Boycott and shown round the dressing room. This was a Boycott who had come a long way since the 1981 England tour of India. As I narrate in *The Nine Waves*, on the tour Boycott had told Raman Subba Row, the England manager, born in this country to an Indian father and a white mother, that 'you are one of them', referring to Indians. Raman took it in his stride, although Chris Tavaré, the Kent batsman, was most upset. Boycott had since got to like India and eagerly supported Yorkshire having overseas players whatever their colour.

But in the years that followed, this historic moment felt like a token gesture, as Rafiq certainly thinks it was, since not many players of colour made it to the dressing room. It was 12 years later, in 2004, that Ismail Dawood, born in Dewsbury, became the first Yorkshire-born Asian to play for Yorkshire. But race was still an issue that touched a raw nerve in the committee.

That year Terry Rooney, the Bradford MP, in a parliamentary debate, accused Yorkshire of 'deep-rooted, embedded racism'. Yorkshire was outraged, and as Rooney would later recall, '[They] said I'd only said it under parliamentary privilege for a headline, wanted to score some votes with Muslim voters, and that I should resign. Nobody actually addressed the issue . . . No recognition of facts that were staring them in the face.' What is fascinating is that *Wisden*, the game's bible, agreed with the county, saying, 'If Rooney's view ever had been accurate, it certainly looked out of date in 2004.'

So, in the light of what Rafiq had said, how do things look for those Asians who have, since the 1960s, been involved in Yorkshire cricket?

Yorkshire go backwards

My first port of call was Solly Adam. I had had dinner at his home with Tendulkar when he was full of hope of the new Yorkshire that would emerge. Now he says sorrowfully, 'I offered my services and said, "If you need anything, sponsorship or any help, I am here." Nobody rang me. I have been waiting five years. Nobody came to me and said, "Can you recommend a good Asian player?" I feel very, very, sad.'

Taj Butt's tone is just as sorrowful. Butt, who is 63, came to this country from Punjab in Pakistan as a 12-year-old. 'I see myself as a proud York-shireman. Unfortunately, the cricket side of Yorkshire is something I have never felt I belonged to. I am not at all surprised by what Azeem Rafiq said and that it took 15 months to explode. Knowing the organisation as we do there is a certain amount of arrogance within Yorkshire cricket.'

It was this arrogance that made Butt set up the Quaid-e-Azam Sunday Cricket League in 1980 and of which he is chairman. 'We want to be main-stream. But the real tragedy is the situation is getting worse.' Yet, for a brief period in the 2010s, Butt did feel things between those who run Yorkshire cricket and the Asian community were coming together:

> 'The problem had been that a lot of our young players were not actu-ally getting nominated for the cricket trials to become part of the system. It was only in the early 2010s that we first started making quite a lot of progress. We started meeting and putting action [plans] in place to make things better for young Asian players. We got them to open up the system. There was still prejudicial thinking on the part of the [white coaches] and unless an Asian lad was absolutely talented, like Adil Rashid who is from inner-city Bradford, he would not get through.'

But there was dialogue and hope for more change. Then, in 2015, the ECB came with grand ideas of making the South Asian community part of cricket, but it was to prove a salutary lesson of how good intentions can backfire. 'The ECB came in with a pot of money but instead of improving the situation it worsened it.' Butt and Yorkshire had set up dialogues on how to broaden the Asian base. The ECB discarded those and implemented its own ideas with multiple forums:

> 'The result was that the pathway for Asian cricketers has gone backwards. Now, in junior teams that represent Yorkshire, there are fewer and fewer Asians. The few that are there are from private schools. We want to play on proper turf wickets. What we are getting is money for non-turf wickets, money for tape ball cricket, devised for Pakistani conditions, which does not make sense here, money to play cricket in mosques and temples. It has reinforced racially segregated cricket in Yorkshire. Things have gone backwards.'

Talking to Solly Adam and Taj Butt it is clear it will require more than ticking boxes marked 'diversity' and a truly revolutionary change in attitudes if the Asian community is to become part of the mainstream.

But what makes this story of racism in English cricket all the more complicated is that there is a great, curious divide between English domestic and international cricket. Cricket in the last two decades has seen a remarkable shift in international power. Cricket may be the most English of games, but England no longer rules the cricketing waves. Power in cricket has passed to India, the first time a non-white nation has got control of an international sport, which is an unprecedented development. For all the changes that have come over sport in the last few decades, power continues to reside with the old white powers, be it Europe or America. But in cricket, India's economic might gives it control of world cricket with all cricketing nations, including England, having to give in to demands from India. Such is the money power of India's IPL T20 tournament, a domestic tournament whose schedule overlaps with the start of the English season, that English cricket allows its top players to miss the early part of the English season including Test matches, to play in the IPL. This would have been unthinkable before the start of this century. So, if England can kowtow, and that is not too strong a word, to a brown country internationally, how is it behaving in a racist manner at home to its brown and black players? Is it because the people who ran, and run, English cricket have always refused to accept that there is racism in the game?

What about reverse racism by non-white people towards white people?

One man who was at the heart of English cricket when power began to shift to India was Tim Lamb. For almost twenty years he had been involved in running English cricket and his leadership had seen various changes that are still part of the cricket scene. The game has honoured him, making him an Honorary Life Member of the MCC, Middlesex and also Durham.

I had often interviewed him, but this was the first time I was talking to him about race. He admitted that 'I'm looking at it from the point of view of a middle-class, white Englishman; some may say I've had a very privileged upbringing, and I certainly did and I'm very fortunate.' Lamb grew up in a village in Cheshire 'that was predominantly white. There weren't many people of colour around. [But] in a family where my mother, who was a liberal thinker, refused to buy South African fruit on principle because she felt so strongly against the apartheid regime.' When I ask him about racism in cricket, Lamb says firmly that he had never found any evidence of racism in cricket. He had played with cricketers of many races, including Imran Khan, Norman Cowans, Neil Williams and Roland Butcher and there had never been any problems.

Yorkshire, he admitted, was 'a bit of an exception partly because at that stage they insisted that everybody who played for Yorkshire had to be born in Yorkshire'. But even here Lamb refused to see this as a racial issue. When I mentioned the Quaid-e-Azam Sunday Cricket League, Lamb immediately said:

> 'Now, there are instances of specific ethnic leagues in other parts of the country. I went to play for Northamptonshire for six years from 1978 to 1983. There was a West Indian team who played on the recreation ground in Northampton, but I honestly don't know whether that's because they chose to be an exclusively black team or whether they felt excluded. Certainly, one or two players who excelled in that league proved their worth and actually got a county contract. The fact of the matter is, rightly or wrongly, even to this day there are Asian cricketers and Asian clubs that feel more comfortable playing with their own kind. I mean there are cultural differences. Maybe there's a drinking culture in recreational cricket, in British sport, not to their liking.'

How did Lamb feel as he witnessed at first hand the Indian takeover of this very English game?

'You couldn't justify the MCC continuing to run cricket. Personally, I don't feel a sense of loss at all. I'm not a colonialist and I have friends all over the world with all sorts of different cultures and shades of skin colour, and I've always taken a wider view of these things.'

But having set out a position his mother would have approved of, he articulated views on the empire which would delight the anti-woke brigade:

'There were many elements of British colonialism that were bad, and certain things the British have done around the world which were dreadful. Rightly or wrongly, it's happened, and the way people have jumped on the bandwagon and want to pull down statues of Cecil Rhodes in Oxford and all this kind of thing [is wrong]. By any stand-ards Cecil Rhodes was a nasty piece of work and an exploitative person, but if you think of him as a 16- or 17-year-old from Bishop's Stortford who went out and made a fortune in South African diamond mining, became extremely wealthy, ended up as prime minister and left a legacy of infrastructure and scholarships. Yes, judging him by twenty-first-century standards, he would not be somebody you would necessarily admire, but he was a product of his age and the same goes for many other people. History is history. It happened. Get over it. Move on. The Chinese have moved on and they were a race that was exploited and badly treated, but they've got over it.'

Given such a view of history it is not a surprise to hear his reaction to what Michael Holding and Ebony Rainford-Brent said of the endemic racism in sport and how blacks had been written out of history:

'I was saddened to read the comments of Michael Holding. I respect Michael very much. He's a very educated, intelligent man and a won-derful bowler in his time, but I was surprised and disappointed to hear what he had to say. I have found it quite difficult that they glorify somebody like Mr [George] Floyd. I don't know whether you heard but there were rumours that he actually died of self-inflicted barbitu-rate poisoning rather than as a result of the actions of the police. Well, it's only a rumour. [Our conversation took place before the Minne-apolis jury found the policeman Derek Chauvin, who had pressed his knee on Floyd's neck, guilty.] What happened to him was totally, abso-lutely wrong, but the Black Lives Matter [movement] was an American phenomenon and I'm sad that there were people in this country who jumped on that bandwagon purifying somebody who, at the end of the day, was a pretty nasty piece of work by all accounts. And I was disappointed that there are certain elements in this country that used the Black Lives Matter movement just to create havoc and deface statues of Churchill.'

During our conversation, Lamb had asked me whether I 'personally have been the victim of racist behaviour'. When I mentioned that I had been racially assaulted, Lamb immediately said, 'But you can be assaulted as a white person walking down the streets in town.'

When I explained that the assault I suffered was clearly racially motivated and asked whether he was saying 'as a white person I could have suffered the same assault', Lamb responded, 'No, I'm saying that I hope you were just, you know, the victim of a random attack.'

It was then that Lamb in response to my question as to whether we can get to a non-racial world said:

> 'Throughout this conversation we've talked about racist behaviour on the part of white people against black people, but I'm sure you wouldn't deny that there is reverse racism by non-white people towards white people. And when people talk about South Africa, it's far too much of a simplification to say that it was blacks and whites when you've got the Asian community, Cape Coloureds and so on.'

Lamb went on to express his anger at what he called Indian 'hypocrisy in terms of the way India led the world, certainly in cricketing terms, in opposing apartheid and yet effectively were imposing a form of apartheid on a section of their own population'.

The reference here was to the Hindu caste system. As I pointed out to Lamb that while there can be no question Hinduism's treatment of the so-called lower castes is its original sin, which has caused untold misery to millions of Indians over many centuries, caste was not based on colour and caste differences could be camouflaged in the way colour cannot be. Some years ago I met a prominent Indian who had done well and was a Dalit, the lowest of Indian castes. However, he asked me not to reveal it as no one outside his family knew. From his colour, which was no different to mine, it would be impossible to say what caste he was. If Lamb putting apartheid South Africa on the same moral plane as other injustices was a surprise, it was an attitude I had encountered often during the 1980s when arguing with those who wanted to resume playing cricket with South Africa. My answer would be that the Indian constitution was written by a Dalit and the Indian constitution reserved educational places and government jobs for Dalits. The moment, I would argue, Nelson Mandela was freed and wrote the South African constitution, cricket relations could resume. And that is in effect what happened. However, this made no impression on supporters of white South Africa, who just refused to come to terms with history. But then that is the story of English cricket as its handling of the South Africa issue shows. On this, the greatest racial issue in the history of cricket, English cricket has always wanted to have its cake and eat it.

Coming to terms with the past

For 80 years, MCC, the body that ran the game, not only allowed cricket to be played at an international level along rigidly segregated colour lines, but accepted dictation from a foreign country, South Africa, as to who should play for England. South Africa, long before apartheid, laid down an iron law which was that South Africa would only play white countries – England, Australia and New Zealand – and that these white countries must only field their white players. England, Australia and New Zealand, keen to maintain links with their white brethren, had no qualms in accepting this diktat.

In 1929 Duleep, nephew of the legendary Ranji, was the country's best batsman. As Leslie Ames, the England wicketkeeper, told me, Duleep would be the first name on the England team sheet. But South Africa forced England to drop Duleep. The MCC argued that by playing with white South Africa they were building bridges. Through the 1950s and 1960s, as there was more opposition to white South African cricket tours of England, the English cricket world kept trying to build bridges. White South Africans, they said, having been reassured by seeing how races mixed in England, would return and feel emboldened to relax apartheid. This was despite the fact that the apartheid laws were often bolstered even as the bridge-building exercise went on.

MCC, which also ran international cricket then, made sure its white brethren were not penalised in 1961 when South Africa left the Commonwealth. The rules of the then Imperial Cricket Conference required that to play Test cricket, the country had to be a member of the Commonwealth. After Indian independence in 1947, India's membership of the ICC had only been resolved after India agreed to stay in the Commonwealth, which India had not originally planned to do. South Africa should have lost its Test status and the first tour after South Africa's withdrawal against New Zealand was initially described as 'unofficial'. But then through a mysterious process that has never been disclosed, it became official and South Africa continued to play Test cricket as if nothing had changed.

In 1968, Test cricket between England and South Africa came to an end, but only because John Vorster, the South African prime minister, who had shown no previous interest in the game, suddenly decided to become an England selector. He vetoed the selection of Basil D'Oliveira, who because of his colour was unable to play for South Africa, had left his homeland to play for England and was part of the England team selected to tour South

Africa. Even then, two years later MCC wanted to welcome the white South African team to this country despite the brilliant protests organised by Peter Hain and his Stop the Seventy Tour. It required the intervention of the Labour Home Secretary James Callaghan to force the MCC to cancel the tour.

The white English, Australian and New Zealand sports administrators were never keen on the boycott and politicians had to get involved leading to the Gleneagles Agreement which called for a total Commonwealth sporting boycott of the apartheid regime. Despite this, many in England tried to revive cricket relations with South Africa. The 1981 England tour of India was very nearly cancelled, because two of the England party, Geoff Boycott and Geoff Cook, had played in South Africa, contrary to Gleneagles. This led to hectic diplomacy with the final decision taken in the unlikely cricket setting of Mexico City, where 'Madam' Indira Gandhi, the Indian prime minister, who was at a conference, discovered a passage in Boycott's recent book of his loathing of apartheid. But while Boycott went to India, he spent much of the time secretly recruiting English players for a rebel cricket tour of South Africa in a plan codenamed 'Operation Chessmatch'. Boycott left the Indian tour halfway through and just a month after the series, he, Graham Gooch, John Emburey and Derek Underwood, who had all toured India, arrived in South Africa for a rebel tour. For those who supported links with apartheid South Africa, these were cricketers expressing their fundamental right to play cricket wherever they could. In 1988 an England tour of India was cancelled because Graham Gooch, captaining the side, and seven other members of his squad, who had all played in South Africa, were refused visas to travel to India.

Nothing, however, could cool the ardour of those who were keen to resume relations. In the 1980s South Africa made cosmetic changes to the apartheid laws seeking to portray itself as very different to the South Africa that had been banned. Many South Africa supporters in this country clamoured for its return to international cricket, arguing that those opposed to playing cricket were bringing politics into sport. In fact, as Ali Bacher – the last captain of white South Africa, who was organising white cricket then – would later tell me, the international cricket that he was hosting was financed by tax handouts from the apartheid government. It was part of a wider political effort by the apartheid South Africa to fool the world into believing it was a normal country. I spent much time debating this issue and what struck me was that despite the moral vacuum at the heart of their argument, the supporters of apartheid South Africa claimed the moral high ground. For them, not playing cricket with white South Africa was an infringement of liberty.

Cricket cannot hope to construct a truly non-racial world unless it is able to look at its history and acknowledge what has happened. Yorkshire believe Darren Gough could be the man and I hope he is, although his appointment has reminded me of an occasion when he did not appear to want to come to terms with Yorkshire's past.

In 2015 there was a benefit dinner held for Devon Malcolm at The Oval, the scene of Malcolm's greatest cricketing triumph, taking 9 for 57 against South Africa in 1994. Malcolm had achieved this feat after being hit on the head while batting and telling the South Africans, 'You are history,' a comment that would become memorable. Gough, who was batting at the other end when Malcolm was hit, was that evening at The Oval on the stage with Malcolm. The two got on very well and were joshing in the way old teammates do. Malcolm talked of how despite being brought up in Sheffield, he could not play for Yorkshire as Yorkshire did not have non-Yorkshire-born players. Gough immediately piped up by saying that Yorkshire had had players born outside Yorkshire suggesting Malcolm had got it all wrong. What he did not mention was that until 1992, when Sachin Tendulkar arrived, they were all white. In effect, Gough's response glossed over the racial bias which had been so long part of Yorkshire cricket. True, the remarks were made in jest and this might have been evidence of Yorkshire's much vaunted humour. But if cricket is to change it will require more than music-hall wit. For real change cricket needs to learn from the American philosopher George Santayana who said, 'Those who cannot remember the past are condemned to repeat it.' Unless his advice is heeded, all the pledges that have been made following the Azeem Rafiq scandal will prove as worthless as the previous diversity initiatives have. Cricket will once again repeat its past.

The media can play a huge part in changing attitudes and has in the last two years been relentless in exposing racism. But in the half century since I became a journalist, how far has the media come in reflecting the diversity of the society we have and which we so often glory in?

THE FROZEN MEDIA WORLD

TWENTY-EIGHT

I DON'T KNOW WHERE YOU WOULD GO TO PRAY, PAL

That was the comment Lawrie McMenemy made to me on the evening of 22 October 1983. That morning McMenemy had taken his Southampton team to Luton with Southampton thinking of winning championships rather than just avoiding relegation, more often their concern in recent years. Southampton finished second that season, three points behind champions Liverpool, and McMenemy could field more than a useful team, including Shilton, Wright, Williams, Moran and Danny Wallace.

However, by the time McMenemy came to the post-match conference he was far from happy. The walk to the corner of the large Hatters Bar, partitioned off for the press conference, must have made him feel he was literally being made to walk the plank – he had had to go along a little iron gangway at the back of the stand to get there – and this was reinforced by the result. A Southampton side that had conceded just one goal in eight league games since the start of the season, that afternoon let in three for a fairly demoralising 3-1 defeat.

McMenemy always has an imposing air about him – not surprising in a man whose six-foot-four-inch height made him such a natural as a Coldstream Guard during his National Service that he stood guard outside both Buckingham Palace and the Bank of England – but that afternoon, as he was ushered in along with David Pleat (in those days managers held joint press conferences), it was Pleat, much the smaller man, who loomed larger. Pleat had the smile of a man who had just slaughtered the world, McMenemy the distracted, subdued air of one who has an unpleasant job to do and wants to do it as quickly as he can and get away.

I felt for him and thought I would do my best to cheer him up. It was to prove a tragic mistake. I had done my runner for the *Sunday Times*, dictating copy as the match went on and which would be in the first edition. I was looking for something more for my considered piece. Now seizing on the fact that despite the 3-1 scoreline against Southampton, they had begun the match well and might even have scored before Luton did, I asked McMenemy if he took comfort from the fact that in patches Southampton had played quite well.

'We played well? What match were you at, pal? Are you sure you are not at the wrong type of game? This is football, pal.' The implication was clear. Only someone with my lack of knowledge of football could have asked such a daft question. My fellow journalists, who at that stage had been struggling to ask McMenemy anything, were quick to laugh at my expense but McMenemy was not finished. The following week Luton were due to visit Liverpool – then in their pomp and glory. Southampton had got a 1-1 draw there and McMenemy was asked what advice he had for Luton. 'Go to church and pray before the match.' Then, turning to me, he said, 'I don't know where you would go to pray, pal.'

This was the cue for my fellow journalists to fall about in merriment; I do not blame them for had the roles been reserved I might have done the same, and McMenemy, his spirits now fully restored, strode out of the press conference looking every inch the giant Coldstream Guardsman who had just quashed the attempt of a midget to get into Buckingham Palace.

As it happens, McMenemy's prediction that Luton would require something divine at Liverpool was a good one. Luton lost 6-0, with Rush scoring five and Dalglish one. McMenemy could say I was being sensitive if I took his remarks in any racial sense. After all did he not, in his diary of a season published way back in 1979, have a photograph showing the four apprentices he had signed that season at The Dell? On one side of McMenemy was Reuben Agboola, who had played that day at Luton and won nine caps for Nigeria, and on the other, Johnny Pang, son of a Chinese restaurant proprietor. If two out of four apprentices were non-white, what more could be asked for? In any case, his crack at me could be seen as the perfect illustration of the Hyde Park Corner orator who takes on a man asking difficult questions and makes him or her the subject of his barbs, so much so that soon the rest of the audience are laughing at the intruder instead of the speaker.

Only one man at the press conference was outraged. That was Pleat. In the years to come I have met him often and, whenever the subject of race has come up, he has mentioned what McMenemy said, the sorrow in his voice conveying how he felt. I did not know then that Pleat was of Jewish origin and understood how McMenemy, with a few choice words, had made me feel an outsider. The difference between Pleat and me was that Pleat could hide his Jewishness but I could not hide my brown skin. In a sea of white faces I stood out and McMenemy could make me feel I did not belong to that exclusive white club. He may not have meant to but it is how it came over to me and Pleat.

Over the years, I have often heard white people say non-whites have misinterpreted what they have said; McMenemy would no doubt argue that. But, in this instance, the meaning seemed very clear. over the years I have written about this episode a few times in my football reporting career. But now we are four decades on and I mention it to a Chinese-born journalist, from whom we shall hear more later, who has covered football for most of our major national papers, and ask whether he has ever had an experience like the one I had with McMenemy that evening.

The journalist says, 'No, nothing like that.' Then he mentions two incidents.

Mauricio Pochettino, then manager of Tottenham, once said to him. 'Ah, you are the guy who always comes to ask about Sonny,' a reference to Tottenham's Korean player Son Heung-min. 'I asked Wenger how many languages he speaks and he said, 'I speak your language.'

In 1983 it was unimaginable that two of this country's greatest clubs would be managed by a former Argentinian international, who had played against England in a crucial World Cup match, and a Frenchman. But if the world of football has changed so dramatically, how much has the world of journalism, which when I was reporting football matches was uniformly white, changed?

TWENTY-NINE

CONFRONTING
MEDIA WHITENESS

On 13 December 2018 Matt Hughes, then the deputy football correspondent of *The Times*, wrote an article which was headlined 'Racism would be far worse without football'. Hughes made a remarkable confession:

'A shocking realisation: of the hundreds of numbers in my phone, the only ones belonging to black people were those of individuals working in football. Despite living and working in one of the most cosmopolitan cities in the world, with about 40 per cent of London's population classing themselves as black minority ethnic according to the Greater London Assembly, my social and professional circle is "hideously white", to borrow a phrase once used by Greg Dyke to describe the BBC. Without having the good fortune to work in football it would be even whiter still . . . A quick glance at our wedding photograph from over a decade ago confirmed this was not a recent phenomenon – among 150 guests there is my Sikh mate and Chinese sister-in-law . . . How can the media – and indeed other powerful industries – guard against the unconscious racism correctly identified by [Raheem] Sterling when it is so lacking in diversity, both in terms of its composition and the social circles of its participants? . . . In retrospect I can barely recall seeing a black face at the posh university I somehow scraped into, and from where the majority of my best mates are drawn, and other than through football I have not made enduring friendships with anyone who is black since, despite having

234

spent years living in such diverse areas of London as New Cross and Brixton. There were no black students on the post-graduate journalism course I attended in London and the vast majority of the relationships I have developed since have come through work . . . A personal view is that the unfair treatment of [Raheem] Sterling by various news desks over the years is the product of click-chasing, crass scapegoating and vindictive bullying in the worst tabloid traditions, rather than him being deliberately targeted because of the colour of his skin, but if there were more black people working in the media one would hope that news editors would think twice about how their actions could be perceived and their role in reinforcing negative stereotypes. If journalists do not know any black people – or poor, or old or disabled people for that matter – how can they write about and/ or for them fairly?'

I had never read anything like that by a white writer on the sports pages. It made me realise that the world had moved on since the mid eighties when I had considerably upset a white female colleague by my remark that, apart from me, the only non-white she knew was the waiter at her Indian restaurant. When we spoke, Hughes, who has since moved to the *Daily Mail*, said, 'If I wasn't working in the football industry I wouldn't have any black friends.'

However, while admitting that the composition of 'the British press is largely white males,' he did say, 'But it doesn't mean we are not highlighting the issues and trying to expose wrongdoing wherever we see it. Ten or 15 years ago if you were at a match and you heard a monkey chant it wasn't really a story. It wouldn't have been reported. Now anything like that is called out. That is progress. The fact the abuse has migrated largely online where it is anonymous, while unacceptable, is also a sign of progress. You wouldn't have people being racially abused in person any more. I know Raheem Sterling has had occasional monkey chants at a match which is obviously totally wrong, but again it's one or two people at most and it's pretty rare. I was at a game three years ago where one fan threw a banana on the pitch. And that was back-page news for about a week. And he was eventually charged. He claimed he wasn't thinking and it wasn't racist. But the fact was it was highlighted. That became the story of the day. Twenty years ago, as you know, that would have been pretty common [and not reported].'

Indeed, it would not have been as I well know. In fact, a racist incident on a football pitch would have been reported as something else entirely.

In 1989, Tottenham went to Tranmere to play in a League Cup match. It was a dark winter's night. Gascoigne and Lineker were playing but so was

Mitchell Thomas. The moment he touched the ball, the Tranmere crowd, as if on cue, start grunting: ugh, ugh, ugh, ugh, ugh. I was taken aback but only for a moment. Thomas was the only black player on the park, and it was clear the grunts were directed at him. However, this was soon accepted as background noise, inevitable in the game, and we were all taken by the ebb and flow of the match. Gascoigne scored; Tranmere scored twice, then right at the end Tottenham drew level which we in the press box, without the benefit of TV replays, thought was a Lineker goal, but turned out to be an own goal.

However, when it came to the match reports, while a journalist mentioned that Thomas had been booed, he did not mention it was racial but said that it started after he had committed a foul on a Tranmere player. He, like me, would have known that the booing started long before that: the moment he touched the ball for the first time, some minutes before the foul. What the journalist had done was turn a racist incident into an everyday story of football fans reacting to a visiting player fouling one of their players. After the game, as Paddy Barclay, then with the *Independent*, drove me back to my hotel in Liverpool, I mentioned how the journalist had decided to ignore the racism that was so evident. But Paddy seemed very sceptical. Then he told me a story. In another match he had written that a black player had been booed because of his colour and received shoals of letters denying that and saying it was because he had fouled their favourite player and played a dirty game. I argued with Barclay, one of our most perceptive writers on the game, but not too forcefully. I, too, knew of letters which always denied that there was any racism in the English game and saw any attempt to write about it as an act of betrayal, or worse. Over the years, whenever I have written about racism in football, I have met with abuse. I have never received a single letter which accepts that there may be a problem, let alone that I may be making any worthwhile points.

This denial was vividly brought home to me in August 1993, just before the start of the football season, when I wrote a piece on racism in football. The Commission for Racial Equality joined the Professional Footballers Association to launch a campaign called 'Let's Kick Racism Out of Football'. Their aim was to put more black people in the stands, and in the boardrooms.

I wrote a think piece for the next day's *Daily Telegraph*, briefly mentioning my own problems at football and highlighting the fact that before blacks began to be targeted by football crowds, Jews had been the target. My *Telegraph* piece was meant to raise questions about how effective this campaign might prove, given the FA and the Premier League, convinced racism was a problem the game had dealt with, were very reluctant to back it. However, the mere fact that I had narrated some of my experiences of racism proved too much for some *Telegraph* readers. But, unlike the cranky postcards and anonymous letters, often written in green ink, that I received when writing on controversial subjects, this time the writers clearly identified themselves – providing addresses and telephone numbers. One man even sent me what amounted to a racist booklet arguing how since the Second World War, following the loss of the colonies and the arrival of 'coloured' people in Britain, the white man had lost power. Their hatred for people who were not white was so palpable that it was very disturbing.

So, if the media attitude to reporting race has changed, how do those who now work in this still largely white media world feel about the changes? I spoke to a few of them and found that the individual stories of the journalists who dominate our sports pages reveal a world far more complex than a simple description of the sports media being 'hideously white' would convey.

Barney Ronay has worked for the *Guardian* since 2004. I have admired his writing and, while I was intrigued by the name Ronay, looking at his picture byline I had no reason to think he was anything other than white. However, as we begin our conversation he tells me:

> 'I had an Indian grandfather, but you could not really tell by looking at me. What happens to me is people will say to me in the winter, "Have you been on holiday?" They ask me if I've been skiing, and it has got to the point now where I say, "No, that's the colour of my skin." My mother is quite dark. She grew up in Nottingham, and she experienced racism. She was always being told to scrub that off and all this kind of stuff. This was in the fifties and sixties. But my father was Hungarian and quite white so we are just a little bit darker than your average. Funnily enough, when I've been to India to cover cricket, I have felt quite at home. I also felt that people in India do see me as looking a little bit more Indian than they do in England. Somehow some part of me adapts a bit over there. And I started looking a little bit more native. I certainly feel more at home than I might have done.'

Ronay's grandfather was of mixed Indian and Dutch stock, with a Dutch name Van Spall:

> 'He was a very educated man but he couldn't get a job in this country because he was not the right colour. He was unable to join the bar in London because he was "coloured". He moved to Nottingham to get away from London. He had all sorts of other jobs as a salesman but it didn't work out there and he became very poor as a result. My

grandfather, who had ideas about his status, became a very unhappy man. I grew up with stories about what can happen as a result of the colour of your skin. In India, he would have been seen as an educated, probably quite light-skinned, cultured person.'

The one person who in this country accepted Barney's grandfather was his wife, a white woman, who, says Ronay, 'couldn't have had a more English name, Havercroft'. By the time Barney was born in 1973 his grandfather had died, but he remembers his grandmother well:

'She would try to cook my grandfather curries. She embraced that side of it. She did her best but they were terrible curries, where she would just bung a load of curry powder into some meat. And she made chutneys and things and tried to create what she imagined to be Indian food which she was still making when I was a kid. I would never claim to have suffered discrimination myself, but I had a family one half of which did suffer that. They were Jewish and were exterminated in the German death camps. My father's family came from Vienna when he was five and I found it really strange going to Vienna for the Euros in 2008. I had never been there before and while in the city I thought that the same people who knocked on the doors to tip off the SS about my family were probably still alive.'

But for a long time because he 'came through such an English sort of establishment upbringing, in many ways I never really had to think about it [racism]. I've actually started to think about these things a lot more since society has begun to think about them in the last few years.'

His establishment upbringing means that while he has one thing in common with Marcus Rashford – 'I had a single mother and we were pretty impoverished; we literally had no money at all.' – in one, crucial, respect his life was different:

'I was more sort of a middle-class kind of boy than him, which always helps. I had certain advantages. My parents went to university, and that kind of thing makes a huge difference in this country. It means you're much more likely to be yourself university educated. I was able to get a scholarship to a private school. I got an old-fashioned state bursary – they used to do them at Dulwich College – and ended up with the fees paid to Oxford University so I had that privilege. We lived in Lewisham and a lot of boys got these government bursaries. And that was quite an eye-opener for me. It sort of changed the way I spoke and the trajectory of my whole life.'

But Ronay accepts that, 'On the other hand, if you have an Oxbridge education and you're the wrong colour, you are still going to experience prejudice.'

Lewisham in the seventies and eighties was:

'Really a hotbed óf National Front activity. I remember the marches against the National Front in the early eighties. We had a whole group of local travelling kind of lefties, communists and activists come and stay in our house in order to go and stand on the front line for those marches. I remember the police camping out on Hilly fields just around the corner from our house. And I remember the Battle of Lewisham when the National Front was fought off. And those forces are still there. But maybe they are not as prominent and perhaps not as deep-layered as they might have been in the seventies and eighties.'

Ronay has vivid memories of racism in football in the eighties:

'There was open hostility and racism at football matches then that was shocking to see, but nobody really cared enough to stop it. It has definitely changed. It's changed so much since the Black Lives Matter movement. There was an extraordinary situation at my local club, Millwall. I have always gone there. I talk about Millwall being on the front line in that regard. I always feel that that is the place where these issues should be confronted because there's no point in preaching to the converted. If you really want to talk about racism in society you have to go to places where this problem has been experienced. I believe racism comes from social problems. It comes from people feeling stretched and poor and threatened by new things and [people] who don't look like them. I'd say that that is what has happened in some of the poor areas of London.'

The murder of George Floyd and Black Lives Matter have led to a veritable tsunami of stories about race on the sports pages, but Ronay is not sure how sincere this interest in racism is:

'I have to say, there's a certain amount of hypocrisy in that I'm reading stories in newspapers and by journalists who have been in this business for 30 years, and didn't give the slightest toss about discrimination, racism and all the rest until they became this kind of hot-button issue. Maybe they've had an epiphany. Maybe they always wanted to write about these topics but were not allowed. Maybe their eyes have been opened by that which is a good thing. People change, people realise actually this isn't fair and also society changes and there's more need for diversity, that we really need to sort this out. We've reached a stage now where racism isn't just calling people bad names, it's excluding them from the structures of power and maybe people are understanding that more. But it is slightly galling when you see these calls for equality in the same media that have been promoting that kind of structural racism for quite a long time. I find that hard to understand. People change, editors change, journalists change and if that's progress, then that's a good thing.'

But while Ronay accepts the media is still largely white, that does not mean the recruitment process is institutionally racist:

'What's happened is that journalism has gone through this very strange period where nobody is hired. The *Guardian* is desperate for people to leave, so they can hire new people, but people don't leave. And it's incredibly unionised. So, most of the people there are still the same people who were there when I joined. It's just not been expanding.'

Ronay agrees with me that editors often hire people they know or have the same background as themselves rather than people with diverse backgrounds:

'That's probably true and that was certainly the case. It has completely flipped on its head now. There's a huge pressure to change. So, every single hire at the *Guardian* from now on will be someone who is not white.'

I say to him that he must feel that it is wrong. 'I don't really. Part of me feels that's probably going too much the other way.'

He laughs softly as if he is saying something he should not.

'How good do you have to be to work for the *Guardian*? You have to be pretty good. So, there are probably good people who are white and good people who are from South Asian communities and good people who are black. I would rather we hired on merit and you ended up with a true reflection of the society you're reporting on. That's where we want to end up.'

There is one *Guardian* journalist who fits that bill perfectly and it is one whom Barney Ronay had to defend when he had a very public row with Jonathan Agnew, the BBC cricket correspondent.

Jonathan Liew, like me, a Tottenham Hotspur supporter, is the Chinese-born journalist I referred to earlier, and, like me, he worked for the *Daily Telegraph* although he joined in 2009, three years after I had left to become

BBC sports editor. 'I started doing a lot of news, investigations and things like that.' The editor who hired him, he says, 'wanted me to be the next you'. But then a new sports editor came in and Liew had 'his sliding door moment. He saw me as someone who could write funny, irreverent copy, do features and interviews'. His career took off and after the *Telegraph* he moved to the *Independent* and then the *Guardian* and is rightly regarded as one of our best sports writers.

Both of us are classified as part of the BAME community, but his background could not be more different, emphasising how these labels can not only mean so little but are often misleading. Liew's mother was born in China, his father is Malaysian Chinese and they met in Whitechapel in the 1980s. 'Actually, my dad was renting a flat from my mom in Whitechapel.' The racial experiences he suffered at Greenford were minor and have left no scars:

'Very few. Occasionally. There was an estate round the corner from where I lived and when I walked to the shops occasionally the kids there were would make slanty eyes at me. And sometimes the kids would say go back to India. I was seven or eight which I thought was quite funny. I never got sat down by my parents and given the racism talk. I was always brought up to think that anybody who dared to utter a racist thought was simply not worth the time of day and quite clearly intellectually inferior. So, it never really impinged on my childhood in a way I think it does for a lot of black children, for example. I guess school kids are just mischievous and they will find any kind of way of getting somebody. So, there were all kinds of racist abuse flying around the playground. It felt like just the whole part of pushing and shoving and the joshing of childhood, rather than anything more sinister. Fortunately, I was never the only Asian or person of Chinese descent in any of the schools I went to. They were mixed schools of various backgrounds, incredibly diverse schools. Obviously growing up in London you'd expect that. And so there was no real outsider status.'

This process of integration meant although he has a Chinese name, Chung Yao, it is one he never uses:

'Jonathan is my name. And again this might be an integration thing but a lot of British Chinese families do seem to love old English names. I know so many Brians and Howards. My dad and my mom both adopted English first names when they arrived in this country. My mother is Susanna, and my dad is Jeffrey. They had Chinese names but we never used them at home or anywhere else. Maybe, and I am speculating, Chinese people have been emigrating around the world for centuries and they really tried to assimilate into whatever culture they moved to. And part of that is giving their children English names. I was not only given an English name, I was given an English schooling. That was always very important to my parents.'

And while his mother's side of the family are Mormons, he was not expected to be a Mormon or a Buddhist or follow the Confucius system of belief.

Jeff Randall, an old colleague, and the first business editor of the BBC, would always tell me that the Chinese community didn't dwell on any racial problems they may have had, while the South Asian and the black community made too much of their racial situation. Liew accepts that, 'the Chinese community has historically encountered less racism than the black and Asian communities. I certainly don't think it's accurate to say that race is less of an issue for us. We were made extremely aware of our background, who we were, where we came from and the fact that we were different, a different kind of ethnicity.'

He went to Chinese school on Sunday. 'My parents tried unsuccessfully to teach me Chinese. I cannot really speak Chinese. I can understand and I can say a few words but it wasn't really a successful experiment.'

What mattered to Liew was not speaking Chinese but to make sure nobody could fault how he spoke English. 'I was very keen on integrating because my mom had a bit of an accent. And my dad had a little bit of an accent, even though they're both smart people. I wanted to speak English like the English.'

As he says this I think of Peter Sellers and how he patented an Indian accent that all Indians were supposed to have. Did he know, I ask him, that Indians find it very difficult to pronounce the letter V? It sounds like W. 'My parents never seemed to struggle with V or W but often the Rs and the Ls get mixed.'

What is fascinating is what his mother told him about the English. 'My mother taught me English people were slightly', he pauses, repeats 'very slightly', then says 'classless. Class not in the sense of the class of society but as in lacking class. She thought the Chinese were far superior to anybody else. My mum used to say the English just drink. They drink and drink and drink. That is what their society is based on. She always told me, "Don't marry an English girl." Unfortunately, I married an English girl. I didn't take her advice in that respect.' But his mother approved the union:

'My wife is half-Finnish, half-English. I have got a girl called Astrid and she will be two in June. She's a quarter-English, quarter-Finnish, quarter-Chinese and quarter-Malaysian Chinese. Her grandparents were born in this country.'

When I say his daughter, who does not have a Chinese first name, will be the right person for this new world, he says, 'Exactly.'

Liew feels more British than Chinese and for him the much-debated question of who is British and who is English is not an issue:

'I feel more English at home. When I go abroad, I become British. I am Jonathan first and then my passport is a British passport and I have Chinese ethnicity and Asian background and all these things seem to be true at once.'

But like almost all persons of colour, is he asked, 'Where do you really come from?'

'Oh, all the time. I react now a lot worse, with a lot more hostility than I used to because I'm more aware of what is behind that. When you were 12 years old, if someone asked where you are really from, it is a question like any other. It is like where do you live? Who are your favourite footballers? Because you're not aware of the impulses that lie behind that question. Whereas now you know what it is – an attempt, however ham-fisted, to make it clear that I don't look like I'm from here. That you are an outsider. I react quite strongly and try and particularly annoy people. When they say, "Where are you from?" I will say Brixton. Then they say, "I want to know where you are originally from?" Ah, well I grew up in Greenford. And then they will say, and this is like in a coded way, "Where are your parents from?" Ah, well they met in Whitechapel. When I ask people are you talking about race, they back away as they don't want to admit that they're really talking about it.'

In one sense his parents, particularly his mother, lived up to the Asian stereotype:

'She wanted me to be an accountant or work at a bank or some kind of respectable job. A lot of Chinese kids get pushed into things like maths. I was terrible at maths, and science and engineering and medicine. That's probably why you don't see many British Asian, or British East Asian journalists, especially in sports journalism. I always wanted to write. My dad used to get *The Times* and the *Independent* and I would lay them out on the living-room floor. And I would just lie on the floor and read the newspapers and go straight to the back page. I would have been about seven or eight and I remember saying to him, "These people who write the articles, do they go to football matches for free?" "Yeah," he said. I thought, I want to do that. I think that was where the seed was planted, quite early. I was always obsessed with sport. I love cricket and football and that seemed like the dream job to me.'

In the decade he has been in the press box it has, 'changed more in terms of the gender balance than the ethnic balance but certainly in terms of the issues that we cover, the journalists coming through today need to be so much more aware of issues like representation, diversity and racism as well. It is difficult to be a sports journalist and not have a keen ear for this sort of stuff.'

What has surprised Liew is the tsunami of stories of racism that has emerged as a result of George Floyd's death and the Black Lives Matter movement. 'Amongst marginal communities there is a real strength of feeling that has always been there and it is only now being voiced. It has got the outlet to voice it.'

This coverage has seen another, important, change:

'Even when non-white voices were given a platform in the past, whether it was through the media or through politics or whatever, it was still mediated through a white lens. So, whatever it was that non-white people had to say it was almost inevitable that white society was still the gatekeeper in many ways. What non-white people are saying is, "I am done having my voices mediated or mitigated by these gate-keepers that I don't recognise. I don't want to be there. I am going to speak without any fear or favour without moderating it for an imagined audience or imagined standards." '

Liew's upbringing has meant he has 'never felt any kind of inferiority complex'. And this was dramatically demonstrated when Henry Blofeld retired as the *Test Match Special* commentator in September 2017:

'I remember sitting in the Lord's press box next to Nick Hoult while Henry Blofeld was doing his stuff in the outfield at Lord's and saying I want to write a column about Henry Blofeld and white privilege. Nick burst out laughing. He said, "I dare you to write that in the *Telegraph*." And I did.'

Just as the *Telegraph* readers were expecting a warm, glowing piece about Blofeld, Liew wrote a withering piece entitled, 'Henry Blofeld is a much-loved character, but surely we can do a little better than this example of privilege over performance':

Only the privileged white man has this luxury: of being cast as a 'love-able eccentric', 'a distinctive voice', 'a bit of a character'. The young female commentator who keeps misidentifying fielders will not last long. Nor will the working-class black commentator who frequently gets the score wrong and refers to Jonny Bairstow as 'David'. This is the gift of privilege: you need only be half as good as another to earn twice the acclaim.

The result was:

'An utter shit storm. A lot of the readers went "phew". For a lot of them it would have been the first time any of them would have been confronted with the very idea of white privilege. Piers Morgan referred to it on his TV show. The point is not that Blofeld was a bad broad-caster. I wished him a happy and peaceful retirement. The point was he enjoyed opportunities that a female broadcaster or a broadcaster of colour would not enjoy. His foibles, his mispronunciation, his misi-dentification of players became folded into this happy-go-lucky persona in a way that is not available to Ebony Rainford-Brent. If Ebony Rainford-Brent mispronounces a fielder, she will be seen as incompetent, whereas Henry Blofeld will be seen as charming. And that is white privilege.'

The original unedited article might have caused an even bigger explosion.

'My original version was a little bit more like goodbye and good riddance. Unusually John Mullin, who was on the desk, asked me to tone it down a little bit and I did. He thought, and this was good editing, the piece would work a lot better if it was I wish him well, give my warm regards to him. That this was not vindictive but I was just pointing out the privileges that he enjoyed along the way. I think it was a more nuanced and effective piece as a result. Nobody said I can't write it because I was generally allowed to write what I wanted.'

Liew is certain, 'If Chris Evans the editor had known about the piece before it was printed, I don't think he would have allowed it. They went pretty potty afterwards.'

The *Telegraph* asked Oliver Brown, who is now their chief feature writer, to interview Blofeld. Brown says, 'The sports editor asked me to go and talk to him. We saw the need to repair relationships.'

By then Liew had left the *Telegraph*, having written the piece after handing in his notice:

'I think they felt it was probably like throwing a grenade over your shoulder and waiting for the explosion. I would have argued the same had I intended to carry on working there. It was important to say those kinds of things to a *Telegraph* audience.'

There was to be more trouble when Liew took on Jonathan Agnew, the BBC cricket correspondent:

'I wrote a column for the *Independent* about the selection of Jofra Archer and the way his potential selection was being received in English cricket. I quoted Trevor Bayliss, the coach, and I also quoted Jonathan Agnew. I highlighted the different ways in which Agnew had reacted to the initial selection of Gary Ballance, a white Zimbabwean, and the potential selection of Jofra Archer, a Barbados-born fast bowler. Whereas Ballance was seen as a good player who would improve the sport, Jofra Archer was described as a potential threat to team cohesion and morale. This is kind of the coded ways in which individuals or certain groups are othered. And cast as the outsider. The citation of what Agnew said was just one line in a 1,300–1,400 word column. He took great exception to this. My piece appeared on the internet on Friday afternoon sometime. That Sunday evening he sent me a series of Twitter direct messages, increasingly angry. He said that I had called him a racist. Although the piece itself did not mention race or racism, or racist, at all, he was certain I was calling him a racist. He was outraged at this perceived slight. He began sending quite abusive messages along the lines of everybody in the press box thinks you are a cunt. You are a cunt. You are the real racist. For which he was later forced to apologise. Later he elected to delete his Twitter account. It's not there any more. He resigned from the Cricket Writers' Club because I think he felt he was not getting support from the Cricket Writers' Club.'

Liew's article received support from many in the press ranging from Simon Kelner to Barney Ronay who devoted a column in the *Guardian* to it:

'I received a lot of support from colleagues, even from people I didn't know, defending my right to write it without being abused. What we have seen over the last decade or two amongst white society is this idea that race is something that you don't mention. That we are living in a post-racial society. That even to bring up race is not acceptable. This was the crux of what Agnew was saying to me. It was indecorous of me. It was impolite of me to bring up race. We are over that. It got solved. And there are any number of metrics you can point to that show we are absolutely not living in a post-racial society in terms of opportunity, or economics or anything like that. So as long as these inequities persist, it will always be the right thing to do, to look at this from a racial lens and I think it will always be fiercely resisted. People who tell you to keep politics out of sport are probably the people who are winning the politics.'

Liew thinks we will still be searching for answers to race and diversity if I revisit the subject in another ten years. 'These things take generations.' However, there is one note of progress: 'The number of female sports journalists 20 years ago would be almost none; now it is slightly higher than none but still not very high at all.'

In 1973, Julie Welch became the first female football reporter. But in the half century since, not many have followed her. Alyson Rudd is the great exception and quite the most distinguished of our football writers who happens to be female. As it happened, I knew Alyson long before she had started writing on football as she subbed a financial column I wrote for *Post* magazine, a publication that catered to the insurance market.

I start my conversation with Alyson by saying that it must have been terrible to sub my copy. I am hoping for a compliment and she sweetly provides one saying, 'It wasn't, I am sure.'

'Did you always want to write about football?'
'No, it took me ages to work out you could actually combine your career with your passion.' Then, laughing loudly, she adds, 'Didn't realise you could earn money doing something you liked.'
'But you always wanted to be a writer?'
'Oh God, yeah, yeah, yeah, yeah.'

Alyson's move from the *Post* to *The Times* meant:

'Moonlighting for a little bit. I was working nine to fiveish and then going off and doing evening matches. That was exhausting. And I had to take a big salary drop, leave full-time employment, become free-lance, and then work my way back up.'
'So, how difficult was the journey from subbing at *Post* magazine to writing on football for *The Times*?'
'I haven't found it difficult myself, because I wanted to do it. That overrode any nastiness I might have encountered. I didn't have a plan of action to deal with it. I think I must have just dealt with it in the right way by accident.'

Walking into a press box as the lone female reporter was not a problem:

'It didn't really bother me very much. What I thought about was the football. And the fact that I had to write to a deadline. And that was enough for my brain to handle without the fact that there was no other woman in the room.'

But there was one male reporter who could not believe a female could possibly report football:

'One of my very first matches for *The Times* I was in the press box and one of the older guys, a rather large guy, said, "With all due respect, how can you write about football? If you don't play football, if you're not a man?"'

Alyson laughs:

'I was very polite. I said that that morning I was training with my female football team. And two days earlier, I was playing in the match with my male football team. I play football with men and women, train a lot, play lots of matches. "Do you play? Did you play this week-end?" I knew he didn't. He went, "Oh, Oh, Oh, Oh." I think it must have been around 26 years ago. It must have got around because then people started saying, "Oh, Alyson is the exception to the rule." Brian Glanville actually wrote a column saying that he didn't think women could write about football adequately. But then he said Alyson Rudd is the exception to the rule because she writes well and because she played football for so many years. I think that probably annoyed quite a few people. I don't know what it feels like to play in front of 50,000 people, but I know what a striker feels like when he misses a sitter. And that day in the press box I sat next to a bloke who hadn't played for 30 years. So, who knows best?'

That world Alyson encountered has gone:

'Honestly, Mihir, in my quarter of a century of doing it, that mood has completely changed. I was at the *Sunday Telegraph* for two years. I walked into a meeting and it was all white, middle-aged men. I was writing for the paper; my opinion should have mattered. They should have wanted me to be as productive and happy as possible. But they just stared at me as if to say, "Oh God, is she part of the team?" It wasn't really a meeting at all, it was more about catching up on gossip and then going off to the pub afterwards. I just wasn't made to feel part of the group. It didn't put me off. I just didn't bother going to those meetings. It is very different now; it is a very welcoming place. Now I can often be the only woman in the room, but I am never made to feel that I shouldn't be there. In fact, probably, I'm too bossy and tell people what to do. There really wouldn't be a problem if someone different walked into a press room now.'

But she accepts, 'It's still difficult for anyone who's in the minority to walk in.'

That may explain why in the quarter of a century that Alyson established herself, not too many more have followed in her illustrious footsteps:

'I get shadowed by women who want to be sports writers. And they never come back. Because they walk into the press room with me and they see a sea of male faces. And they just think this isn't for me. That I can't possibly operate in that environment. I'll say to them, "Oh, it looks a bit daunting. But this is a really nice group of guys. Welcoming, and they're not sexist at all. They will be really helpful if you're on your own here. And if they knew you were new they wouldn't treat you differently because you're a woman. They're nice to new young male reporters and they're nice to new young female reporters; it would be absolutely fine." But they never come back. They just see it as not for them.'

Alyson is well aware that as a white person she cannot talk of the black experience:

'I don't know what it feels like to walk into a football stadium as a black person, a black fan or a black player. I don't know what it's like to go shopping as a black person. When I talk to friends of mine who are black about this it's a difficult conversation. I've been happy that my children went to a state school, which in London was, obviously, incredibly diverse. They grew up not noticing difference, which meant I always knew they would never be bigoted in any way. I think what you want is that a white person meets a black stranger and acknowledges the difference without any negativity, celebrate that there is difference. And then it's another step to go from that to thinking, "Actually I am allowed to treat you differently, because you're black. But the way I'm treating you different is completely out of respect for your cultural upbringing and where you're from." And that is incredibly nuanced. And I don't fully understand it because I'm not black. I do know the fundamental thing is most black people don't want to walk down the street and people are assuming things about them. So, police don't assume they might have stolen whatever is the nice thing in their possessions. Or that little old lady thinks "They're going to mug me because of their colour." We make assumptions all the time. But because we're pack animals, we probably make negative assumptions about everything we see. A woman is heavily made up and has blonde hair and high heels and there will be an assumption she's stupid. Because people are protective they protect their own and outsiders are not welcome. Education is the answer, diversity is the answer. A perfect world? It might happen in 8,000 years.'

Jonathan Northcroft, the *Sunday Times* football correspondent is from a long line of Scots who have been prominent in Fleet Street. What makes him exceptional is that he became football correspondent because of the intervention of another Scot who had nothing to do with journalism or the *Sunday Times*. Northcroft, who after an English degree in Edinburgh started with the *Glasgow Herald* as a news reporter, had after the 1998 World Cup become the *Sunday Times* Scottish football correspondent. He got moved to the Premier League in 2001:

'I got my move because Fergie [Alex Ferguson] banned Joe Lovejoy [the paper's football correspondent]. This was at the height of the Fergie versus Wenger enmity. Joe attended a Sunday briefing at Carrington [the Manchester United training round] where Fergie, at the end of the briefing, basically went off about Wenger and about Arsenal and that they portray themselves as this and that but that actually you know Dennis Bergkamp is a terrible cheat. He is always trying to hurt people but gets away with it. Wenger encourages it. It was off the record but Joe thought that was such a good story that he would just put it in the paper. It was too good a story to miss. He was banned for that. And it became a bit problematic for the paper with Manchester United.'

Northcroft became football correspondent in 2009, more than a decade after I had left the paper to move to the *Daily Telegraph*.

But if Northcroft carries on the great Scottish tradition, he is aware that the British sports media has remained white:

'I find it astonishing. I have lived through a period of enormous changes in football, in the media and one of the things that hasn't really changed is that scenario that you pose, looking around the press box and seeing nearly exclusively white faces. It is still quite skewed towards public schools, educated middle class; sports writers are university educated. I think broadcasting has changed. I think digital journalism has changed things. And now a lot more black and Asian sports writers are using digital platforms and are being given opportunities placing their stories. But at an England game or an FA Cup final, or one of the major Premier League games, things haven't changed that much. That does really surprise me. Having started in Scotland, which is much less diverse as a country, I would have expected to see more diversity in journalism in England. There hasn't been, not enough anyway.'

Why is that?

'There are a number of things going on. There's undoubtedly unconscious bias. There's still a leaning towards giving positions to people who are from the kind of safe backgrounds as the editors see it, i.e. the same boat as themselves or other writers that they've already got. But I think there is also that aspect that maybe editors aren't sure to find talent, or are conservative about looking for talent, not to be open-minded about where talent might come from.'

But he has noticed that in the last ten years:

'At least editors will speak about wanting to change, which they wouldn't have done ten years ago. But actions aren't following words at the moment, and this has come around exactly the time that the number of jobs in journalism has started to decrease. I speak to editors and they say they want to make opportunities but there aren't any jobs going. We are just not hiring. There has been very little movement in journalism in the last ten to 15 years. The guys I sit with at the game are probably the same guys who were there ten to 15 years ago.'

What has changed for Northcroft is the role of the football writer:

'In my generation, being a football writer is about a lot more than football now. It's about engaging with the world: social, political and wider issues. To me, that kind of started around about 2011. It was partly as a product of being in a mixed-race marriage, because we've talked about these subjects quite a lot. We were living in Liverpool surrounded by Liverpool fans, friends were Liverpool fans when Luis Suárez abused Patrice Evra. [Suarez called him a Negrito on 25 October 2011 in a game between Liverpool and Manchester United. Suárez in his autobiography would say the word in Spanish does not have the same meaning as in English and that he was not a racist.]

'And that became a very big debate between Liverpool and Manchester United. It was the first moment I found myself as a football journalist writing about really big, proper stuff and not just football.

And I appeared on [Sky's] *Sunday Supplement* and gave my opinion about why Liverpool supporters were wrong to back Suárez which got quite a bit of blowback from them. And then there was John Terry and Anton Ferdinand quite soon after that. From that point onwards there's always been another dimension to the job. In football in the last year I had to write about Black Lives Matter and understand properly the whole context and debate. To get my head round food poverty and understand Marcus Rashford and his activism, understand gambling and gambling laws. That's a difference, I would say, between the first ten years of my career and the last ten years. Raheem Sterling raising a debate about media bias and unconscious bias is certainly something that my generation of football writers are willing to engage with. I suspect that in a previous time, he might have been shouted down, but it did cause a lot of soul-searching among my generation.'

Northcroft's reference to his mixed-race marriage is significant:

'My wife Janice is second generation. Both her parents come from Montserrat. Her dad came over to the UK in the early sixties and ended up in the British Army and worked for the BBC. Her mom came over from Montserrat in the seventies.'

Northcroft, himself, is of 'mixed heritage' but of a very British kind. 'My father was English. He came to Scotland when he was 15. England has been a factor in my life because my dad had always hated Scottish nationalism. And I had many arguments with him."

Northcroft is well aware the younger generation think differently, as was illustrated by what David Walsh, Northcroft's *Sunday Times* colleague, and the chief sports correspondent of the *Sunday Times*, wrote soon after the death of George Floyd. Walsh wrote an article entitled: 'Reaction to death of George Floyd shows how little understanding sport and white society has of what it takes to eradicate racial iniquities'. In the article, he spoke to Edwin Moses, a great black American Olympic athlete, about his experience of racism. Walsh said that when he told his youngest son that he was speaking to Moses, his son said: 'So you, the privileged white writer, call up the former black athlete, effectively getting him to write your column. You then get paid for reproducing the insight he gives and that's your contribution to the debate?' Moses actually welcomed his call. Walsh concluded his piece saying: 'The deaths of George Floyd, Breonna Taylor and Ahmaud Arbery in America were wholly avoidable tragedies. They happened in part because we haven't been listening when black people talk about police brutality and racism. It is a cliché now but nevertheless true – silence is no longer an option.'

'It was', says Northcroft, 'very well put by David. That's the younger generation holding our generation to account.'

Northcroft has two daughters, eight and six:

'They are at an age now where they are conscious of race, conscious of being mixed race. That hasn't been an issue that's caused them any negatives. A couple of things at school but nothing much. And to look at the young generation, or just 20-year-olds in general, I think they are leaving a lot of stuff behind. I really do. And things like the empire don't mean anything symbolic. I do think it would be a much better world. Maybe that is optimism.'

What Northcroft cannot say is whether that better world will mean that the 'hideously white' media will change and become more representative of our society. One where a successor to McMenemy would find it impossible to make the comments he made to me all those years ago, without being challenged by the media.

TOWARDS A NEW JERUSALEM

THIRTY

THE THREE SPORTING MUSKETEERS OF CHANGE

Great sporting moments are etched in our memories by a single deed on the playing field. Jonny Wilkinson's drop goal with 26 seconds left which won England the 2003 Rugby World Cup in Sydney. Or the super-over drama at Lord's in 2019 which won England the 50-over white ball Cricket World Cup. These victories live on in people's memories as I found when in 2007, as BBC sports editor, I covered the Rugby World Cup final between England and South Africa. I heard women say they would like to have Wilkinson's babies. It was, undoubtedly, in jest, but it showed how such victories resonate. There are still men who vividly recall where they were when Geoff Hurst's hat-trick won England their only football World Cup in 1966. But between December 2018 and July 2020, Raheem Sterling, Marcus Rashford and Lewis Hamilton said and did things which, while having no bearing on the field of play, have resonated and defined a new kind of sports activism. This was previously a field dominated by Americans such as Muhammad Ali, and John Carlos and Tommie Smith giving the black power salute at the 1968 Olympics. Sterling, Rashford and Hamilton provided a unique British dimension to sportsmen making a stand against injustice and, in Rashford's case, taking it to a height which not even the Americans can claim to have reached.

And uncannily, for all the differences that distinguish these three, there is much common ground.

All three of them were brought up by single parents. Sterling by his mother, Nadine, in St Raphael's estate in the Stonebridge ward of Brent in North London, in the shadow of Wembley. Life was so hard that Sterling accompanied his mother at five in the morning every day as she went to clean lavatories at a hotel in Stonebridge. A Bounty bar from a vending machine was often his breakfast. The poverty meant that when he joined Queens Park Rangers, he and his sister Kima-lee would catch three buses, the Nos 18, 182 and 140, to make it to the QPR training ground near Heathrow and often not return home until 11 p.m.

Rashford was brought up more than 200 miles away, in the working-class area of Wythenshawe in Manchester, where his mother, Melanie, like Nadine a single mother, also worked as a cleaner. To feed her family she had three jobs: as a cashier at Ladbrokes, where she also cleaned, and then another cleaning job at weekends. Melanie would sometimes not eat so Rashford and his brothers and sisters could, but disguised it in such a way that Rashford and his siblings did not know. Rashford had to take two buses across Manchester to get to Carrington, Manchester United's training ground. Dwaine Maynard, Rashford's older brother, describes their upbringing: 'It wasn't a mum, a dad and the children. We didn't really have a father figure. We didn't even have anyone who was driving.'

This may explain why Marcus Rashford has always been driven, even as a 12-year-old. His teacher at Button Lane Primary school, Simon Payne, recalls that once, on a trip to the Lake District, Rashford wanted to set the alarm before everyone else got up. When Payne reassured him the teachers would wake him so he would not miss breakfast, Rashford said he wanted to finish the push-ups and sit-ups he always did before others got up.

Hamilton did not grow up in the great historic cities of England but in Stevenage, which became the first of the post-war new towns in 1946 but, like the other two, he knows all about the pain of growing up in a single-parent household. Born to a white mother and a Grenadian-British father, he lived with his white mother, Carmen, from the age of two to 12 and then from the age of 12 with Anthony, his father. In order to support his son's racing ambitions, Hamilton's father worked in various jobs, including dishwashing.

Up until December 2018, all three had made their presence spectacularly felt in their sports: Hamilton was quite the most outstanding, after winning five World Championships (now seven), and Sterling and Rashford were crucial players for Manchester City and Manchester United respectively and England internationals. Yet none of them had done anything to mark them out as special outside their sport. All that was about to change. Sterling was the first one to move, in December 2018. On 8 December, playing for Manchester City at Stamford Bridge and with the game 37 minutes old, in front of the Matthew Harding Stand he went to retrieve the ball when a Chelsea fan leant over and racially abused him. Sterling laughed. As we have seen, he behaved then no differently to how black players for almost 50 years had reacted when confronted with racism in English stadiums. It is what Sterling did the next day that set him apart.

On Instagram, Sterling commented on how *Mail Online* had dealt with two players buying houses for their mothers. The white player Phil Foden was seen as just doing the thing a loving son would do, while the black player Tosin Adarabioyo's action was reported much more unfavourably. Sterling wrote, 'For all the newspapers that don't understand why people are racist in this day and age, all I have to say is have a second thought about fair publicity and give all players an equal chance.' A clear message to the media about the subconsciously racist ways they reported on such stories.

Sterling had come to this after some years trying to cope with media mockery. After Euro 2016 there was criticism of him for showing off the house he had bought his mother and shopping in Poundland. He felt so alienated that he called himself 'the Hated One'. Before the 2018 World Cup there was more hatred directed at him. This arose from the fact that he had a tattoo of an assault rifle on his leg, which unleashed much media indignation. Sterling had to explain that he was not advertising guns but actually warning against their use in memory of his father. When Raheem was 18 months old, his father Phillip Slayter was murdered in Kingston, Jamaica, where his family then lived, by a gang. It was this tragedy that motivated his mother to move to England and bring Raheem to this country when he was five. As a child he had promised not to use guns.

Justifying his Instagram post he would say:

'That was just me having had enough of the media coverage over the years and trying to find a reason for that coverage. I was getting hate when it was not like I was running around the streets doing the craziest stuff. I wanted to inform that this does have an effect on how people see black players.'

Sterling was the first of the modern generation to realise how social media could be exploited to turn the tables on his tormentors, a power at the disposal of the modern black player that was not available to Ricky Hill or Cyrille Regis.

So successful was Sterling that on 8 June 2020, as the statue of Edward Colston was brought down in Bristol and Black Lives Matter protests swept the nation, he gave a 21-minute interview to Emily Maitlis on *Newsnight* in which he said that, '[Racism] is the most important thing at this moment in time because it [has been] happening for years and years.' That racism more than coronavirus was 'the disease right now we are fighting'. It was widely seen as a seminal moment both for football and this country's discussion of racism. By the time Sterling made this dramatic appearance, Rashford had already shown how the modern player, provided he is willing to engage, can scale over any barrier, however insurmountable it may seem.

The Rashford story had begun three months earlier on 18 March 2020 when the government announced that the pandemic meant schools would be closing. The next day Rashford tweeted, 'To anyone reading who can spare a few £s, you could make a big difference . . . And to the food industry, we know it's a challenging time, but we ask you to please send any product you can . . .' He had a partnership with FareShare and by April this had raised £20 million. In June that year, when the government announced there would be no food voucher scheme over the summer holidays, Rashford went one step further and wrote an open letter to all MPs asking for the policy to be reversed. His letter explained how he knew what it was like to go hungry: 'The system was not built for families like mine to succeed, regardless of how hard my mum worked. As a family, we relied on breakfast clubs, free school meals, and the kind actions of neighbours and coaches. Food banks and soup kitchens were not alien to us.' The next day, Boris Johnson did a U-turn and it meant 1.3 million children in England would receive their meal vouchers during the holidays. An elated Rashford tweeted, 'I don't even know what to say. Just look at what we can do when we come together. This is England in 2020.' He went on to say, 'I stand proud today knowing that we have listened, and we have done what is right. There is still a long way to go but I am thankful to you all that we have given these families just one less thing to worry about tonight.'

There was indeed a long way to go, but Rashford was on his way. It came in October 2020 when, five days after the news of his being awarded the MBE broke, he took up the cause of ending child poverty and making sure that until Easter 2021 there were out-of-term free school meals to all children from households that got Universal Credit or its equivalent. Rashford's petition was signed by more than two million. The prime minister showed no sign of giving in and extending the free school meals programme. Parliament voted 322 to 261 in support of him.

But Rashford was building up steam and, despite attacks on social media, with one comment saying that his mother 'shouldn't have five kids if you can't afford to bring them up', he would not be deterred. And eventually, having just got back from a match, he was told Boris Johnson wanted to speak to him. The documentary *Feeding Britain's Children* would record the conversation with Rashford at his end sounding as if he is speaking to a friend: 'Yeah, man, yeah, yeah, yeah, go on, can you say that again please . . . yeah, that will be the perfect situation for me . . . Thank you on behalf of the families. They'll really appreciate it. Speak to you soon.'

So Rashford, twice in the space of four months, had forced the government to reverse its policy on free school meals for the country's children most in need. In footballing terms, Rashford was the forward who twice nutmegged defender Boris Johnson and left him flat on his bottom as he sped past to bulge the net. Two-nil to Rashford. What made it even more dramatic was that at this stage, Rashford, while a major figure at Manchester United, was not even sure he would always start a match for England. He did not start a match for England in the Euro 2020 tournament that followed and as I write his form for Manchester United in the 2021-22 season has raised many questions about how long he may remain at Old Trafford. But the man educated at Eton and Oxford, who often quoted Cicero, a first-century BC Roman statesman, lawyer, scholar, philosopher and academic sceptic, had been bested by a 23-year-old footballer who only started reading properly when he was 17. Nothing like this has ever been seen before in British political life.

Lewis Hamilton's moment came in the events that followed the death of George Floyd. Until then nothing he had done outside sport would suggest his ambitions lay beyond driving a Formula One car better than anybody had ever driven before. Growing up in Stevenage as a mixed-race child who identified himself as black, he had suffered racism and was subjected to racial taunts and bullying. He would get beaten up. When he went go-karting, white kids would throw things at him. To make it worse, his white mother, while loving, couldn't, as he says, 'fully understand the impact of the things I was experiencing at school'. His father was 'quite tough', and Lewis kept quiet. But he learned boxing and karate to defend himself. When he went go-karting he was the only non-white and his reaction to being pushed around was to be cleverer than his tormentors so that he could beat them. His father's advice echoed those of the parents of many black footballers: 'Always do your talking on the track.' So, like the Chris Hughton generation of black football players, Hamilton turned the other cheek.

As a racing driver, even his successes did not stop the racism. In Newcastle people shouted, 'Go back to your country.' In Spain in 2008, at one of his first Formula One races, people blackened their faces, put on wigs and wore white T-shirts on which was written 'Hamilton's Family'. This felt like something out of *The Black and White Minstrel Show* and a cruel mockery of Hamilton's racial origins. Formula One said nothing.

Hamilton also found it was dangerous to joke about race. In 2011 he was penalised for two collisions in Monaco. When he was asked if he felt he was targeted, he joked, 'Maybe it's because I'm black. That's what Ali G says. I don't know.' The *Daily Telegraph* reported the story under the headline 'Lewis risks disciplinary action after astonishing outburst'. All this made Hamilton even more reluctant to talk about race. As he would explain to Gary Younge:

'It often felt that maybe I didn't speak about [race] in the right way, or wasn't great at explaining it, or maybe educated enough to talk about it. Either way, I got a lot of pushback and it seemed like more hassle than it was worth. So, I reverted to just doing my talking on the track.'

Hamilton had followed what American sportsmen had done to demonstrate their fight against injustice. Back in 2017, after Colin Kaepernick had knelt at the start of an NFL match while the American national anthem was being played, Hamilton had spoken to him before the US Grand Prix. He had a helmet made in red with his number on top and thought of taking the knee. 'But I was silenced and told to back down. I supported that decision, which I regret.' Towards the end of 2019, looking at team photos of Formula One teams, he was struck by how few black people were there. That was hardly surprising as of the 40,000 people working in Formula One, only 1 per cent are black. In 2010 he had invested his own money and teamed up with the Royal Academy of Engineering to set up the Hamilton Commission to examine why there were so few blacks employed by Formula One teams. The commission reported that Formula One needed to be more diverse and made recommendations about how it could be so.

Then, on 25 May 2020, George Floyd was murdered in Minneapolis. It was the 'deep pain, anguish and frustration' caused by the murder that made him speak out publicly. On 21 June 2020, in the *Sunday Times* he set out his thinking in an article that was spread over two pages with the headline: 'I won't keep quiet about the unspoken racism in this country.' He revealed that it had 'awakened some of my memories of the racial abuse that I had experienced as a child'. He had decided to speak out because people he respected had said nothing.

'I'm used to being one of very few people of colour on my teams and, more than that, I'm used to the idea that no one will speak up for me when I face racism, because no one personally feels or understands my experience. Most of the time, they don't even see it and if they do, they let their fear of saying the wrong thing get in the way. The unchanged make-up of the F1 community throughout my career makes it feel like only a certain type of person is truly welcome in this sport, one who looks a certain way, comes from a certain background, fits a particular mould and plays by certain unwritten rules. Even now, the media ask me different questions than they do my competitors and make accusations directly and indirectly – you're not British enough, not humble enough, not loved enough by the public. Being the first black "anything" is a proud and lonely walk.'

He also highlighted British silence on race: 'As a nation we're quick to condemn monkey noises and bananas thrown at black footballers, but when it comes to addressing structural racial issues, the people in power stay silent. Injustice prevails when you remain neutral.'

Hamilton was determined not to remain neutral and before the Austrian Grand Prix, on 5 July 2020, donned a Black Lives Matter T-shirt and took the knee. The other drivers, all of them white, were far from happy. But after Hamilton had said, 'Silence is complicit,' they all wore End Racism T-shirts and 14 of the drivers took the knee with him while six stood behind. On winning the Styrian Grand Prix, also held in Austria, he gave the black power salute and commented on those of his fellow drivers who had said nothing. Hamilton was also critical of teams that did nothing, in particular Ferrari: 'I've heard no word from Ferrari saying they hold themselves accountable. We need teams to do that.'

Hamilton now felt he was on a journey:

'I remember not being able to be myself. Of not being able to speak the way I want to speak. That's the point of all this inclusivity: including people and not asking them to change in order to fit. I remember feeling that I had to be a different shape. The entry point to my sport was a square and I was like a hexagon, and I thought, "I'm never going to fit through that bloody thing." So I had to morph my way in order to fit into that world and then try and get back into the shape I was before.'

Both Rashford and Sterling have also been on such a journey of discovery. Like Hamilton, Sterling has launched his foundation to help people like those in Stonebridge where he grew up and where 47 per cent of the population is black. Many of them have never made the six-mile journey to central London, preferring to shop in Brent Cross. He would like to change that. Rashford would like to help 383,000 children in the UK who have never owned a book to read. He has become an author of a self-help book for children *You Are a Champion: How to Be the Best You Can Be,* written with football journalist Carl Anka, which is meant to show how people can fulfil their dreams, and has teamed up with the publisher Macmillan Children's Books to start a book club which will give 50,000 fiction titles to 850 primary schools.

Of course, it helps that all three players have resources they can draw on to further their plans. As the highest-paid English player, Sterling has an estimated income of £15 million a year. The fund for his foundation could exceed £10 million. Hamilton can fund a commission to find out what is happening in Formula One. The previous generation of black players just would not have been able to command such financial resources.

What is fascinating is how Rashford has used the means now at the disposal of high-profile players. He can call on the services of Roc Nation, a global agency founded by rapper and self-made billionaire Jay-Z. The effect of this is very striking. On the same weekend of May 2021 Rashford featured in two weekend magazines. The *Guardian Weekend* magazine of 22 May had a cover story about him headlined 'Top of the Class' and showing him going back to his school, Button Lane Primary in Wythenshawe. The front cover of the magazine showed him posing with four kids, one black girl, two white girls and one white boy. That Saturday's *Times* weekend magazine had a story about Tom Kerridge, a popular celebrity chef, who had just published a new cookbook, *Outdoor Cooking: The Ultimate Modern Barbecue Bible* and who had teamed up with Rashford after he had said he had never peeled a potato. Kerridge, who was also brought up by a single mum, contacted Rashford who had launched a social media home-cooking campaign called 'Full Time'. This involved posting on Instagram 'How to Cook' videos which had very simple dishes like chicken satay or tortilla pizza. When Kerridge went to film at Rashford's home, he found that despite earning £200,000 a week, Rashford did not possess a kettle, and Kerridge ordered one for him from John Lewis. The story was headlined 'Marcus doesn't even own a kettle. I had to order him one from John Lewis', accompanied by pictures of the two men, both smiling.

All this was rounded off by a feature on Rashford in the *Wall Street Journal* magazine entitled 'Level the Playing Field'. The seven-page article on him came as a pull-out with four pages devoted to the text. Three pages had black-and-white pictures of Rashford. One showed him with his eyes closed and his face turned upwards. The headline was 'Upright Citizen' and the caption quoted Lindsay Boswell, chief executive of FareShare, describing how Rashford could talk in such a way about hunger and what needs to be done that it 'makes other people shut up and listen'. On the final page of the pull-out, there was another picture of Rashford, again bare-chested, but this time some of the writing on his right breast could be read. It began, 'Nobody can judge me, only God.' Rashford, who is a devoted Christian, said, 'If you could see our lives 15 to 20 years ago to where we are now, it's impossible not to have faith in God and all he does for us.' In the photograph he is shown balancing a ball on his head and looking at it.

The pull-out also had a photograph of a banner that had been hung on a sign welcoming visitors to Wythenshawe which read 'Rashford 1 Boris 0'. The article, addressed to an American audience, had James Corden, a West Ham supporter, explain football and quoted Serena Williams saying, when she was shooting alongside Corden, 'So, tell me about Marcus Rashford.'

Such has been Rashford's dramatic impact that GCSE media students will learn about his use of social media to change government policy on child poverty. The course was added by the exam board AQA in the hope that pupils can learn about the social and race issues raised.

Of course, that does not mean that Rashford would no longer be racially abused, which he was after missing a penalty that meant England lost the Euro 2020 final to Italy. But what it showed was that a modern black footballer had moved on to a different sphere. This was demonstrated when Rashford heard that the *Spectator* planned to write a negative article on 'how I have benefited commercially in the last 18 months'. Informing his five million Twitter followers of that, Rashford asked, 'Why has there always got to be a motive? Why can't we just do the right thing?'

The *Spectator* never wrote the story. Instead, Rashford wrote the magazine's weekly 'Diary' page, in which he took on critics in the right-wing media who had advised him to stick to football. 'I don't stick with football,' he said, adding, 'With a shared focus, people from different cultures, nationalities, races, sexual orientations, political affiliations and religions can unite to achieve incredible things.' The 23-year-old also said he would 'be doing [my] community and my family a disservice if I did not use my platform to speak on behalf of the millions whose voices are not being heard'.

And Rashford is a figure who politicians are aware of and to whom they have to pay attention – although the attempt by Gavin Williamson, the then Education Secretary, to do so resulted in dreadful embarrassment for him. He claimed he had spoken to Marcus Rashford on Zoom when he had actually spoken to Maro Itoje. They are both black, both England internationals and both clients of Roc Nation. But Itoje is a rugby international. Itoje tweeted, 'Due to recent speculation I thought it was necessary to confirm that I am not Marcus Rashford . . . And whilst we are here my name is not Mario either!! Just a simple Maro Itoje will do . . . Much love, Marcu . . . I mean Maro Itoje.' It prompted Matt to draw a cartoon in the *Daily Telegraph* showing a club official coming into the office of the chairman on whose wall was a picture of a jersey bearing Rashford's name and telling him, 'There's been an awful mix-up. We've bought Gavin Williamson for £100m.'

However, while the media mocked Williamson, the episode further emphasised that a whole new generation of black sportspeople has emerged who are breaking the shackles that have for so long limited the debate about creating a non-racial world.

THIRTY-ONE

EMPIRE, SLAVERY, RACE AND SPORT

John Barnes, the footballer, has always been an iconoclast on and off the field. On the field his attitude is enshrined in a memorable YouTube clip which shows the goal he scored for England on 10 June 1984 at the Maracanã Stadium, the home of Brazilian football. Brazil had not lost in their fortress for 27 years; England had never won there. Just before half-time, with the score 0-0, Barnes receives the ball wide on the left wing, chests it down and 30 yards from goal goes on a run. He is thinking of passing, but as he glides through the Brazilian defenders, he carries on and then, with a feint past the goalkeeper, Roberto Costa, scores. It has taken him eight seconds, 11 touches and he has beaten six Brazilian players. This is the sort of goal that Brazilians – the keepers of the world's beautiful game, as Pelé, their greatest player, described foot-ball – are supposed to specialise in, not England's roast-beef brigade, who rely on strength and a bulldog never-say-die spirit. The astonished Brazil-ians rise to applaud. England go on to win the game.

Barnes that day fulfilled the dream that many had had that when sons of black immigrants finally play for England, they would bring some of the exotic overseas styles of play: the mazy dribbles, the intricate passing, the delightful ball control, the unexpected that we had always admired in the Brazilians, the Hungarians and the Dutch.

But one group of Englishmen refused to accept that the goal counted, because Barnes was black. He later recalled to me:

'The National Front supporters were on the plane with us, sitting at the back of the plane. They had their National Front flag. I don't know if you remember the old guy who used to dress up in the England kit; he must have been about 80, and he had a picture taken with the National Front supporters. There were a lot of reporters who were on that plane. They never said a word. Bobby Robson, the manager, said, "Well, just get on with it; don't worry about that." Listen, when I first started playing, your own teammates would call you "nigger". You would hear them talk to other players during the game, calling them "nigger". If you stood up to it or you fought against it, you were told you had a chip on your shoulder. Back then it was accepted as just part of society. Now all of a sudden, because it's become de rigueur to be hard down on all the anti-racist thing, the same people who were there, who never said a word, are now writing stories on anti-racism. Wasn't it wrong back then?'

Three years after the Maracanã goal, in his first season for Liverpool in 1987 and playing in a match against Everton, every time he got the ball he was loudly booed. He took corner kicks in a hail of spit, and a large section of Everton's fans sang, 'Niggerpool, Niggerpool, Niggerpool!' and 'Everton are white! Everton are white!'

The Barnes I am talking to now has aged. The 20-year-old Maracanã wonder boy has lost his Afro hair and his wispy beard is streaked with grey, but as we talk it is evident that just as he astonished with a ball at his feet, so he also does when expressing views on the issues of the day. So, Barnes does not agree that players should boycott social media because of the racist abuse they receive:

'These are people to be ignored and if you ignore those people, they will go away. From a social media perspective, the more we actually highlight it, the more they'll do it. These people on social media . . . if I was to meet them in the street, they'd keep their mouth shut. Football fans are the same. When I got racially abused by hundreds of fans, if I met any one of them in the street when they weren't there with the tribal mentality, they'd say, "Oh, hiya, Barnesy, how's it going, blah, blah, blah, all right?" By giving them such a big profile and making such a big deal about these sad, insignificant people, it emboldens them, and they feel that they have a life. These are people who are just hiding behind a keyboard in their bedrooms.'

That Barnes has been prepared to dissent from mainstream thinking is not new. What is interesting is how he is now casting his net much wider and raising questions that few in sports have ever done:

'My whole take on this is that this is the legacy of the empire. The empire created this myth of racial inferiority. The myth of racial inferiority was created because that's what they had to do to then say to the people, "We're going to Africa; we're going to steal the wealth. We're going to steal all their money." If they were regarded as equal or normal, then even normal English people would have said, "No, this is wrong." So, there's a myth of racial inferiority that had to be created, fostered, perpetuated for years. These people are less than us. They're not like us people so therefore it is okay to rob them. And that is how racism came along. That's what we have to challenge.'

He says with heavy irony, 'Of course the empire was fantastic, wasn't it?' When I laugh, he adds, 'And what it did to India was great.'

For Barnes, the focus on colonialism is more important than slavery:

'Colonialism did more to make people racist than slavery did. The average person in England didn't know about slavery because they didn't see when Africans were taken from Africa to the Caribbean. If they had seen that, then they may have said, "This is wrong." What they saw was the goods that came from the Caribbean to help build factories, help in the development of the country's Industrial Revolution, get people jobs, have sugar.'

But Barnes would not remove statues like the one of Edward Colston in Bristol that was pulled down in 2020 as part of the Black Lives Matter movement:

'What is the point of removing a statue? If Colston's statue is removed, then tear down all of those buildings, the old institutions and all of those schools that he also built with the money from slavery. Go to Trafalgar Square and look at Nelson and look at all the great British heroes who were part of the slave trade and tear them down as well. Where do you draw the line? It's a waste of time. So what we have to do is acknowledge what he did, and we have to discuss that what he did was accepted by everybody. Do you not think everybody in the 1800s or in the 1700s wanted to be a slave trader and make money from slavery? I mean 100 per cent of the people in England would have done that. So, it's not a thing that all of these people who are talking about [these statues] that their forefathers would have been any better than Colston. They would have felt Colston was lucky, and they would have loved to have done the same thing. Colston wasn't unique. What are the benefits of the slave trade or the colonisation of India? The benefit was the whole of Britain being built. So, therefore where do you draw the line? If you want to say to the Bank of England,

"Give all the money back," where does the Bank of England start? Barclays – all of these institutions – were linked to exploitation through the empire and through the slave trade. You can't just look at the ones who were the slave traders. What about the ones who actually gave them the laws to do it, or who bought stuff from them, who brought the sugar, or the tobacco, who built the factories, who built the schools? They are all part of it. If you want to start talking about people who benefited from the slave trade, you'd have to dismantle all of England. England became great because of India and because of Africa. The people who are English and who are white, 80 per cent of them, how can they then say, "Oh, we're not happy with that," because it made them what they are. That's why when we're looking back at history, what we have to understand is more the legacy of it. Reparation for that is never going to happen.'

What Barnes wants is to change the perception we have of people who are different from us:

'Racism, sexism, homophobia, it's a perception we have of different groups of people based on what we have been unconsciously taught over the years. Individual people have to know where these perceptions come from and change their perceptions. We shouldn't be too hard on ourselves because this is how we have been conditioned to think. That's what we have to challenge.'

Barnes is quick to point out that it is not just white people who have to change their perceptions:

'It's not about blaming white people for being racist. You can't blame Muslims for hating Hindus because of what they [Muslims] have been wrongly told about them. It's the way we have been conditioned. Black [people] want to talk about racism, but how about the way that a lot of black people feel about homosexuals? We want people to be our allies in our fight for racial equality because we know it's wrong. Homosexuals say we want black people, who are homophobic, to be our allies. Some black people who are homophobic would not think about that. How can we expect people to be on our side in this [fight against racism] when we are not on the other people's side?'

In Barnes's view, our ingrained perceptions affect everyone, including the most revered:

'We can talk about whether Winston Churchill was great or not. Mahatma Gandhi. What did Gandhi think about black South Africans?

[Gandhi in his early days of living in South Africa thought blacks were inferior although he later changed his mind.] I don't blame Gandhi, because this is how he had been conditioned to think. He's a lawyer, he's been brought up in a Western country and he's an elite person, so therefore he can't help the way he sees, because this is what he has been wrongly told. So, great as Gandhi was, a great freedom fighter for equality for his own people, if even he is conditioned to think that black people are inferior, what chance has the average person got in not thinking the same thing? That's why I have no problem with racists at all. I tackle the environment that made them think that way because I am a prejudiced person. If I see a male referee and a female referee, before I can see the quality that they have, I'm going to think the man's better because of the way I've been conditioned.'

This is one reason why Barnes rarely appears as a pundit on television, because he would disagree with his fellow commentators, mostly former players, making glib anti-racist comments:

'All of these football pundits are saying, "Oh the fight for racial equality. It's a disgrace." Do you not think they all racially abused people when they played? One hundred per cent. But, of course, they never got caught and now they're saying it's a disgrace, and anybody who does it should be killed.'

This perspective at looking at things meant that Barnes was the only one to raise the question why, following Jose Mourinho's sacking in April 2021, Tottenham appointed Ryan Mason, a white ex-player of the club, as caretaker manager. Tottenham did not consider the two black coaches in their ranks, Chris Powell and Ledley King. Both had better credentials. Powell had managed several clubs before, something Mason had not, and is also assistant to Gareth Southgate, the England manager, and King is an iconic figure at Tottenham.

'It's nothing to do with Tottenham, it's to do with the general way football is. You look at Sky and every single day they talk about, "I'm into the fight against racial inequality." And they're highlighting every incident whereby some fan from Bulgaria or some working-class man from Grimsby or whatever [has made racist comments]. But no one is ever talking about how come there are no black managers. They were talking about black managers when I was a player, and now they're saying it for Raheem Sterling's [generation], but nothing will change because we're not even addressing that issue. That's the elephant in the room. How many black people are working in the high echelons of Sky? It's okay to have a token black person, a token woman, in these positions which really don't carry any power and say we are fighting for equality. That doesn't change anything.'

Barnes, showing his radical, iconoclastic streak, also raises the question of what black players themselves are doing about the lack of black managers: 'Why are all the black players playing for a [Premier] League with no black managers? Because it doesn't affect them, and until something affects them, they're not interested. Very much like the black perspective with homophobia, a female perspective towards blacks; everyone is looking after themselves.'

But surely this generation of players like Raheem Sterling are really different. The moment I ask the question Barnes shoots back:

'Why are they different? What have they been doing? Raheem hit out against the media and what has happened? Are they still stabbing people in London? Can black people still get jobs? Marcus Rashford is the only [one] who has spoken about being underprivileged. He used his platform to talk about people less well off than himself. And he's changed government policy. Every other black player, every other black pundit, every other black elite person is talking about needing more black elite people. No, we don't. We need more respect for the black working classes, the black underprivileged people. For hundreds of years, we have had black, female, Muslim, Indian elite people who are doing very well, thank you. But nothing has changed for the masses, and that's what we're trying to do again now. We're not talking about problems in the inner cities, are we? We're just talking about we need more black people in the boardroom, and more black owners. And that's not the solution to the problem, because that will only help a very small percentage and that's been happening to us for years.'

If this makes Barnes sound like a socialist, perhaps I should not be surprised. Back in 2010 during the South African World Cup, I had interviewed him, and he had told me:

'I am a bit of a socialist when it comes to football. Football is a socialist sport. Financially, some may receive more rewards than others, but from a footballing perspective for 90 minutes, regardless of whether you are Lionel Messi or the substitute right back for Argentina, you are all working to the same end. The teams who embrace the socialist ideology rather than having superstars are the teams that are successful. Or if there are superstars, they don't perceive themselves to be that. That's why I use Lionel Messi as an example. As much as he's a superstar, he respects his teammates and their collective efforts as much as the substitutes, if you like.'

Assault without words

In the years since then, Barnes, who has always liked reading history books, has moved from being a socialist on the field of play to questioning the very tenets of what is generally regarded as universal historical truth:

'The French Revolution, the American Revolution, the civil rights movement, has never been about the people. It has always been about getting more elite people into power. That is what has been happening throughout history. For hundreds of years, nothing has changed for 90 per cent of the people. The French Revolution was never about the people, it was about a group of elite people wanting more power from the king, so therefore they lobbied the people and said, "It's on your behalf." Their [the elite's] lives got better, but nothing changed. The American Revolution was the exact same. The Haitian Revolution was [supposedly] about freeing black people [when it was] about mixed-race people who wanted more power, and they used slavery as an excuse. And we're still doing the exact same thing that we've done for a long time, saying, "Let us get more black people into high posi- tions." And that never worked. Frank Rijkaard won the Champions League with Barcelona, a black manager. How come they didn't get any more black managers? Because they had an elite black manager who was acceptable. We had Obama who was the president, so how come things haven't changed in America? Because it's within the system; you cannot change the system by putting individuals within that system to change it. You have to change the system. You can't get involved in an existing capitalist system that has been around for 500 years and change it from within. That's like beating yourself up. Black people are saying, "Let us get into the system and we can change it for ourselves." We can't. We have to stop pretending that the solution is to get into the system.'

For Barnes this is illustrated by the government setting up a committee headed by Tony Sewell, a black man, to report on race and diversity which concluded there was no institutional racism in this country:

'When he comes out and says there's no systemic racism, how can black people then complain if a black man is saying that? You can't have people coming into the system and changing it from within. If you just say, "Let's put a woman on the board, let's put a black man on the board," nothing will change within the existing system as it stands now. We're wasting our time doing anything like that. What I want to do is change the perception of the average black person, of the average woman, of the average Muslim. What we're doing now in football is wanting to have more black elite in positions of power. We have to stop this elitism.'

Barnes has been criticised for saying the greatest thing about being a black footballer now is that he earns 'the same amount of money as a white footballer and some of them are crap. The point I was making was: in which other job can you have a crap black person making the same money as a crap white person?'

It comes as no surprise that Barnes is not in favour of players who have been racially abused walking off the pitch:

'Because black people can't walk off the field of life; they're racially abused every day, silently. Jordan Henderson [the Liverpool captain] said, "Racism is an assault with words." The assault with words is the most insignificant part of racism; it is the assault without words. That's why black kids can't get jobs, they're stabbing each other, and they can't get access to social care. And women can't get positions of power and gay people can't do what they want to do because it's assault without words. And that is the most important thing. People who throw bananas or shout racist abuse, that's an easy, obvious one that we can actually point at and challenge. It's the unseen and unspoken racism that's affecting their lives, not the idiots who shout out. Rather [than] trying to work from the top down, work from the bottom up. You have to make a better environment for the average person.'

What is depressing for the many, like myself, who believe in the power of sport, is that Barnes has no belief that sport can play a part in that:

'Sport can't play a part in it at all. Only society. Do you think, apart from Manchester City fans, other football fans are listening to Raheem Sterling? Because that's the tribalism of football. Everybody else is always going to think he's just played the race card. So this whole idea that footballers can make a difference, no we can't. Society has to make a difference.'

The result of his reading and reflecting on things emerged when the book he has spent the past five years writing, *The Uncomfortable Truth about*

Racism, was published in October 2021. But he is not optimistic that his book will start the debate. 'Well, John Barnes is not the John Barnes he was 25 years ago. I haven't got that profile any more; people are more interested in the present superstars.'

If that strikes a sad note, he ends our conversation by saying with some pride 'It is not ghost-written.' Barnes was right in being pessimistic about the book. It only got mentioned in the Brief Review section of the *Observer* book pages on 14 November 2021 with the reviewer saying, "this book feels uncomfortable but important too". The review ended "Passionate, confrontational stuff". It got 14 lines and was one of three books in that section that week but it did not merit the top spot even in the brief review section. That went to a book of essays, titled *My Body*, by model and actor Emily Ratajkowski, the star of Robin Thicke's controversial *Blurred Lines* video.

It would be easy to say that Barnes, for all his anti-elitist talk, is himself very much part of the elite, with a very different background to most Afro-Caribbean players. He is the son of middle-class Jamaican parents who came to England when he was 13, and his background and upbringing helped him cope with the racism he faced. One of the most iconic and revealing pictures of a player confronted by racism is of Barnes back-heeling a banana thrown at him when he was playing for Liverpool. But when I have asked him about it, he has said, 'I've seen a picture of it, but I can't remember doing it. You see, growing up in Jamaica, because I was fully empowered by my parents, I've never felt inferior at all.'

But even as Barnes finished his book, another son of Jamaica in the summer of 2020 would set the cricket world alight by his views on the very subjects Barnes has been meditating on and all triggered by a death many thousands of miles away, totally unrelated to the sport in which this Jamaican had made his great name.

THIRTY-TWO

AN AMERICAN DEATH
AND CRICKET

O n 8 July 2020, the start of the Test series between England and the West Indies was held up by rain. But instead of showing clips from old Test matches featuring the two teams as they would normally do, Sky Sports showed a film where two of their commentators – Michael Holding, perhaps the most respected commentator, and Ebony Rainford-Brent, the first black woman to play for the England women's team and a World Cup winner in 2009 – spoke about race. After the film, Ian Ward, the presenter, standing on the balcony overlooking the Southampton ground, interviewed Holding, Nasser Hussain and Ebony Rainford-Brent, all of them sporting Black Lives Matter insignia. I could not believe what I was seeing and was intrigued Sky had presented such a programme. So were the cricket writers present at the ground. Paul Newman, the *Daily Mail* cricket correspondent, rang his colleague Lawrence Booth, who is also editor of *Wisden Cricketers' Almanack*, and asked, 'Are you watching? It is incredible.' A few months later, when I spoke to Rainford-Brent, what led to this extraordinary programme, which had a far-reaching effect, turned out to be even more amazing:

'It basically came about because I broke down in a Sky team meeting held two or three weeks [before the Test series started]. Michael Atherton was there, all the producers, directors, people like that. I had been going to all the Black Lives Matter rallies. I was in a sort of emotional place basically. I was asked in the team meeting did I want to talk about my thoughts, and I said, "Yeah, no problem, I'll be fine to talk." And then as I started speaking at the meeting I really broke down. I just talked about the fact that you walk into many rooms and you're the only one of colour. [I said] in this industry you may be in front of a screen but often you go behind the scenes – I've been 25 years in the game – and it is all white. I also said I didn't expect to ever see a black director, to work with a black director or black PA or a black producer. I just didn't imagine that could happen because I know how the world operates. I think it just shocked everybody. And the head of Sky said, "I think we should put this on. Would you and Mikey [the affectionate nickname Sky's fellow commentators have for Holding] be prepared to talk about how you feel?" Mikey wasn't in the meeting actually. He got told about it and he messaged me straight-away that evening and said, "Let's speak." '

Rainford-Brent was surprised when I told her about the tremendous reaction to the film: 'Is it the way it was filmed? You know, I thought the reaction would be negative.'

For Rainford-Brent to be the only black woman in a world of white men and women was not a new experience. She had also felt very alone when she had made her England debut in Chennai [Madras] against India in 2007. It should have been a special moment as Charlotte Edwards, the England captain, handed her the cap. But then a woman called Imogen told her she was the first black person to play for England and for all the pride she felt wearing the cap, she also felt 'uncomfortable. And it took me a long time to really feel comfortable.' Much as she wanted to play for England, she did not want to be the only one 'and it's something that I still feel a little bit plagued by now.'

The tears that flowed at the Sky meeting had been building up ever since Rainford-Brent, lying in bed at home, turned on her phone on 26 May 2020, and the first thing that came up was the video showing the policeman with his knee on a prostrate George Floyd's neck. The first thing she heard was Floyd saying, 'I can't breathe.' She could not bear to watch and clicked off. She later did watch the full eight minutes and told Sky viewers, 'I burst into tears.' Reliving her feelings with me, she said:

'I watched the whole thing. I felt absolutely sick for two to three weeks. It was too much for me. You know that cannot be ignored. And that's the difference now. It is hard to deny what has been denied for a long time. The pandemic in that sense helped because we all watched it. Normally that would have been a quick jaunt, a quick story, and then it all got back to everything else. Whereas now it was a time to reflect on something really, really important.'

Rainford-Brent went on three Black Lives Matter marches:

'I was fed up that racism is a huge elephant in the room. I know it exists. Unconscious bias exists. All these inequalities exist, but it wasn't recognised. That was a moment for me where the world was recognising an issue that needs to be dealt with, and I needed to be out there with everybody walking, in supporting the cause and helping make as many people aware as possible. For me marching wasn't a big thing, it was just, if your friends are going and this is an important issue, it's important to be there.'

She had herself tested [for Covid] privately, and feeling that London was pretty much virus-free, she went:

'Oh, it was really interesting being at marches and then seeing them reported on the news because they felt almost like completely different events. Sometimes they [the media] would be reporting saying it was full of trouble. They were really peaceful. They were so peaceful and very diverse. There were white people there and black people. I would say 50-50. That was what was nice because I grew up in London and my friends were multicultural – black, white, Asian, Greek. And that's how it was and that's what was really nice about it.'

Before the killing of George Floyd, she had not felt bold enough to come out and talk about race, worried she might not be supported, and admits she was embarrassed she did not. But even now, when I ask her about her racial experiences, she seems reluctant to talk: 'Because I mean, when it comes to talking about race in cricket, I don't know how to put it. I am so exhausted.' This is maybe because unlike many people of colour, she did not grow up experiencing racial prejudice.

Rainford-Brent, born in 1983, grew up in South London: Brixton and Herne Hill. This was the heyday of the National Front, who were particularly active in that part of London, but the National Front had no impact on her life. 'I wasn't maybe reading the news as such. I was going to school, which was multicultural. In my schooling years all the way up to 18, I never experienced anything that made me even question colour. In that environment nobody called me names. It was quite a low socio-economic area, so for everyone the biggest challenge was money.'

Her mother, who is from Jamaica, came to England when she was 13 and she says with pride, 'I've got the Jamaican culture at home, but born and bred in South London.' It was her mother, working in two jobs, the NHS and a supermarket, who brought her up, and Rainford-Brent's childhood is the classic story of the deprivation and anguish single-parent families often suffer. When she was five, her eldest brother was killed in a knife crime which had a devastating effect on her two other brothers, who had problems with alcoholism and drugs, and her youngest is still in a prison in Kent. But despite that, she says 'in my whole school experience' she was never made to feel she was different. 'The cricket world was my introduction to realising that I was different.'

This was through a constant stream of hurtful comments. Her mother, who came to watch her play, would sometimes fall asleep, and this would make some of the players and coaches laugh, not realising that she worked at night to put food on the table for her children. For the players and coaches from a more affluent, often middle-class background, this would have been an alien world. There were comments that the food she ate stank. Rainford-Brent's skin colour, body parts and hair – 'especially the derriere' – also caused comments. One of the players asked, 'Do you wash your skin?' While Rainford-Brent did not treat this as malicious, others were more vicious.

More wounding, given how her brother died, was to be told that in her area people get stabbed. And she was made aware by white coaches that as far as they were concerned she was not an individual but part of a black group. One coach told her at one match that people watching the match did not like her 'lot', and she had better not play. On the Sky film she would reveal:

'When things that happened like Barack Obama becoming president in the US, having a paper thrown down in front of my face. And saying, "You lot must be happy." It is the constant drip-drip [that] was tough. And I'm not surprised that people who come into the environment don't want to deal with that. I question myself why I stayed sometimes so long. I love the game. I think it has so much more to offer. But it can be really difficult dealing with it [at this point she begins to cry, she stops, and then says] day in, day out.'

In some ways, most revealing was what happened to her at one of her first trials. Her full name is Ebony-Jewel Cora-Lee Camellia Rosamond Rainford-Brent and this was just too irresistible for a white girl at the trial who said, 'Oh, you are from Brixton, aren't you? Bet your mum doesn't know who your dad is. So, she's just giving you a name for everyone.'

What her white colleague did not know is that Rainford-Brent cannot trace her ancestors.

'I've done my DNA, and my DNA is African. My last name is not my ancestors' last name. I have looked into the Rainford name. It is an

English last name to do with a trader from Liverpool. We don't know the details. The closest we can find is Samuel Rainford, Liverpool. You really think about that. Your last name is not your last name, it belongs to a kind of history.'

The kind of history she is talking about was the very cruel history of slavery that took her African ancestors to the Caribbean. The link to Liverpool, given that it was a port at the centre of the slave trade, suggests that Samuel Rainford may well have been one of the English slave traders who transported Rainford-Brent's African ancestors to Jamaica. Liverpool's prosperity owed much to the slave trade. When she played cricket, she did not talk about all this; she confesses she never had the confidence to do it, internalised it. As we talk, she is still reluctant to draw back the curtain and reveal the historic events that have created her and which are so different from those of her white colleagues.

But in contrast to what happened to her when she started playing cricket, her broadcasting experience has been very different:

'Jonathan Agnew has been great. He was a big supporter of mine. And the producer Adam Mountford. They just made me feel normal, because there could have been a chance that as a woman going into that environment, or a person of colour, that you could have felt uncomfortable. Adam Mountford, in particular, was the key to just introducing me into the industry and making me feel this is the place I belong, that if you put in the work you can progress. I saw Aggers as the kind of God of radio, really, and so to have someone like that show you so much love and respect was really having a nice, warming feeling of "Okay, maybe I'll be all right."'

Now what Rainford-Brent wants to do is make sure the next generation of black cricketers are not lost. The vehicle for that is the African Caribbean Engagement programme (ACE) which she launched in January 2020. 'This is basically the charity I started with Surrey. That is who I work with [she is on the Surrey management board].' The need for such a programme is obvious. In the eighties or nineties there were several black players in the England squad, but now there is only Jofra Archer, who learned his cricket in the West Indies, and the county cricket pipeline has also dried up. The number of black cricketers in county cricket has dropped by 75 per cent since 1990. In 2020 there were only two blacks among the 118 support staff in county cricket. Rainford-Brent says:

'It's gone backwards. Participation is really low, less than 1 per cent. The point of the ACE programme is to reverse that. We are going into black communities, getting engaged with the schools and finding talent. We're trying to accelerate opportunities because we know that in a lot of black communities they didn't go to the right school, or they didn't have the right connections. So, they might have the talent, but they're not being seen or supported enough. We've been really fortunate we've got a lot of funding from government and Sport England. The plan is to go into all the densely populated black communities, and we want to reach five different cities in the next couple of years. What we can do is create opportunities to change the landscape. I'm really seeing a window of opportunity where people are listening, prepared to invest, prepared to make a difference. Kids from our environment do not even engage with cricket. I'm talking of the South London way around The Oval. In Lambeth alone, 40 per cent of young people are from a black background. The option for them is football, and even rugby has improved. Rugby is still not as diverse as it needs to be, but that's a better option for a kid as a path because there are more people who kind of look like you. But schools are not playing cricket. That is why we are going into more schools.'

Despite the long journey ahead, Rainford-Brent is:

'More optimistic than I have been for 25 years of the game, and that's because people are listening. What I'm seeing now is so many people reaching out to say, "Okay, how can we make a change? What do we do to open up the game?" You can't eliminate racism, but there could be enough systems and structures in place that provide opportunities for people of colour. Denial [claiming that racism does not exist] is not going to cut it any more. I think that's what the marches and the movement has done. You can't deny what you've just seen on your TV. You cannot deny what happened to George Floyd.'

It was also the killing of George Floyd that had made Michael Holding finally break his silence on race.

If Rainford-Brent's journey to her Sky broadcast was a long, emotional one, that made by Michael Holding was even more complicated and, in many ways, much more surprising. Before July 2020 Michael Holding had always given the impression that he was in total command of whatever he did, and everyone knew exactly where he stood. Then, in the course of a couple of days, he twice broke down in tears when talking about race. The day after he had made his Sky film on race, he spoke about his experiences of racism on Sky News to Mark Austin and how his mother's family would not speak to her because his father was too dark, and he broke down. The clip went viral and reached people who had not heard of Holding, who did not even know or care much about cricket. A few days later, narrating a story to Andy Bull of the *Observer* about what his mother told him about race when he was a little boy, he put his fingers to the bridge of his nose, turned away from the screen, and again started to cry. Nothing could have prepared the cricket world for this Michael Holding.

Until the morning of 8 July 2020 when, as we have seen, Holding made the first of his dramatic statements on race on Sky, the image that the cricket world had of him could not have been more different. He was one of the greatest fast bowlers in the history of the game with a very distinctive style. Holding's run-up was so silent and light-footed, yet the destruction he wreaked on batsmen so devastating, that he was christened 'Whispering Death'. Then, as a commentator he made cricketers whom he had often vanquished love him. It was summed up for me by David Gower. Holding was part of the great West Indian teams that beat Gower's England 5-0 in successive home and away series in the eighties. Gower admitted the defeat in 1985–86 was his lowest point as a cricketer: 'The crowd was singing, "Captain, your ship is sinking." I did not enjoy the tour.' Gower, then Sky's cricket presenter when we were talking in June 2014, told me what an undiluted pleasure it was to have Holding as part of the commentary team:

'Mikey has three things going for me: a great fast bowler, one of the great voices, and he is the most honest man you will ever meet in your life. There are women falling apart at the seams listening to Mikey's voice. When things come up which reflect the slightly darker under-side of the game, Michael is your moral arbiter.'

However, Holding had never before talked about race, not even to his family. So much so that his daughter was shocked when she saw the Sky clip. Holding was born in Jamaica in the fifties, eight years before it got independence and six years before the West Indies team had their first black captain, yet racism was something he had heard stories about but never suffered from. This may have been, as he told Sky viewers, probably because he did not go to places 'where I could experience racism'. He heard how Edwin Blake, who lived on the road where Holding grew up, went to a hotel in Kingston that only whites, expats and local white Jamaicans went to. As he dived into the swimming pool, the whites jumped out. The police were called, Edwin Blake was thrown out, and the pool was drained before the white people resumed swimming.

Holding also did not experience much racism while playing cricket and when he did, he brushed it aside. If while he was fielding on the boundary he would hear racist comments, he would dismiss the people making the remarks as sick. Even when in 1976 Tony Greig, the South-African-born England captain, said he would made the West Indians 'grovel', words that had connotations of slavery, Holding did not hold it against Greig. When he came to know him, Holding was convinced he was not a racist. Unlike Viv Richards, Holding never became politically active on race, and when West Indians playing in England told him of their experiences, he said nothing. Even if he heard comments that were upsetting, he would grin, hiding inner feelings of distress.

Holding's reticence to talk about race may also have been influenced by the fact that after his retirement, and having become a commentator, he mixed in a stratum of British society that was very different from that of most sportsmen. One of his great friends was the publisher Tom Rosenthal of André Deutsch, who loved cricket and was an MCC member. Rosenthal never missed a Test at Lord's and often travelled to other grounds to see Test matches. Rosenthal, who also published some of my books, often spoke to me of his close friendship with Holding. 'I met him', Holding told me, 'when he did the Michael Manley book, *A History of West Indies Cricket*. Tom was responsible for my first book, *Whispering Death*, that Tony Cozier wrote. He wasn't just my publisher. We built up a friendship. He would come to cricket whenever we were in London, and we would go out and have a meal sometimes. He was a good man.' Holding, along with me, was present at Rosenthal's memorial service and I was struck by the fact that many of Rosenthal's arty friends did not know who Holding was. For them, Rosenthal was the publisher of authors like the Nobel Prize winner V.S. Naipaul or Gore Vidal. That he could have admired a cricketer like Holding seemed remote to them, and in her eulogy Joan Bakewell confessed that she could not speak of Rosenthal's love of cricket. Holding, for whom relaxation is following horses, is also a good friend of Sir Michael Stoute, a Barbadian Briton, who left the island at the age of 19 and whose father was chief of police there. 'Whenever I'm away from cricket,' Holding told me, 'I'm in Newmarket. I'm out on the heath with Michael Stoute every morning, and that's my fun and relaxation. Well, he has won the championship ten times now [we were talking in 2014]. He has won almost every important race in England. I think he's a great trainer.' In such an England of publishers and racehorse trainers, the racism that many of his fellow West Indians living in England experienced did not touch Holding.

The video of George Floyd dying jolted Holding, making him aware that he had been selfish for too long, allowing racism suffered by others to bounce off him. Seeing blacks and whites march together in the Black Lives Matter rallies touched him, for this was in stark contrast to marches organised by Martin Luther King during the American civil rights struggle, when it was largely black:

'Everyone is now coming alive and seeing the difference in treatment of people. And we're all human beings. So, I hope that people will recognise that this Black Lives Matter movement is not trying to get black people above white people or above anyone else. It's all about equality. When you say to somebody, "Black Lives Matter," and they tell you, "All lives matter," or "White lives matter," please, we black people know white lives matter. I don't think you will know that black lives matter. So don't shout back at us about "All lives matter." It is obvious the evidence is clear, linear, that white lives matter. We want black lives to matter now. Simple as that.'

In the discussion with Ian Ward that followed, he spoke about teaching white people about black history that they knew nothing about and about how everything was seen from a white perspective. Then, having said with a laugh that he was not religious, he became very serious:

'Look at Jesus Christ, the image that they give you of Jesus Christ. A pale skin, blond hair, blue eyes; where Jesus came from, who in that part of the world looks that way? But again, that's a brainwashing to show you this is what perfection is. This is what the image of perfection is. If you look at the plays of those days, Judas who betrayed Jesus, he's a black man. Again, brainwashing people in the thing. 'Oh, he is a black man. He is the bad man.' Go through history, Wardy . . . I was never taught anything good about black people. And you cannot have a society that is brought up like that, both white and black, that only teach what's convenient to the teacher. History is written by the conqueror, not by those that are conquered. History is written by the people who do the harm, not by the people who get harmed. And we need to go back and teach both sides of history. And until we do that, and educate the entire human race, this thing will not stop. They keep on telling me there's nothing called white privilege. Give me a break. I don't see any white people going into a store in Oxford Street and being followed. A black man walks in, somebody is following him everywhere he goes. That is basic white privilege. Whether that white person ended up robbing the place or not, he's not going to be thought of that way. And things like that have to change.'

As he said those words, Holding's voice seemed to break, as if he was about to cry. There was a pause. Ward seemed stunned by what he had heard. He said, 'We will leave it there and come back to this.' Then, turning to Nasser, he asked, 'Have you experienced racism in your time as a cricketer – or otherwise?'

Nasser, standing next to Holding, responded:

'Of course I have. With my surname, growing up in south Essex, East London, with an Indian dad and an English mum, probably getting it a little bit from both sides, you know, fielding on a boundary in various parts of the world and people saying, "Oh, he is Saddam; why don't you eff off back to wherever you came from."'

Hussain, like Holding, spoke about how he had been affected by watching the George Floyd murder:

'I felt something inside me saying, "Nas, you've been looking away too long. We've all been looking away too long." The players should be proud of wearing these [Black Lives Matter] badges . . . [It's] 2020 and we have to wear a badge saying Black Lives Matter. Really? That should be a given, Wardy.'

Nothing could better illustrate how Hussain had changed. His father, Jawed, was an Indian Muslim whom everyone called 'Joe', and his mother Shireen, an English girl from Cornwall, converted to Islam. Nasser is nominally Muslim – but in his autobiography *Playing with Fire* he hardly mentions race. Paul Newman, who ghosted the book, told me, 'Nasser had not been badly treated. He had had no racial abuse and felt the battle had been won. He had not been a victim. His view is, 'I am proud of my Indian side, but I am English.'

That book was written in 2004. Having heard Holding and Rainford-Brent, the Hussain of 2020 was a different man when it came to race. Nothing could better emphasise the impact of Floyd's death and the rise of the Black Lives Matter movement.

Almost exactly 50 years before Holding made his dramatic speech, another sportsman had also spoken of how the white man had made the world in his own image. In 1971, when Holding was 17 years old, Muhammad Ali told a British television audience how he had asked his mother why everything was white. Ali had asked her why Jesus is white with blond hair and blue eyes. But unlike Holding, Ali was appearing on *Parkinson* and he was trying to act the court jester. Every Ali sally about the world being white was received with gales of laughter from the almost uniformly white audience. The black man was making fun of 'whitey', and the whites were enjoying it. It would not mean the world would change, and it didn't in fact change. Holding was on a different mission. He was trying to change the world. The danger is that, for all the seriousness and tears with which Holding and Rainford-Brent made their points, in another 50 years another black sportsman or woman may have to make the same points. If that happens, the words, actions, marching and gestures will not have changed the old world one jot. However, there are signs that a new world is emerging that is determined to see the sports world changed.

THIRTY-THREE

INCHING TOWARDS A NON-RACIAL SPORTS WORLD

In October 2018 I was a panellist in a discussion in front of an audience entitled 'From the Cricket Test to Three Lions: Sport and Identity' at that year's Battle of Ideas Festival. England had surprised themselves by reaching the semi-finals of football's World Cup and the organisers thought this would be a good time to talk about the role of sport in national identity.

My fellow panellists were a Manchester United season-ticket holder, a London-based Celtic supporter and an academic. During the discussion, the Manchester United season-ticket holder said a little bit of racist chanting at football grounds did not matter. The Celtic fan, who was sitting next to me, and who until then had been quite amiable now got quite angry and said that there was no problem with racism in football: it was all dreamt up by Kick It Out and the organisation should be disbanded. Both the Manchester United season-ticket holder and the Celtic fan were white. While I was aware that some people held such views, that they would publicly air them at a seminar astonished me.

To my surprise, the uniformly white audience, far from supporting my argument of how unacceptable and dangerous such views were, did not find anything objectionable in what they had said. As regards the experiences I had of racism while covering football matches, the response of a young white man was that football was a working-class sport that had been appropriated by the middle classes, which made me feel the world had not changed much since I had suffered my assault by Chelsea fans in 1981. Then, as I have recounted earlier, one football supporter wrote to me claiming it was not a racist attack but because I was travelling first class. A more middle-aged white man in the discussion audience said that as a Luton supporter he had often received abuse from fans of other clubs, but when I put it to him that he could always conceal his Luton identity while I could not conceal my colour, he did not seem to understand. My lone supporter was a white woman who felt I deserved a hearing. The third of my fellow panellists, who apart from me was the only other non-white in the room, said nothing, but when I spoke to him afterwards, he shook his head sadly and said he had heard such views and was not surprised.

After the discussion had finished, the Manchester United season-ticket holder, who was sitting on the other side of the rostrum, came round to my side, smiled and offered me her hand. Was it supposed to mean that she, a white woman, was prepared to shake the hand of a brown man? Was it meant to show that while she might not mind a bit of racist chanting, she herself was not a racist? I took her hand but thought that when it came to race, no amount of handshaking could conceal that some white people in these islands and I were still living in two different worlds. I had gone to the meeting thinking in 2018 we could have a discussion about race and identity and agree on certain basic things. I left the meeting with the definite impression there was white fatigue. The whites were tired of hearing all this talk of race. What the people in that meeting were, in effect, saying was, 'You non-whites should get over the past, stop moaning and move on. We are already living in a post-racial world where nobody is bothered about the colour of your skin.'

The world since then has changed, or at least the public discourse. Indeed we are now discussing issues of history and race that sport has never discussed before. But how far this takes us down the long, painful road to a non-racial sports world is more difficult to say.

It is November 2021, and I am talking on Zoom to Lilian Thuram whose football career could not be more glorious. A World Cup winner with France in 1998, winner of the Euros in 2000, most appearances for France – 142 – and outstanding defender for Monaco, Parma, Juventus and Barcelona. He is in his office in the centre of Paris wearing what looks like a Nehru jacket. When I tell him he laughs and says it has a zip, which a Nehru jacket does not. In 2008 at the end of his career he set up his Lilian Thuram Foundation and surrounded himself with what they call in France a scientific committee – a group of intellectuals and academics and his office bears testimony to that. It is filled with books these learned men have written. Thuram has tried to learn from them to get to the roots of racism. He tells me he is just back from a visit to Corsica where he was giving a talk to future civil servants at one of those very French training schools where people go to get into the famed French civil service.

During the talk he asked a young man in his mid-20s how long he had been white. The man said, 'Well, I am 25, so 25 years.' Thuram took a white sheet of paper and said, 'Are you white like this sheet of paper? Obviously not. Well, why do you say you are white? You are clearly not white in the same way this sheet of paper is white.' Thuram tells me:

'Whiteness is a completely constructed identity. People who consider themselves white need to understand what it means to be white. White people need to begin to question that identity. Once white people start to question that identity and come to terms with it, then they can start to see what it is like to be a person of colour. And to suffer discrimination.'

Thuram had talked about something that had also intrigued me. Like Thuram I have been described as a person of 'colour' or one of the 'visible minorities'. But then what does that make my white wife? A person of no colour. Part of an invisible majority. White has become the world's default colour.

Our conversation has come about because Thuram has written a book called *White Thinking: Behind the Mask of Racial Identity*. The inside cover has a map of the world known as the Peter's projection where the traditional map has been turned upside down with Europe no longer on the top. The Thuram Foundation seeks to educate young people on racism and when Thuram goes to schools and shows them the map, the kids say, 'Oh, it's upside down. Turn it the other way.' Thuram tells them, 'It is a globe, a circle; you can look at it from any perspective.' Thuram's overall conclusion is, 'Racism is primarily a problem for white people. We always look at it the other way round. White people need to understand they are the ones practising racism. How does that come about? That is what the book is trying to get at.' The work, a historical study of slavery and colonialism and how this has underpinned racism, is heavily footnoted with quotes from academic studies, a rarity in most sports books. For Thuram this is very necessary:

'If you want to challenge racism, you need to look into the history behind it. Looking into the history of racism we come back to slavery and colonialism. And that takes people to uncomfortable places. That is why we are having such complicated debates about these things. Basically, white people need to understand their own history, the violence of colonialism and slavery. White identity has been constructed on the basis of that violence. If you talk to French people about racist laws they go, "That's America. We don't have anything like that." The French want to talk about the grandeur of their history, not the negatives. They can't face up to the trauma of their past. This undermines the positive construction of their own identity. I imagine the situation is the same in Britain; that white people do not like to be categorised as white because a lot of the history of the past centuries is of the domination of the non-whites by the white people where bad things happened.'

The 'bad thing' happened to Thurman when, as a nine-year-old, he was brought to France from Guadeloupe in the French Caribbean. Kids at his school called him 'sale noir': 'dirty black'. When he asked his mother why, she said, 'It's just like that.' He says with a laugh that his mum 'gave a very bad answer. A lot of my thinking is to come up with a better answer. I have spent a lot of my life since then to discover what it is that led white kids to call a black child "dirty black", and more widely as to the roots of racism. Why do people think in these categories?'

His search for the answers has made him conclude that 'it is a lie when in the French republic you are told the colour of your skin doesn't matter. That you are a citizen.' Thuram has taught his own kids that 'society will perceive you as black. And that has a meaning.' White domination, he argues, has had such a profound effect on non-whites that it has led to 'non-white self-loathing', and he illustrates this with examples of behaviour of black players in the dressing room. He recounts how in the showers light-skinned blacks would preen themselves and pointing to a darker player say, 'Look how black you are,' as if to say they were better-looking. His most telling example of this self-loathing is how black men feel towards black and white women.

When he was an 18-year-old in AS Monaco's youth academy, his girlfriend Sandra, now the mother of his two children, came to visit him. He, along with black friends, went to pick her up at the airport and when they saw she was black they said, 'Erm . . . your girlfriend is black.' Later, one of them said, 'She looks like she's your sister.' Throughout his playing career his black teammates would joke, 'Lilian is into black women,' and they would even ask, 'Don't you like white women? Are you racist?' Thuram has no doubts that 'this ribbing revealed a staggering contempt for black women'. As far as his fellow black players were concerned, he had 'money, a big house, a big car and a big gold watch. You marry a white woman.' This is part of the process of 'whitening' himself, the white mask that black men wear.

Thuram, who first encountered racism in a football ground when he moved to Italy and heard monkey chants, regrets he did not speak out during his playing career, particularly when he was captain:

'If there had been a racist incident [we needed] to get the players together to leave the pitch. And say, "We are not playing on." I could have used my authority as captain to make a statement about these things. Even today there are lots of black players who behind the scenes will talk about racism. But they are afraid to speak out publicly. It is inscribed in the collective unconscious in many ways. This fear is because there is this legacy within the global black community that for people who speak out against racism, bad things will happen to them. When I first started speaking out against racism, my mum, fearful of what would happen to me, asked me to stop speaking out. And that is why we only see a tiny proportion of players speaking out about racism.

But while Thuram draws encouragement from gestures like 'taking the knee', which Thuram strongly supports, he warns, 'Racism has very deep roots. Things won't change as fast as we would like. We won't see the end of these problems.'

An almost identical note of pessimism is struck by another famous sportsman:

'One day, people of colour might have equality. It will be the gene-ration, young and hopeful and fierce, who marched together in 2020 that will propel us to that point . . . And listen, I don't expect to be around to see the fruits of that labour of love. I will be long gone by the time we have a genuine level playing field, a day when the black person is not stuck on first base and the white person is on third. It is going to take time.'

These are the concluding words of Michael Holding's book *Why We Kneel, How We Rise,* which was published a few months after Thuram's book was published in France. Like Thuram's book, Holding's is packed with his-torical references on racism by institutions and includes a discussion of slavery and how the idea that black people were inferior developed. And like Thuram, Holding's mission is to highlight 'uncomfortable and unedited history that has been ignored for far too long'. His book shows how atro-cities committed on blacks, like the lynchings in America, or the contribution that black soldiers made during the World Wars, were ignored in history books written by whites. His book ends with an 11-page 'Black History Timeline' which starts in AD 1–33 'Life of Jesus Christ; born in the Middle East and certainly not white as portrayed.' This is followed by four other entries mentioning Septimius Severus, the black Roman emperor; the foundation of the Kingdom of Ghana, 'One of the earliest and most advanced civilisations in history'; the beginnings of African–Indian trade; and the seventh-century North African-born scholar Hadrian becoming an abbot in Canterbury Cathedral, but turning down the opportunity to be Archbishop of Canterbury. Other major non-white events are recorded in the way they rarely are in the timelines of history books written by Europeans with the names of several of the black Americans murdered by white US policemen also mentioned.

Some of what both Thuram and Holding say has been said before. That racism is a white problem is not new; other non-white writers have made this point like James Baldwin, one of Thuram's heroes, but it has never been done by a professional sportsman. And very rarely have the greats of international sports written books that have virtually nothing about the sports they excelled in but are about the much wider question of race and society, extending the discussion far beyond sport. And both books touched a nerve. Thuram was invited to London to speak to the House of Commons, although Covid meant he spoke in a room above a pub near the Commons to just one MP.

Holding was featured in the prestigious *Financial Times* slot called 'Lunch with the FT', the lunch hosted by Murad Ahmed, then the FT's sports editor who is of Bangladeshi origin. Just as Thuram had spoken about the shades of colour, so did Holding. Ahmed mentioned how fair-skinned women were more highly prized by the Bengalis. Holding's response was, 'That all stems from racism. From white people preaching to the world that they are superior. So, the darker-skinned people want to get lighter, to match them, to feel they belong.' He then recited a Bob Marley song: 'Emancipate yourself from mental slavery . . . None but ourselves can free our minds.'

But apart from the public attention Thuram and Holding have received what these two books, (along with that of John Barnes, published a few months after Holding's), show is a dramatic new development in the writing on racism by sports personalities that has taken the debate on racism on to a new level. Just how radical this can best be judged if we compare books by these three sportsmen with the one written by another man like them also from the Caribbean. He is the writer C.L.R. James, described by one of his biographers as 'Cricket's Philosopher King'. A friend of Learie Constantine, he wrote about cricket for the *Guardian* in the 1930s. But he had a huge life beyond cricket and his belief in Marxism – he was a Trotskyite – earned him the title 'The Cricketing Marxist'. One of the leading black intellectuals of the twentieth century he was a mentor both to a whole generation of African leaders who fought for their countries' independence from colonial rule and to many black activists who emerged in the 1960s in Britain. In 1963 he published *Beyond a Boundary*. When it came out as a paperback in 1986 it had a foreword by Mike Brearley in which he mentioned how the book advances the argument of the role sport and, in particular, cricket can play in society. 'The book is a classic of cricket literature and, more than that, a fascinating contribution to aesthetics and social history.'

James was a great campaigner for West Indian freedom from colonial rule and wrote a seminal book on the eighteenth-century black revolt in Haiti, *The Black Jacobins*. Yet, unlike Thuram and Holding, *Beyond a Boundary* has nothing about slavery, let alone the need to understand the history of slavery. For him all that is needed for people to come together is to go back to the ideas of ancient Greece. Greeks for him not only 'laid the intellectual foundations of the Western world' but 'were the most fanatical players and organisers of games that the world has ever known'.

Yet observe how very differently Thuram sees ancient Greece. He tells the story of how, when he was invited to speak at Harvard, 'a Greek delegate, who seemed very proud of his origins, told us that his country had "a long time ago, invented democracy" . . . But who enjoyed the benefits of this democracy? A handful of male citizens. Women and slaves were entirely excluded. In other words, most of the Greek population.' For Thuram, who wants to offer the oppressed a voice and help them 'free themselves from bondage', ancient Greece has no lessons to offer. As for James' fellow West Indian Holding, ancient Greece and its wonder are not even worth considering. This change in sports attitude could not be better timed for almost every day we have examples of how sport can show a way to the world in helping create a non-racial world. So, for people seeking to create a non-racial world, sport provides a better platform than any other form of human activity. I am writing this as the producers of a film called *I Love Lucy* have been criticised for casting a Spanish actor to play Desi Arnaz who was a Cuban. This is seen as stealing the Cuban heritage. Such a question would never arise in sport.

Sport has many advantages compared to other human activities. It can supply some of the ingredients associated with religious observance: theatre, ritual, beauty, belonging, a source of hope and belief and a space to express extreme feelings, a sense of right and wrong – even a glimpse of another kind of existence. A visit with fellow supporters to an important fixture away from home, especially overseas, has some of the character of a medieval pilgrimage. In certain respects, belief in a team or an athlete is a 'safer' investment than belief in a religious faith. You may not take your feelings quite as far as religious fervour, but supporting a team or player gives you multiple ways to put some meaning into your life and to express your identity.

In sport you receive regular, indisputable evidence of the quality of your favourites and the rationality of your beliefs. Sport has become a rare source of trusted news in a sceptical world where more and more information arrives either in the form of hearsay and rumour or as planted propaganda. There is no room to argue over the facts recorded on the sports pages, and on those pages there is always a clear distinction between fact and interpretation or opinion.

Sport is simultaneously a global language and a marker of personal and local identity. A contest in a popular sport is one of the few experiences which can be understood by, and excite passion in, people all over the world regardless of language or culture or intellect. You do not have to know Portuguese, or indeed anything about Brazil the country, to appreciate Brazilian football. It also helps that all the people who play a popular sport perform essentially the same activity. Some do it with more skill than others, and with better equipment and facilities and rewards for success, but they still share a common experience.

Sport's only rival could have been music. But the musical traditions of the West are very different from that of music in India, China and the Arab world. Musicians, or at least some of them, have a global following, but there is no common set of rules, conventions and implements which allows any particular kind of music to become a global activity. Quite the opposite: music has very different conventions across the world, in terms of fundamental structure, tempo, melody, harmony, tone colour and much more. Western music, especially at a popular level, may be the most pervasive and the most commercially successful, but that is largely a product of technology and conquest. It has been assimilated by other cultures (and influenced by them), but it does not form part of a global experience in the same way as global sport.

Sport has a tendency to codify – to invent rules and conditions to create a common experience. If you give 20 footballers a football each, most of them will instantly do the same things with it. If you give 20 pianists a piano, each will play it in a different way – some classical, some jazz, some rock, some completely improvisational.

That points to another important difference between sport and music. In any sport, even the most indifferent player occasionally matches the performance of the greatest. The park footballer produces a dribble like Lionel Messi, the park cricketer uncorks a shot to match Sachin Tendulkar. For the great ones, such performance is routine; for the park player it happens once in a lifetime, but the emotional impact can be permanent and life-changing.

Sport is the one enduring and unifying force in the modern world.

However, for sport to act as an agent of change, institutions that run sport need to go through a fundamental change. In recent months, as this book has shown, people who run many of these institutions have admitted they are institutionally racist and promised to radically change the way they operate. This, of course, is a huge advance when for decades they argued nothing needed changing. Indeed, until well into the 1990s the Football Association did not believe there was any need for an anti-racist organisation; and until the Azeem Rafiq scandal broke, both Yorkshire and English cricket could claim racism was not a problem facing the game.

But this change needs to be more than symbolic. It is not a question of non-whites being brought in to make the boards that run these organisations look more diverse. That has been Yorkshire's response to the Azeem Rafiq crisis with the club advertising for non-executive directors who come from 'a range of backgrounds', code words for non-white people. The danger with that approach is what you have is an organisation that looks different but whose nature has not changed. What Angela Davies said is, 'The difference that brings no difference and the change that brings no change.' A good example of this is the current British Cabinet. It is by far the most racially and religiously diverse cabinet in British history with two Hindus – Rishi Sunak and Priti Patel – holding two of the highest offices in the land, Chancellor and Home Secretary, and two Muslims – Sajid Javid and Nadhim Zahawi – one as Health Secretary and the other as Education Secretary. But as Gary Younge has put it, 'Organisations looking different, even if they act the same, end up not with equal opportunities but photo opportunities.'

The danger with photo opportunity is the debate on race develops into who said what to whom and what a word means. This was well illustrated in the aftermath of the Azeem Rafiq testimony. After Rafiq had spoken about being called a 'Paki', there were many whites who felt this was acceptable banter and no different to an English person being called a 'Pommie'. I was asked about it on GB News and could not convince the presenter that while Pommie is not a racial slur, as an English person of whatever colour could be a Pommie, 'Paki' was a racial term invented in post-war Britain to denote people from the subcontinent, shorthand for Pakistani and applied to brown people even if they had never been to Pakistan or had any connection with the country. As we have seen, the boys and the Chelsea mob, who back in 1981 called me 'Paki', knew it was a racist term and were using it as such. The idea that they were indulging in banter with me is so ridiculous as to be not worth discussing. This emphasised the point that Thuram, Holding and Barnes were making about the huge historical gap that still exists between many whites and non-whites.

For change to come there must be white people willing to respond to what Thuram, Holding and Barnes are saying and not dismiss it as woke culture which threatens Western civilisation and Western values. Thuram has been very critical of white people saying 'white people, even if they are not openly racist themselves, and maybe people of goodwill, they just can't see what is happening round them.' Thuram's French experience may lead him to such a conclusion but in Britain there are now white men and women who are not only aware of racism but know how they can help combat it. The outstanding among them is undoubtedly Gareth Southgate, the England football manager.

As we have seen, Southgate came into football when many whites who ran the English game were convinced blacks could never play football. But, as manager of England, he has shown an awareness of race which is exemplary. In September 2021, just after England had beaten Hungary in Budapest 4-0, Hungarian fans shouted monkey chants at Raheem Sterling, who had scored England's first goal, and Jude Bellingham, a young black player. Southgate condemned the Hungarian fans. But, and this is significant, he also warned that English football could not afford to take the moral high ground as it also had problems in this area. Southgate was not taking shelter in English exceptionalism.

It could be, and has been, argued that English exceptionalism is not a cliché but has real meaning. Many in English sport have always contrasted England's tolerant attitude to race compared to that of America or Australia, let alone white South Africa. In America, blacks were excluded from playing Major League Baseball, so had to form their own 'Negro Leagues', and it was only in 1947 that Jackie Robinson became the first black man to play Major League Baseball. As it happened, that was also the year that India got freedom. Yet half a century earlier, Ranji, an Indian, had made his debut for England, and would become one of the greatest stars of what is called the 'Golden Era of the Game'. Yet in selecting Ranji cricket still remained a white world, it was just that it had opened a window for some, very select, non-whites. Ranji would go on to rule an Indian princely state, and the racism was not as stark as in America or in white South Africa. Non-whites were accommodated as long as they knew their place, which was below stairs.

For Southgate not to shelter under English exceptionalism shows a remarkably refreshing sense of self-introspection and a willingness to admit the issues that still need to be resolved. Nor does he show signs of being fatigued by talk of the racism. What makes Southgate exceptional is that as a white man he not only acknowledges that he has not experienced racism, but that racism cannot be put on the same moral plane as other forms of discrimination, which is the argument that Thuram, Holding and Barnes make. This is something that non-whites feel strongly about, and Southgate is very aware of that and acts on that.

There can be little doubt that his leadership has had a profound impact on the England team. This was well illustrated when Raheem Sterling was selected as one of the guest editors for Radio 4's *Today* programme during the 2021 Christmas period, itself a significant moment. Sterling interviewed Southgate who said Floyd's death had 'educated me a lot'. He then went on to explain how he had begun to change his views on racism in football and how the team had come together on the issue as a result of the racial abuse Danny Rose and Sterling had suffered during the match against Montenegro in 2019.

'I wasn't aware of it until the very close to the end when Danny got booked and there was a reaction from the crowd. So, when we got to the changing room I am having a go at Danny for being booked, and I had to apologise on the plane because it emerged that this [abuse] had been going on during the game. I didn't like the fact that the boys felt they couldn't mention it in the changing room at half-time or report it. For me it was like: "God this is awful. How is this an environment where our players are allowed to be abused on the pitch and they don't even feel comfortable to report it or that anything is going to happen?" This had to be a team where we were united in how we saw it and we could send a message to young kids watching. I think the lads didn't think how powerful that would be and they wanted to be judged on the football. I wanted to represent the players in the best way I could.'

Southgate would go on to say how he felt 'hurt' that Rashford, Jadon Sancho and Bukayo Saka were racially abused on social media for missing penalties against Italy in the final of Euro2020 which led to England's defeat.

'What really hurt me was that this was a group of players who had brought everybody together for 30 days, and then the first time that we have a defeat, now all of a sudden we're going to allow that division to happen – I wasn't happy about that at all.'

Southgate's leadership, as Sterling says, has been instrumental in England's white players joining their black teammates in taking the knee as a collective entity and, as Sterling reveals, 'There have been times when we have sat down and said, "Is the message still powerful?" and we've said, "Yes", as a collective.'

This is crucial for as Thuram had said, 'White players can be part of the solution. To remain neutral is part of the problem.' Jordan Henderson and his white teammates understand that. Not for them turning their faces away, or having tears in their eyes when their black teammates, like the 17-year-old Ricky Hill away at Burnley, were racially abused, but doing nothing to stop it. It marks a seminal change from the grim eighties and nineties.

There have always been white men and women who have been able to see that non-whites would feel differently about race. When I asked John Gosden, one of our most celebrated flat trainers, about how he reacted to people who say there is white privilege his answer was:

'You really have to read James Baldwin, *The Fire Next Time* and Franz Fannon on the European colonial powers. Inevitably, if you lived in the Congo, you wouldn't be in love with the mineral companies who financed the Belgian government. Obviously, I read them when I was younger but the point is that, you know, European colonialism, inevitably leads to that feeling and justifiably so.'

It was an answer that would surprise Lilian Thuram who also admires Franz Fannon and quotes him in his book. What has changed is until recently Gosden was a lone voice, there were few who thought like him in sport as a whole let alone racing. Now Southgate and the views of the England football team show that they are not quite an isolated minority.

Emma Raducanu, an 18-year-old Bromley schoolgirl, made history by becoming the first qualifier to win a tennis Grand Slam tournament, the US Open. The Queen wrote to her, and her achievements dominated the British media for days. Given Raducanu's unprecedented achievement, she featured not just in the sports pages but also in the news pages. One little story on the bottom of page three in the *Sunday Telegraph* stood out for me. It was headlined 'Raducanu: Chinese heritage taught me to believe in myself'. The article was jointly written by a white journalist based in Britain and a Chinese journalist in Beijing. Raducanu's mother is Chinese, and the article said she regularly travelled to her mother's home city of Shenyang in northeast China, that she understands Chinese, and attributes her drive and discipline 'in large part thanks to her mother's family. My mum comes from a Chinese background – they have very good self-belief. It's not necessarily about telling everyone how good you are, but it's about believing it within yourself. I really respect that about the culture.' And while other British schoolgirls looked up to British tennis players, Raducanu's idol was China's tennis idol, the former world number two, Li Na. 'Even though Li Na has retired,' said Raducanu, 'I've watched lots of her matches on YouTube, because she was really aggressive.'

What makes this interesting is how Raducanu, despite her non-white origins, is being treated. While her achievements are exceptional, there have also been in the past very distinctive non-white female tennis stars such as Althea Gibson and Evonne Goolagong, and in the case of Gibson, she had to break through American racist laws to even get on a tennis court against white opponents. But while they were lauded, nothing was made of their non-white culture and how it contributed to their success. Their achievements were seen as the triumph of white cultural values civilising their native cultures. Raducanu, in contrast, can not only retain her heritage but even broadcast it. Michael Johnson had told Michael Holding that as black people got more opportunities and there was equality between the races, 'a lot of young white people or young white men now have to compete, and they don't like it. It doesn't feel good. So, they are afraid.' The way Raducanu's success has been received suggests that the dominant white culture of the world now feels less threatened by the rise of non-white culture, of its capacity to shape and influence non-whites who live in the West.

Also, part of the change process is the way Holding's book came about. This showed that, at least in Britain, the discourse on race is now being encouraged by the white publishing industry. Holding's views on race, aired so dramatically on Sky in 2020, had caused such a sensation in the publishing world that British publishers waged a bidding war to sign him up for a book. He was rumoured to have been paid a £50,000 advance. In the past such a book might have been ignored, but now Holding was invited to appear on *Desert Island Discs*. The book went on to win the William Hill Sports Book of the Year, the Booker of sports book awards.

In some ways, just as significant was what Troy Deeney, the Birmingham City striker, who led the campaign to take the knee, decided on doing after talking to his young daughter. His daughter told him that at school she had learnt about same-sex couples becoming parents and there was discussion on mental health issues. This set him wondering about how empowered teachers were in tackling a diverse curriculum. He commissioned a YouGov survey of 1,000 primary and secondary teachers and its findings were very disturbing: 93 per cent of ethnic minority teachers and 54 per cent of all respondents thought there was a racial bias in the national curriculum; only 12 per cent felt empowered to teach diverse topics. Another 64 per cent said they were not given enough support about teaching a culturally diverse curriculum and 72 per cent said the government should do more to make sure schoolchildren, whatever their background, have a balanced and inclusive understanding of Britain's past. 'Yet,' says Deeney, 'the teaching of black, Asian and ethnic minority histories and experiences in school still remains optional. Is it that people are scared how it might paint the British Empire? That old quote about history being written by the victors. But the world has different lenses and we need to give teachers a platform where they feel comfortable to teach.'

For Deeney, the fact that a mere 12 per cent of teachers feel they are able to teach a diverse curriculum in history and science, 'That alone warrants a conversation'. How much of a conversation there will be remains to be seen, but that the call has been made emphasises how this generation of black footballers feel. They are not going to be silenced.

However, to read into all this a revolution that will sweep away the old system and usher in a non-racial sports world would be too optimistic. But, to borrow Harold Macmillan's phrase, the winds of change are blowing and seem to be blowing in the right direction. Not only has the nature of the discourse on sport and race changed, but more people from very diverse backgrounds are willing to participate. They give every impression they will not be deflected or seduced by cheap promises, in creating a sports world that is diverse and truly reflects our society. This is a huge change that needs to be applauded.

Macmillan was talking in the early 1960s of European colonialism being blown away from Africa. It took time and almost three decades before South Africa, in whose white parliament he made the speech, was free. So, a non-racial sports world will take time but, just as Macmillan's speech marked the first step towards the end of colonial rule, all the signs are that the first steps towards a truly non-racial sports world have been laid.

INDEX

Wycombe Wanderers FC 94

xenophobia 60–1

Yeovil Town FC 68, 97–101

Yorkshire County Cricket
    Club 215–22, 223, 228, 295

Younge, Gary 295

Zahawi, Nadhim 295